D0908325

THE
CANARIS
CONSPIRACY

THE
CANARIS
CONSPIRACY

THE SECRET RESISTANCE TO HITLER
IN THE GERMAN ARMY

ROGER MANVELL AND HEINRICH FRAENKEL

Skyhorse Publishing

CONTENTS

v

PART THREE

Acknowledgments

Contact has been made by the authors with every principal survivor of the resistance movement within the Abwehr, the department of German Military Intelligence during the Hitler régime, as well as with the families of those leaders who were arrested and executed. During 1965 Heinrich Fraenkel learned of the survival of Hans von Dohnanyi's private letters and memoranda, which were smuggled out of prison and which his widow, who died in 1966, fortunately preserved. They are now in the hands of Pastor Eberhard Bethge, Bonhoeffer's close friend and biographer, who has most generously put this completely new material at our disposal with the permission of members of Dohnanyi's family. The more we studied the subject, the more we came to the conclusion that the heroic Dohnanyi represents one of the principal links in the network of German resistance, both civilian and military, prior to the sudden emergence of Stauffenberg as the youthful leader of the July plot of 1944.

Much new material has come to light since 1953, when Sir John Wheeler-Bennett wrote *The Nemesis of Power,* his comprehensive study of resistance in the German Army, and since the publication, in 1949 and 1951 respectively, of the pioneer biographies of Canaris by Abshagen and Colvin. (The book formerly considered the authority on the subject, *The Downfall of the German Secret Service* (1956) by the late Karl Bartz, has proved to be nothing but a whitewash for Wilhelm Schmidhuber, the man whose interrogation led to that downfall.) In compiling our book, we have drawn on this new material, adding it to the detailed valuable evidence which the survivors themselves of the inner circle of the German resistance movement— have been able to give us, in particular Josef Müller,

Achim Oster (son of General Oster), Frau Anni Oster, Otto John, members of the Dohnanyi family, and Dr. W. W. Schrader (son of Colonel Werner Schrader). We have also taken statements from the former Nazi officials Dr. Werner Best and Dr. Manfred Roeder. Much unpublished documentation, including the records of the Gestapo's examination of suspected persons after the attempt on Hitler's life in 1944, and the affidavits made after the war before and during the investigations of Roeder and the successive trials of Huppenkothen and Sonderegger has been put at our disposal. In addition, through the courtesy of the Freiburg Military Archives certain of the then unpublished Grosscurth papers were made available to us whilst we were writing this book.

We are deeply indebted to Professor Harold C. Deutsch of the Department of History, University of Minnesota, who, when our book was already completed, allowed us to study the typescript of his own recently finished work, *The Conspiracy against Hitler during the Twilight War.* This most scholarly and detailed study covers the key years in the German resistance movement, 1938-1940, and is the result of some ten years' research. In particular, Professor Deutsch has sifted the details of Dr. Josef Müller's negotiations at the Vatican and was able to discuss them with the late Father Leiber. Although Dr. Müller has over a period of years given us similar evidence, we benefited greatly from being able to read Professor Deutsch's meticulous elucidation of fact and conjecture.

We would like to express our gratitude to all those who have helped us; in addition to those named above, we should like to thank Dr. Hoch of the *Institut für Zeitgeschichte* at Munich, Dr. Arenz of the Military Archives at Freiburg, Mrs. Anette Pringle at the Wiener Library in London, and Mrs. Patricia Newnham of William Heinemann Ltd.

ROGER MANVELL
HEINRICH FRAENKEL

The Principals

involved in this story of the German resistance to Hitler:

The Abwehr (Amtsgruppe Ausland/Abwehr), *German Military Intelligence:*

CANARIS, Admiral Wilhelm (1887-1945). From 1935 to 1944 Chief of Military Intelligence attached to the High Command. Leading member of the resistance; arrested 23 July 1944, and hanged in Flossenbürg concentration camp 9 April 1945.

DOHNANYI, Hans von (1902-45). Dietrich Bonhoeffer's brother-in-law. Introduced into the Abwehr by Canaris in August 1939, and became leading administrator in the resistance and its legal adviser. Arrested April 1943; executed April 1945.

OSTER, Major-General Hans (1895-1945), Chief of Staff at the Abwehr and a principal organizer of the resistance. Suspended from duty in April 1943; arrested after the bomb attempt of 20 July 1944 and executed 9 April 1945.

Principal agents attached to the Abwehr for the purpose of resistance:

BETHGE, Pastor Eberhard. Closely linked through marriage to the Bonhoeffer family. Arrested in September 1944; liberated in May 1945 at the end of the war.

BONHOEFFER, Pastor Dietrich (1906-45). Eminent scholar and teacher. Attempted to make contact with the British on behalf of the resistance through Bishop Bell of Chichester in Sweden, May 1942. Arrested April 1943; executed April 1945.

MÜLLER, Josef (b. 1898). A lawyer, and one of the leading Catholic agents of the conspiracy. Used his connections at the Vatican in an attempt to enlist Allied support during the early stages of the war. Imprisoned from 1943 until his liberation at the end of the war.

The Army: the principal malcontents:

BECK, Colonel-General Ludwig (1880-1944). Chief of the Army General Staff until his resignation in 1938 in protest against Hitler's policy. Recognized by all as head of the resistance, and nominated to become Head of State after the *coup d'état*. Died, following an attempt at suicide, 20 July 1944.

HALDER, Colonel-General Franz (b. 1884). Chief of the Army General Staff 1938-42. In touch with the resistance, though he gradually withdrew from direct contact during the war period. Arrested July 1944, but not brought to trial. Liberated at the end of the war.

KLUGE, Field-Marshal Guenther von (1882-1944). After a command on the Eastern front, became Army Group Commander in France. In spite of the uncertainty of his support for the resistance, it was hoped to the end that he would come out on the side of the conspirators. Finally refused his support when Hitler survived the attempt of July 1944. Fearing arrest, committed suicide on 19 August of that year.

OLBRICHT, Colonel-General Friedrich (1886-1944). Head of the supply section of the Reserve Army; principal administrator of the *coup d'état* of 20 July 1944. Executed by his senior officer, Colonel-General Fromm, after a summary court-martial the same night.

SCHLABRENDORFF, Lieutenant Fabian von (b. 1907). A lawyer; appointed staff officer working with Tresckow on the Eastern Front, shared his liaison with the resistance circle in Berlin. Arrested 1944, tried and finally acquitted, although kept in confinement until the end of the war. His memoirs, published after the war, are a principal source of information.

STAUFFENBERG, Colonel Claus von, Count (1907-44). Chief of Staff to Fromm, Commander of the Reserve Army. Developed Tresckow's Valkyrie plan and became principal instigator of the revolt of the younger generation in the Army. Planted the bomb at Hitler's East Prussian headquarters on 20 July 1944. Executed by Fromm that same night after a summary court-martial.

STUELPNAGEL, Colonel-General Heinrich von (1886-1944). Military Governor in France 1942-44, and the principal instigator of the *coup d'état* in France. Failed in his attempt to commit suicide. Arrested, tried and executed in August 1944.

THOMAS, Colonel-General Georg. Chief of the armaments section of O.K.W. and a member of the resistance. Arrested July 1944. Liberated at the end of the war.

TRESCKOW, Major-General Henning von (1901-44). Chief of Staff in the Central Army Group on the Eastern Front, and a leading member of the resistance among the younger generation in the Army. Initiated the Valkyrie plan for the 1944 *coup d'état*. Committed suicide on 21 July 1944, after its failure.

WITZLEBEN, Field-Marshal Erwin von (1881-1944). Retired from active service in 1942. One of the oldest members of the resistance, he was nominated to become Commander-in-Chief of the German Army after the *coup d'état*. Tried and executed August 1944.

Some principal members of the civilian resistance in touch with Canaris and his associates:

GISEVIUS, Hans Bernd (b. 1903). Trapped in Germany for several months after 20 July 1944. Escaped to Switzerland January 1945. His memoirs are an important source of information about the resistance.

GOERDELER, Carl (1884-1945). Former Mayor of Leipzig and for a while Price Control Commissioner in Hitler's government. From 1937 the principal advocate of resistance among the older generation and a tireless propagandist for a new, government to replace that of Hitler. Arrested August 1944 and executed February 1945.

HASSELL, ULRICH von (1881-1944). Formerly German ambassador in Rome; became with Beck and Goerdeler a leading member of the resistance among the older generation. Arrested 28 July and executed September 1944. His diary is a principal source of information for the resistance from 1938.

JOHN, Otto. Chief of the legal Department of Lufthansa, and a prominent member of the resistance. Escaped by air to Madrid on 24 July 1944, and became a contact of the British Secret Service, travelling to London via Lisbon.

LEBER, Julius (1891-1945). Social Democrat Member of the Reichstag 1924-33. After four years in concentration camps, became from 1937, together with Theodor Haubach, Wilhelm Leuschner and Adolf Reichwein, one of the most important members of the socialist element in the resistance. Was to have been Minister of the Interior after the *coup d'état*. Arrested July 1944; executed 5 January 1945.

MOLTKE, Count Helmuth von (1907-45). The leading figure of the section of the resistance which advocated nonviolence. Head of the so-called Kreisau circle. Tried by Freisler, with whom he staged a battle of words, and executed 24 January 1945.

SCHACHT, Hjalmar (b. 1877). Minister for Economic Affairs for Hitler 1934-37. Minister without Portfolio until 1943. President of the Reichsbank until 1939. In close touch with the resistance; arrested 23 July 1944, but not brought to trial. Survived the war in confinement; later brought to trial and acquitted by the International Military Tribunal at Nuremberg 1945-46.

TROTT zu Solz, Adam von (1909-44). Attached to the Foreign Office, and a close friend of Moltke. Executed August 1944.

Service Abbreviations and Ranks

GESTAPO: the Secret State Police (*Geheime Staatspolizei*).

O.K.H.: High Command of the Army (*Oberkommando des Heeres*).

O.K.W.: High Command of the Armed Forces (*Oberkommando der Wehrmacht*).

S.D.: the Security Service (*Sicherheitsdienst*).

S.S.: literally, Protection Squads, derived from the original duties of this special force (*Schutzstaffeln*).

ARMY RANKS: In the German Army Major-General was the equivalent of a Brigadier-General; the order of seniority then was as follows: Lieutenant-General, General, Colonel-General, Field-Marshal.

INTRODUCTION

Was it Resistance?

Patriots or Traitors: Morality of a Coup d'État

The question is often put: can the resistance inside Nazi
Germany be considered a real resistance movement? The
people who ask this are thinking, naturally enough, about
the forms of resistance which developed in the countries
occupied by Hitler's armies and Himmler's secret police.
They recall courageous acts of sabotage, the networks of
espionage, the tenuous contact maintained through mobile
transmitters, the circulation of clandestine information, the
rescue of Allied servicemen, the constant, often subtle
opposition which the enemy encountered in day-to-day
affairs which stultified the efficient conduct of the occupation. Against this sometimes romanticized image of the
saboteur, darting from cover to cover in the night, his
mission ending successfully with a loud explosion as he
slips back into the darkness, what image has the German
opposition to Hitler to offer. Nothing, say the accusers, but
talk.

To make any direct comparison between the resistance
movement inside Hitler's Germany and those that grow up
outside is to start off on the wrong foot. In the first place,
saboteurs in the occupied countries were patriots; more
than this, they were great patriots, which meant that they
had the right to call on the respect and, when necessary,
the active help of their fellow-countrymen, who were, one
might say, merely inactive patriots. To maintain their
position, all they had to do was avoid contact with the
Germans themselves, avoid known collaborators, and keep
their own counsel as far as possible. But they enjoyed,
broadly speaking, the approval of the general population,
and this was in itself an immense advantage and encourag-

ing to their morale. If they were caught, they became patriot martyrs in the eyes of the majority of their fellow-countrymen.

To be a member of the German opposition inside Nazi Germany was to be, in the first place, a traitor. You could count on the understanding, support and sympathy of none but those whom you were certain shared your views that Hitler was a destroyer, not the creator of a new Germany. The last near-free vote of the German nation which had put Hitler on the central path to absolute power had represented less than half the electorate (43 per cent in March 1933, after Hitler had already become Chancellor). Yet there can be no doubt that the great majority of Germans by 1938—the year of the Munich agreement and a key one in the establishment of Hitler's prestige in his own eyes, in the eyes of the German people and of the world as a whole—saw Hitler as a kind of national savior endowed, according to your beliefs, with God's grace or the kind of luck that sticks. The unorthodox, uncanny skill of the man, and the seeming prosperity he had brought to a nation so recently oppressed by economic difficulty and the national humiliation represented by the Versailles treaty, resolved whatever doubts may have lingered that this visionary with the loud mouth, the bad breath and the support of a dangerous rabble in the streets was unacceptable as the Chancellor of a great nation. By 1938, men and women alike who still dared to oppose the Führer were compelled either to keep their views entirely to themselves, or to express them in whispers among intimate associates who thought as they did.

To enter into any form of organization that sought actively to rid Germany of Hitler meant even as early as 1933 supporting a *coup d'état*. The Enabling Act of March 1933, the so-called "Law for Removing the Distress of People and Reich" which Hitler introduced in the Reichstag after the elections, changed the constitution of Germany and gave him the absolute powers that were to form the legal basis for his tyranny. After this maneuver, no opposing political party had any effective existence: Germany became a one-party state. The only way to oust Hitler from power was to form an underground, secret force with sufficient strength of number and determination to enter his presence and arrest him, at the same time declaring some form of temporary government to replace the authoritarian régime that had become the sole administration in Germany.

Certain aspects of this problem should by now be clear even to the severest critics of the German resistance movement. With the vast majority of the people, military and civilian alike, holding their tyrant to be their hero, the aftermath to any overthrow of Hitler needed the most careful pre-planning. Trusted men must be ready to step into the breach, men who could quickly and effectively call the nation to order and reason after announcing the sudden disappearance of the leader who had hypnotized a substantial part of the German nation into a state of abject adulation.

To dismiss a régime which, after February 1933, had infiltrated its supporters into positions of power in the public administration with such ruthless efficiency, was not simply a matter of removing Hitler; it was a matter of being in a position suddenly to supplant the top men of his administration (Göring, Goebbels, Himmler, Ribbentrop, Heydrich, at the very least) at the same time as Hitler himself, and place them beyond the immediate reach of their supporters. And it must all be done without the slightest hitch within a matter of hours. Surprise, of course, was essential.

It was for this reason that organized opposition to Hitler had to be concentrated within the Army. The Army was the only active force left in Germany not actually created by the Nazis, or fully infiltrated by them. However, it is also true that the Army hierarchy came directly under Hitler's control; immediately on the death of President Hindenburg in August 1934, Hitler created himself Head of State and Supreme Commander-in-Chief of the Armed Forces of the Reich. The constitutional offices of President and Chancellor were thus simultaneously merged and abolished.

But the Army was to remain a constant source of

anxiety to Hitler. His initial power had stemmed not from the Army but from the mass of unemployed men whom he had clothed in brown shirts and turned into violent gangs of demonstrators marching the streets, browbeating all opposition, and supplying millions of votes at the polls. Once in power, Hitler recognized that his new-found prestige could no longer brook such unseemly support. Accordingly, after 30 June 1934, the so-called night of the long knives when many of the S.A. Stormtrooper leaders were arrested and executed, the S.A. brownshirts lost significance. Nevertheless the established, armed forces of the State had to be absorbed into Hitler's service, since the State and he were now, in his own eyes and those of many Germans, one and the same. But any partnership between Hitler, the divine corporal, and the Army hierarchy, product for the most part of an extreme and often aristocratic right-wing school, could only be uneasy. In these forces, therefore, lay what hopes there might be for discovering the men to lead an effective *coup d'état.*

Hitler, of course, knew this, and with typical psychological acuity, imposed on every man in uniform an oath of personal loyalty to himself. On the very day he became Head of State, the Führer and Supreme Commander-in-Chief of the Armed Forces, every man in uniform, from field-marshal to private soldier, was required without prior warning solemnly to swear this oath:

'I swear by God this holy oath: I will render unconditional obedience to the Führer of the German Reich and People, Adolf Hitler, the Supreme Commander of the Armed Forces, and will be ready, as a brave soldier, to stake my life at any time to this oath.'

This astute move by Hitler was to prove a constant embarrassment to those who sought means to overthrow the Leader to whom every man they approached, unless he were a civilian, was under so direct an oath of personal allegiance.

The very people on whom the opposition placed its greatest dependence were men with a highly developed moral sense, men who for the most part, either as Catholics or Protestants, held traditional Christian beliefs. It will be necessary later to describe in some detail the very varied and interesting characters of the leading members of the complex German resistance; for the moment it is sufficient to mention only a few in this particular connection. Within the Army, the titular head of the opposition from 1938 to the collapse in 1944 was Colonel-General Ludwig Beck, a staff officer of the highest principles who, as Chief of the Army General Staff, openly opposed Hitler to his face over his plans for aggression, and resigned his position in August 1938 as an act of protest. He was a devout Christian and a Protestant. Closely associated with Beck was Admiral Wilhelm Canaris, who as Chief of Military Intelligence (the Abwehr) from 1935 to 1944, centralized opposition within the Army after Beck's retirement largely through the activities of his two closest colleagues, Major-General Hans Oster, his Chief of Staff, who was to be suspended from duty in April 1943, and a brilliant young civilian recruit from the Ministry of Justice, the lawyer Dr. Hans von Dohnanyi. All three were traditionally-minded, practicing Christians and Protestants, though Canaris and Oster were also, in their different ways, men of the world compared with the more strictly moral Beck and Dohnanyi. Dohnanyi was the brother-in-law of the distinguished Protestant pastor Dietrich Bonhoeffer, all the more a dedicated Christian because of his fresh and unorthodox approach to his faith. On the other hand, the man who struck the final blow for the opposition against Hitler, the gallant and phenomenally brave young officer Colonel Count Claus von Stauffenberg, bearer of the bomb on 20 July 1944, was a devout Catholic. Major-General Henning von Tresckow, the man who led the opposition within the armies of the Eastern Front and who made an earlier attempt on Hitler's life with a time-bomb, was another Christian idealist, and so was Colonel-General Heinrich von Stuelpnagel, later to become leader of the revolt in the German Army on the Western Front in France, and, in effect, the man who came nearest to achieving a successful *coup d'état* against Hitler in July 1944.

Yet the very nobility of spirit in most, if not all, of these highly-placed officers and civilians, their idealism and their Christian beliefs and background, lessened their effectiveness as conspirators. It has often been said that the worst thing about Nazism was that it required Nazi methods to destroy it. For the most part they approached their fearful task as idealists seeking to restore the lost honor of their country and not as realists seeking the most practical means of overthrowing Hitler, whatever these might be. For instance, the older generation of conspirators—for this is what the resistance men were in Nazi Germany— were for long staunchly against undertaking the assassination of Hitler. It may seem much clearer to us now that to have a group of senior officers attempt his arrest in 1938 and then conduct his trial in public was, to say the least, impractical. Whether the German people wanted war or not, Hitler was an unorthodox diplomat who had got his own way both in the Rhineland and in Austria, and was soon to do so again in the Sudetan territory, without a scratch on a soldier's face. It appeared, therefore, that all the trump cards of diplomacy were in his hand.

The younger generation, represented by Tresckow and Stauffenberg, realized from the start that Hitler had to be assassinated, but their influence in resistance circles did not mature until the war was well advanced and Hitler, never easy for a killer to reach, became even less accessible for either bullet, bomb, knife or poison. Only much later were the older officers in the resistance persuaded that Hitler was not only leading his country to destruction, but was, from the Christian point of view, a kind of devil or anti-Christ, and that the only way to dispose of him, and of his closest followers, was to kill them. But destroying Hitler necessitated forming in advance a temporary form of government consisting of well-known military and civilian personalities whom it was to be hoped the German people, stunned by the sudden loss of their leader, would be prepared to trust.

It becomes readily apparent, then, that the conspirators

in Germany were inhibited, both morally and physically, in a way members of the resistance in the occupied territories were not. In the latter situation the immediate appeal for action was self-evident, and resistance workers did not necessarily have to be idealists to undertake their tasks. Many, indeed, were the very opposite, enjoying the excitement and the violence for its own sake. Anyone joining the resistance in Germany had to go through a painful searching of conscience, determining whether he or she was right to take action against the acknowledged leader of their country. And, if this potential conspirator was in uniform, there was the additional burden to his conscience that he was an *Eidträger* (an 'oath-bearer'), a person who had sworn his individual loyalty to the person of the Führer.

Opposition to Hitler inside Germany took many forms, and existed (as it were) on different levels. There were, undoubtedly, large numbers of men and women who were, as they put it afterwards, 'never Nazis;' however, their opposition amounted to little more than silence and turning an expediently blind eye to anything they might have seen happening which they disliked. They did what they had to do, joined what they had to join, but no more; paid lip service to the régime when they had to do so, but no more. On this plane, according to the degree of your conviction that Hitler was bad for Germany and, of course, the quality of your personal courage, you could withdraw from participation in the universal shout in Hitler's favor and the hard work he exacted once the shouting was through. On the next plane you might begin to show positive opposition, if only by grumbling, voicing criticism (when you dared), and taking as little part as possible in any activity which advanced the cause of Nazism, making "I was never a Nazi" a more or less genuine statement of fact. But only when this led to some form of active demonstration—helping a Jew escape, for instance—did opposition begin to take a truly courageous form. On this level, many people indulged in sporadic public opposition—like the united and ultimately successful opposition of the churches in 1941 to Hitler's disposal of the mentally sick through euthanasia, or the brave German women who demonstrated outside the Moabit prison in 1943 because their Jewish husbands had been arrested.

Individual acts of heroism were, of course, numerous and people of all ages and classes, political backgrounds and beliefs indulged in them as their gesture towards the common good. They usually ended up in prison, in the concentration camps, or at best as cannonfodder on the Eastern Front. Over 21,000 Germans, mostly working-class, were held in the camps before the war, and the numbers were more than doubled by 1942. Only a few highly-placed people whom even the Nazis dared not touch remained at large after any kind of public denunciation of Hitler's works. Such were Bishop Count von Galen, and Michael Faulhaber, Cardinal Archbishop of Bavaria, who preached against Nazi anti-Semitism in 1935.

Important as every individual gesture was to the credit of Germany during this darkest period of her recent history, the only practical thing to do to get rid of Hitler was to plan organized opposition underground and in secret. Whatever the measure of his courage, no individual civilian could achieve a *coup d'état*. From 1939, a bare six years after Hitler's first emergence to power, Nazi Germany was a vast armed camp infiltrated by the secret, political police on the watch for any kind of opposition, let alone active insurrection. The more practical of the civilian leaders, therefore, could only turn to the Army, though their disillusionment grew as the general sank more and more under Hitler's thumb.

Not least of the difficulties for the opposition was the constantly recurring problem of the sudden dismissal, removal or re-assignment of generals throughout the war. This meant that every potential network for action which the conspirators managed to contrive was, like a spider's web, constantly being torn apart and as constantly rewoven. It must often have seemed an all but hopeless task; influential field-marshals and generals who seemed at one moment to be warming to the conspirators' approaches became cold at the next, and no longer wanted to know them. Such in particular was Field-Marshal Guenther von

Kluge, Commander on the Eastern front at the time of Tresckow's bomb attempt in 1943, and Army Group Commander in France at the time of Stauffenberg's attempt in July 1944.

The Opposition Leaders and the Gestapo

The principal civilian conspirators, men like Dr. Karl Goerdeler, the former Mayor of Leipzig, and Ulrich von Hassell, the former German ambassador in Italy, were, therefore, primarily concerned with keeping the influential military men of their acquaintance involved in the coming *coup d'état*. More often than not, they met with resistance of a kind directly opposite to that which they sought. Even those field-marshals and generals who were convinced by 1943 that the war they were conducting on Hitler's behalf must inevitably lead to disaster were loath to risk their lives, their careers, their honors, their rewards by taking a stand against the Führer. The biggest concession they were prepared to make was to be considered a friend of the conspirators once Hitler had fallen; until such time as that happened they wanted as little direct connection with the conspiracy as possible. Their interest was a form of status-insurance against future developments. The relatively decent men among them, such as Kluge, often seemed on the verge of joining in wholeheartedly. On the other hand, the less decent, such as Colonel-General Fritz Fromm, Commander-in-Chief of the Reserve Army based in Germany and Stauffenberg's superior officer at the time of the July plot, were entirely opportunist, and ready to turn savagely against the conspirators the moment they realized that Hitler was not dead. Neither Fromm nor Kluge, however, were to escape Hitler's all-embracing wrath during the punitive trials of autumn 1944.

The leaders of the civilian wing of the conspirators were as idealistic as their military colleagues. Goerdeler, brave to the point of constant indiscretion, stumped the country working on the consciences of influential civilians and generals alike to bring them into line and keep them there. He was the gad-fly of the conspiracy, while Hassell was its committee man. Each acted according to his opportunities and, above all, his individual temperament. Goerdeler, part evangelist and part agitator, could keep neither his mouth shut nor his pen dry. Hassell kept careful watch, and as carefully a record in his celebrated diary, of how each man was blowing now hot, now cold. With Canaris and Beck (a civilian himself from September 1938) at the center of the spider's web, Hassell worked in the shadows to keep everything as much in order as possible, as calm as Goerdeler was excitable. He kept in touch, too, with the outer fringe of the civilian movement, with the distinguished and scholarly members of the so-called Kreisau circle led by Count Helmuth von Moltke, whose estate at Kreisau was the setting for many a wartime discussion on how to achieve a peace. Here the courageous, gentlemanly Anglophiles gathered, including Count Peter Yorck von Wartenburg and the former Rhodes scholar Adam von Trott zu Solz. Their views were initially pacifist; they had done what they could to warn the British of Hitler's impending war during the years preceding 1939. But for the most part they were not in favor of using any form of violence against Hitler, and would never, again on Christian principle, have approved of murdering him.

It may well be wondered by this time how the active conspirators managed to get away with their clandestine activities. What were the Gestapo doing? There was the ubiquitous Goerdeler, openly talking to everyone he could reach about the need to overthrow (but not to assassinate) Hitler; there was Hassell, known to be against the régime, but allowed to move about freely, though he was never to be given another embassy; there was Beck, a sick man from the early years of the war, confined to the shadows of his house on the outskirts of Berlin, constantly being visited by men under one form or another of suspicion; there was Canaris, the most competent head of the Army's Intelligence service, but always cynically ambivalent in the views he expressed and so openly disheartened about the way the war was going that he seemed to be declining into melancholia; there were Oster and Stauffenberg, neither of whom took too much heed of discretion, and who both said what they thought with little care who heard them, at least in more or less sympathetic Army circles. The camaraderie among the Army officers was such that only that minority fanatically devoted to Hitler would think of betraying those who complained about him or spoke even more directly against him. Everyone who thought at all realized that the régime, however firmly established, was a power conspiracy, and that a palace revolution if not an Army *coup* might one day change the situation. If you were not yourself involved in politics, then the thing to do was to keep right out of them. It was only inviting trouble to get involved. "No comment" was the right attitude to adopt. This situation favored the conspirators and kept them remarkably free from actual betrayal by fellow-officers.

This would not explain, however, the seeming inactivity of the Gestapo. The answer lies in their realistic acceptance of the fact there would be dissidents and that it would pay not to pull in those they knew about until they had served their turn and led to the discovery of others about whom the police as yet knew nothing. Exact timing was an accepted part of Gestapo technique. An important man was never arrested until absolutely necessary; to do so would be to place possibly more important individuals on their guard. So long as the danger they represented was remote to Hitler and the régime they were better left at large, though kept under careful surveillance. They could be arrested individually whenever the appropriate moment came. Meanwhile, the dossier against them grew. For example, the Gestapo knew much about Goerdeler. But they had no suspicion about Canaris until 1944; like themselves, Canaris was a professional. In any case, he was in the Army, and it is important to realize that technically the Gestapo had no jurisdiction over men in uniform. They merely reported any supicions they had to the military authorities—and this, as it happened, meant reporting to Canaris himself. Accordingly, as far as Beck, Goerdeler, Hassell and their many civilian associates were concerned, the Gestapo played a game of cat and mouse. The first to fall victim to the vagaries of the Gestapo's methods were Dohnanyi and Bonhoeffer in 1943, and this only happened as a result of a roundabout chain of information concerning minor currency offences commiteed by an associate of their colleague in Munich, Dr. Josef Müller, himself a dedicated member of the resistance.

One of the most absorbing of the many curious situations in this bizarre period of history was the fact that Canaris, for six years at the very center of the conspiracy to remove Hitler, should ultimately be matched against Himmler, like himself a man of complex and ambivalent temperament. Each knew the other comparatively well, each sat at the head of a complex network of Intelligence, each kept a dossier about the other, and about the other's principal associates. The patiently negotiated agreements about the mutual functioning of their two parallel, secret departments were with equal care broken when it suited either of them to do so. Both were men of considerable ability, but inclined to prefer the shadows to the full light of day. Both worried themselves into ill-health, and were subject to prolonged bouts of depression. Both liked power, but preferred to manipulate events through the activities of other, and subordinate, people.

Canaris's particular ambivalence stemmed from a nature that enjoyed intrigue for its own sake and a brain having the kind of intelligence that favored out-maneuvering an enemy rather than confronting him. Canaris was a man of undoubted courage, but he had a deep distaste for violence. It sickened him physically, just as the bloodshed in the concentration camps sickened Himmler. Each loved his country with a special kind of patriotism—Canaris from a traditional, right-wing point of view that regarded Hitler as a destroyer, not a savior, who must at all costs (even violence) be removed; Himmler from the point of view of a racial fanatic, who wanted above all things to see Germany become the central power in a puritan racial block that could eventually rule the world. The difference between them was that Canaris had to keep his pessimistic views more or less to himself and his inner circle of supporters, whereas Himmler was free to preach his bogus idealism to any audience he could induce to listen to him—though he only caused somewhat cynical amusement among Nazis content to have Hitler as master of Europe with plenty of good living for the master-race, pure and impure alike. When it came to direct action, however, neither Canaris nor Himmler was in his element. Himmler was almost pathologically incapable of taking hard decisions; unlike Heydrich, until his assassination in 1942 virtually Himmler's second-in-command and his principal man of action, Himmler always hedged in his efforts to leave loopholes open. Perhaps it was for this reason that at one stage his wavering orbit and that of the conspirators were on the point of crossing. There was to be a brief period when certain of them were deluded enough to think they might induce Himmler to join them.

The status of the organized resistance against Hitler was a perfectly genuine one. A case could even be made that their level of courage was the highest of all, for they faced day by day, week by week, year by year, the hourly danger of betrayal in a society that would, for the most part, have been appalled by what they were planning to do because, in law, as it then existed, they were manifest traitors, not patriots. In the eyes of many Germans today, Stauffenberg, the supreme hero of the German resistance, still remains a traitor because he sought to kill the head of State to whom he had sworn an oath of personal loyalty.

The German resistance, in fact, unlike that of any country occupied by Hitler, had to justify its actions in terms of a higher patriotism, and, if its members were in the armed services, to rationalize their position in relation to the oath which, they could maintain, had been forced upon them against their will under conditions of a mass ritual they were powerless to avoid without being at once court-martialled and shot. On the other hand, those whose feelings were weak could hide behind this oath and do nothing. Correspondingly, the number of active supporters of organized resistance, both military and civilian, though by no means negligible, was necessarily far smaller than in the resistance groups in the occupied countries where, from the strictly patriotic point of view, everyone should have belonged. To judge by the military executions, the active opposition in Germany amounted to some hundreds, though among those brought to Nazi "justice" were many who openly opposed Hitler as individuals, or as isolated groups like that centred round Frau Anna Solf in Berlin, and so were not linked directly to the centralized resistance for which Department Z, the central office of the Abwehr, Canaris's Military Intelligence, was the focal point.

The Army, in fact, remained throughout the war the center for active, planned resistance with which the equally active civilian wing worked closely when it could. We can recognize a number of peak moments when a *coup d'état* seemed imminent—in 1938 before the Munich agreement, in 1940 during the period of the so-called phony war, in 1943 on the Eastern Front, and finally in 1944, with its tragic climax to the bomb-plot of 20 July. After this, all the principal members of the resistance were either dead, under arrest, or gone to earth.

Special Problems of Resistance in Nazi Germany

The charge so often levelled that they did nothing but talk is therefore grossly unfair. Within the limits open to them, one or another section of the inner circle was almost ceaselessly active. There were not many of them at the top; they were, more especially the civilians, under sur-veillance in the latter months and years. If they were in the Army, they had their normal duties to perform as a cover for their more earnest activities. They were subject to a long series of setbacks which were not of their making —Hitler's constant shuffling of his generals and other im-portant officers whose ears, at least, they had gained; the grave difficulty of finding supremely courageous men pre-pared to undertake suicide or near-suicide missions who at the same time had to have access to Hitler's secluded person as the essential qualification for their task; the lack of any support, formal or informal, from the Allied gov-ernments to help them maintain morale and convince the doubters and waverers that the removal of Hitler would lead to a somewhat more favorable peace than could be expected while he remained in power.

Hitler, of course, was fully aware of his own vulnerability and made an assassin's task as difficult as possible. The conspirators did not draw together effectively until 1938, the year in which Hitler began to absent himself from public life and surround himself with spiritless yes-men among whom they would look in vain for collaborators. When Hitler travelled, he seldom moved by a set route or at a set time; for long periods he lived almost inaccessibly in the Chancellery, in his mountain fastness at Berchtesgaden, or, when the Eastern Front opened up, in his various closely-guarded headquarters. None of the key resistance people had regular, direct access to Hitler—except Beck for a very limited period at the beginning of the organized conspiracy in 1938, and Stauffenberg on occasions at the end, in the summer of 1944. Therefore the conspirators were reduced to trying to discover chinks in Hitler's security measures, and inserting whatever would-be assassin they had available into one or other of those chinks. It seemed a hopeless task until, during 1943-4, the captured British time-bombs, with their completely silent fuses, offered new opportunities for a man with steady nerves who could gain admittance to Hitler's staff conferences. This is how Stauffenberg came to be chosen.

In spite of these manifold difficulties and dangers, between 1938 and 1940 a series of definite moves towards a *coup d'état* were in turn set up and in turn frustrated either by sudden changes in circumstance or by the reluctance of the generals, while subsequently, between 1942 and 1944, a series of definite assassination attempts were prepared and carried to the point of actual execution either by means of suicide missions or by means of time-bombs. At the same time, a reasonably effective emergency government had been prepared. Given the backing of a sufficient number of senior officers had Hitler suddenly been killed, there seems no reason to doubt that this government would have been capable of taking temporary control of Germany. But, by an act of sheer chance, Hitler was not killed when the bomb exploded near him on 20 July, and in consequence support for the conspirators quite naturally faded almost instantly. The key men in the resistance died for what they had planned to do but failed to carry out, and their deaths should be recognized as the martyrdom of true patriots.

Nevertheless, it would be foolish not to recognize the internal weaknesses in the German resistance movement, which set itself this almost impossible task. Though there can be no doubt of the high courage and idealism of this small, inner circle of conspirators, of men such as Beck, Canaris, Oster, Dohnanyi, Stuelpnagel, Tresckow, Schlabrendorff, and above all Stauffenberg, they were forced to rely far too much on generals and officers who actually had fighting men at their command and, for one reason or another, they failed to secure the unswerving loyalty of any high-placed officer in this position. This made their plans for a *coup d'état* too directly dependent on imponderables, and on the indifferent loyalty of very secondary and undedicated men who were only prepared to join them if they proved successful. At the same time, they seem to have failed to recognize their own personal weaknesses, though Hassell's diary is full of such comment. Stauffenberg was undoubtedly a man of action who had seen recent active service, but he was also a badly wounded man and a staff officer at the time of his closest association with the conspiracy. The rest were mainly staff officers whose abilities lay in traditional forms of organization rather than in imaginative leadership or the ability to improvise necessary action on the spot. Their fault lay in meticulous over-planning, which lacked flexibility when circumstances did not mature as expected, and when luck turned against them in matters of detail. Beck during 1943-4 was a sick man in his mid-sixties, recovering from an operation for cancer of the stomach, yet ultimate decisions were still allowed to rest on his shoulders. Canaris, in semi-retirement, Oster in disgrace, Dohnanyi in prison were all a sad loss when the final attempt was made in July 1944. Stauffenberg and his close associate, General Olbricht seem to have thought they could conduct by themselves on the telephone the troop movements of the entire *coup d'état*.

There is something of the quality of high tragedy in the action of this inner corps of the German Army resistance, something that calls to mind Shakespeare's *Julius Caesar* and *Hamlet*. The conspirators appear to 'talk' more than they 'do'; as in the case of *Hamlet*; their continuous attempts at action remain overlooked since they were unsuccessful in achieving their most difficult object, the removal of a tyrant. Hamlet finally succeeds in his fatal mission only when his own death is certain; this consolation was denied to Beck and Stauffenberg. Though the conspirators in *Julius Caesar* were entirely successful in their main object, the assassination of Caesar, they, like the conspirators in Germany, were quite unprepared to cope with its aftermath when things did not turn out as they had been planned. There is more than a little of Brutus's unadaptable nobility of character in Beck; he was a philosopher and strategist who lacked the formidable personality of a great leader. The conspirators in Germany became tragic figures because, with the noblest of intentions, they undertook more than their small numbers proved capable of handling. When sheer bad luck frustrated their final, most nearly successful attempt, their resources immediately gave out, and they fell before the overwhelming counter-attack of the tyrant.

Their story is, therefore, one of the greatest interest and importance, psychological as well as historical. It is the story of action conducted doggedly over a period of years in the face of constant rebuff and frustration; and action which immediately was frequently misjudged. Many human weaknesses infiltrate the courage of the conspirators, their pertinacity and extraordinary capacity for unselfish dedication. Their mistakes were made through lack of foresight and imagination, through fool-hardiness and over-confidence, through inability really to understand the depravity of their enemies. They seem, also, to have disregarded, for the most part, the special problems arising out of the need for close co-operation between men of widely differing background and temperament, age and seniority, the dangers of betrayal that came from the neglect of small details. On the other hand, their critics should understand better the moral anguish of men of conscience faced with the need to commit treason and murder for a concept of patriotism the vast majority of their countrymen would not have been prepared either to understand or recognize. All these issues lie behind the story of the Canaris conspiracy, the continuous web of planning and frustrated action which came on a number of occasions nearer to achieving the longed-for *coup d'état* than is usually credited.

PART ONE

I

Focal Point for Conspiracy

The First Alliance: Canaris and Oster

It was January 1935 that Wilhelm Canaris first took his place at the modest desk reserved at that time for the head of German Military Intelligence. He was pleased and excited that at the age of forty-seven he had been so unexpectedly entrusted with this new work. It was very different from what he had been doing in recent years, and it could offer him unlimited scope for his particular skills and fertile imagination. He had been lifted out of the relative backwater of his command at Swinemünde and placed at the very heart of the nation's renewed activity under Hitler. And, to sweeten him still further, he had been promoted. He was now Rear-Admiral.

At Swinemünde Canaris had considered himself in the final phase of his career. This naval base was normally a pre-retirement post, an important but uneventful establishment for a respected senior man. While he was there, Canaris may well have regretted the lost excitements of his youth. Although he hated violence, he had nevertheless always been involved in extraordinary events, and had played some part in a number of strange episodes both during and after the war. He had worked in wartime Naval Intelligence; he had acted as a spy; he had even been accused of involvement in revolution and political murder. This was nothing compared with what was soon to come. But it was enough to make this small, volatile man from Swinemünde, with his love of books and music and solitary riding on horseback, his charm, his occasional melancholy, his ready turn of brilliant conversation and his even greater

37

readiness to listen, the kind of person people talk about.

He was born on 1 January 1887 at Aplerbeck, near Dortmund in Westphalia. The son of an industrialist in the Ruhr, he was used to the comfort of a large house and garden, and he had learned as a boy to play tennis and ride, relaxations to which in maturity he was always to turn for relief when he found the pressures closing in on him more than he could bear. He loved his horses and his dogs. Although his family had a Catholic background, they were now in fact Protestants, and Canaris at one stage in his later life attended Pastor Niemöller's church in Dahlem.

In politics Canaris had been brought up, and remained, a liberal of the right, which meant that he was, and remained, strongly anti-socialist. From his earliest youth he was always a patriot and a monarchist. Although there was no military tradition in the family, he had wanted when only a boy to join the Imperial Navy as an officer cadet. This his father opposed, but on his death in 1904 at the early age of fifty-two, Canaris prevailed on his mother to let him serve in Kiel as a cadet, and his period of training began there in April 1905. It is clear that at least one of the reasons which had attracted him to a career in the German Navy was the escape it represented from a life spent in industry. His nervous, restless disposition, which was to develop in him with age, undoubtedly influenced him too. Canaris always wanted to be on the move.

Although the family had lived in Germany for at least two centuries, young Canaris liked to think that his unusual name was of Mediterranean, perhaps Italian, origin. The family had in fact originated in Lombardy, but it amused Canaris when people assumed he was connected with the celebrated Greek admiral Konstantin Kanaris who had played so great a part in the War of Independence for his country during the previous century. This romantic streak in Canaris's nature survived in his maturity, and made him always take pleasure in the idea of travelling into the Mediterranean sunshine. The southern parts of Europe were his spiritual home; Paul Leverkuehn, who joined the Abwehr during the war, claimed that Canaris was always shivering even in the heat of the summer in Ber-

38

lin, and wore his greatcoat everywhere. He was a very small man, only five foot three inches in height, and had no objection to being known as the little Levantine.

By the beginning of the First World War Canaris was twenty-seven years old and serving as flag lieutenant and Intelligence officer on the cruiser *Dresden,* the battleship which under Captain Lüdecke distinguished itself during the celebrated naval action off the Falkland Islands. Canaris was by now fluent in Spanish and could also speak tolerable English; he had become something of a student of Latin-American affairs, knowledge which was to prove most useful. The *Dresden* was the only ship in the Graf von Spee's squadron to escape from the punitive expedition sent by Winston Churchill, as First Lord of the British Admiralty, to avenge the initial victory of the German naval forces over those of the British of Coronel, Chile, in November 1914. In December von Spee was caught off the Falkland Islands and his squadron, except the *Dresden,* sunk. The ship on which Canaris was serving managed to slip away in the mist and refuel off Punta Arenas before passing through the Straits of Magellan and hiding in the numerous inlets along the Chilean coast. Here, following many conflicting reports of her position which may well have originated from Canaris, she was pursued by the cruisers *Glasgow* and *Kent,* which did not finally fetch up with her until March 1915. It was Canaris, his reputation for wily diplomacy already well established in the ship, who was sent by Lüdecke to parley with the British. Faced with a demand for unconditional surrender, Lüdecke scuttled his ship and allowed the internment of his officers and crew. Canaris, resourceful as ever, escaped internment on the island of Quiriquina in Chile, obtained for himself a Chilean passport and, posing as a businessman called Rosas, sailed for Europe and eventually reached Holland. From there he made his way to Germany in the spring of 1916.[1]

Later Canaris served for a while in Madrid, collecting together intelligence information concerning the movements of ships for the naval attaché at the German Embassy, an officer called von Krohn. He had been landed in Spain by a German submarine and while there he continued to use his Chilean passport and identity. According to Colonel Friedrich Wilhelm Heinz, one of his associates during the Second World War, Canaris had some acquaintance with Mata Hari in Madrid. He told Colonel Heinz that this woman was a complete failure, and that espionage in the twentieth century needed greater technical qualifications than mere glamour.[2] Canaris also went on a mission to Italy, where he was arrested by the Italians on suspicion of being a German spy. So, for the benefit of the Italians, he posed as a tubercular patient on his way to a Swiss sanatorium. He would bite his lip hard in order to spit blood convincingly. Finally, through the intervention of Spanish friends he travelled back to Spain and, it seems at his own request, returned by submarine to Germany in order to take up more active service. Experienced by now in underwater travel, he secured himself the command of a U-boat. He saw comparatively little action while serving in Mediterranean waters and, returning home in time to avoid taking part in the German naval mutiny, immediately undertook special anti-Communist activities for the *Reichswehr,* or German Army, with the various nationalist movements, including the *Freikorps* commandos.[3]

Although Canaris was involved in what came to be known as the *Kapp Putsch* against the Weimar Republic in March 1920, he managed to avoid dismissal and ended up in 1922 as a first lieutenant on the training cruiser, the *Berlin*; it was here that he met and befriended a young naval cadet, Reinhard Heydrich. For Heydrich, like Canaris, Intelligence work was later to become one of the dangers in his life.

Everything which has come to light about Canaris's career expresses directly his personal character. On the one hand he was active, astute, volatile, highly intelligent and insatiably curious, with a pronounced sense of humor which illuminated all these other aspects of his nature. It amused as well as absorbed him to undertake the devious things which his duties thrust upon him. In his own particular way he was outstandingly courageous, provided he

40

was convinced what he was doing was right; otherwise, he quickly became nervous, preoccupied by doubts and persistently evasive. In appearance he grew kindly, even benevolent, with age, his complexion rubicund but youthful, though his hair became prematurely white. With the war disposed of, in November 1919 he married Erika Waag, the daughter of an industrialist. He was never to lack the money to maintain a comfortable and cultured life at home. Frau Canaris enjoyed playing the violin and was later in the habit of inviting that handsome young naval officer, Lieutenant Reinhard Heydrich, to join her string quartet.

Canaris quietly prospered. He had suffered a brief, difficult period in 1926 when, during the Reichstag Commission of Inquiry into the conduct of the war, an attempt was made to associate him with the murder in 1919 of the socialist leaders Karl Liebknecht and Rosa Luxemburg.[4] It was alleged that he had helped the murderers to escape by issuing them with false passports. Canaris's way with any accusation was always to evade the issue adroitly, smile in such a way as to be considered enigmatic, and then pass by quietly on the other side. So eventually nothing happened to hinder his modest progress: in 1924, staff officer in the German Admiralty on frequent and very welcome missions to sunny Spain; in 1928, first-lieutenant on the *Schlesien*; in 1929, promoted commander; from 1930-2, Chief of Staff, North Sea Naval Base; and in 1932, captain of the *Schlesien*. In 1933 he received Hitler, as the new German Chancellor, on board his ship; soon afterwards he was made commander of the naval base at Swinemünde. It was from here that he finally moved in January 1935 to take charge of the *Abwehr,* the Military Intelligence Service, a section of the Ministry of War.[5]

The man immediately responsible for this entirely new development in Canaris's career was the retiring head of the Abwehr service, Captain (later Admiral) Conrad Patzig, who had been a former colleague of Canaris. Patzig's position was somewhat delicate. The Abwehr, a relatively small department at this time (its initial annual budget was a mere 100,000 marks) was nevertheless one of growing

41

military importance. Patzig, like Canaris a career naval officer, had been in charge only a few months. He was unable to see eye to eye with the new kind of men he found moving into the business of Intelligence in departments elsewhere in the service—in particular the rapidly increasing staff of that renegade Heydrich. Now, emerging as the head of security for Himmler's S.S., Heydrich was boasting of fresh powers which not only rivalled those of the traditional Intelligence service, but even threatened to supplant them. Patzig, anxious to return to active service, because of his inability to practice the diplomacy required of him, put forward Canaris's name to his naval superiors, the Grand Admirals Raeder and Doenitz. He recognized in Canaris the kind of man who would best know how to handle the situation to the advantage of the naval authorities, who were naturally concerned to keep this small but influential department within the branch of the Armed Services, more especially since Patzig's predecessor had been an Army man. The Abwehr, in any case, had originated with the Navy after the First World War. The fact that Canaris had at some time been friendly with Heydrich might, in the circumstances now prevailing, prove most opportune. Raeder and Doenitz were forced to agree that Canaris seemed hand-picked for the job. Patzig, about whom the admirals had received many complaints from Himmler that he was uncooperative, retired happily to take command of a battle cruiser. It was work much more to his taste.

When in 1935 Canaris, as a rear-admiral, took charge of the Abwehr, he was a nationalist fully prepared to see in Hitler a firm and even a desirable head of State. The photograph of Hitler as Chancellor coming aboard the *Schlesien* hung on the walls of Canaris's home in Berlin. To Hitler there was little doubt that Canaris, a noted anti-Bolshevist and former supporter of the Freikorps, should appear especially suitable to handle Intelligence. To Werner von Blomberg, the Commander-in-Chief of the Armed Forces, the new head of the Abwehr had appeared an "untransparent character," but he accepted Raeder's recommendation because he wanted to be rid of Patzig. So on 5 January Canaris took charge of the Abwehr offices, Numbers 74-76 on the Tirpitz Ufer in Berlin. His ambitions were now to be fully stretched. He was forty-seven.

When Canaris took over, the Abwehr organization was small and simple. There were three main departments: the first collected information through appointed agents, both German and non-German, in foreign parts; the second was concerned with sabotage; the third conducted counterespionage in Germany itself. The Abwehr was, moreover, in the fortunate position that it did not have to report direct to Hitler, but only to the various Service chiefs. In addition, military Intelligence had the responsibility of supervising all foreign military attachés on the staff of embassies in Berlin and acting in liaison with the German military attachés serving abroad.

It was not long, however, before Canaris's new work brought him into direct contact with Hitler. He soon discovered, too, that his particular manner, unemphatic and suave, suited the needs of Hitler's demanding moodiness. Canaris was a born listener; observation was a necessary part of his technique. Hitler, a compulsive talker, always wanted a good listener. Before long Canaris became one of the men Hitler used as an occasional adviser. He trusted him, and soon encouraged him to increase the size and scope of his department.

Hans Oster

When Canaris, lifted so suddenly from the backwaters of Swinemünde, found himself placed at the very heart of affairs, he was quick to learn. Being a man who combined his curiosity with a natural diplomacy, Intelligence work suited him far better than physical action. But he stood in need of a senior colleague who possessed the temperament of a man of action. This colleague he found in Colonel (later, in 1943, Major-General) Hans Oster, who became his effective (though not official) deputy at the Abwehr. When the department was enlarged under Canaris at the beginning of the war, Oster became officially head of the

43

Central Office (*Zentralabteilung*), known quite simply as Department Z.

Oster had already been in the Abwher for over a year. Born in 1888, the son of a Protestant pastor, he had served in the First World War and had stayed in the Army during the Weimar Republic. A cavalry officer, Oster had been dismissed the service in December 1932 following a "scandalous" love affair with the wife of a prominent officer. But with the support of General Halder he had been reinstated and appointed to the Abwehr, where he had first served under Patzig's predecessor, Major-General Kurt von Bredow, a victim of the Roehm bloodbath in 1934. Von Bredow's death alone would have been enough to turn Oster against the Nazis, had this in any case been necessary, which it was not. Oster had been repelled from the start by the ruthlessness of the régime, and he was convinced that the Army would become contaminated by the continued existence of the S.S. and the brownshirts.

Though thin and pale, Oster was strikingly handsome, wore elegant uniforms, used a monocle, and was always gallant and responsive to the ladies. Politically he was right-wing, a dedicated monarchist and, for this reason, among others, opposed from the first to the Hitler régime. He always felt more closely bound by his original oath of loyalty to the Kaiser than he ever felt bound by oath to Hitler. Some people found him cold, even arrogant, and mannered in his speech to the point of over-refinement.

Oster was only a year younger than his new chief. Unlike Canaris, he lacked natural guile or any proper sense of caution; his courage was of a quite different order. Volatile and active, Oster took a quick, almost light-headed delight in reaching decisions. He was a rash and pleasure-loving man, delighting in elegant living, society women and riding his horses. He was always cheerful and seldom set back by the endless frustrations which resistance was to bring. But he was sometimes indiscreet about his opinions, thinking that his scathing references to "Emil," his name for Hitler, would pass unnoticed by his political enemies.

During the years following 1935, and especially in 1938

when, as we shall see, the crisis in the High Command became acute over the Blomberg and Fritsch affairs, Canaris's opposition to Hitler hardened, and he grew closer to Oster. This was, of course, the period of Hitler's most striking consolidation of power: in military and diplomatic terms it included the unopposed occupation of the demilitarized Rhineland (March 1936), the formation of the anti-Comintern Pact with Japan and Italy (1936-7), and the Austrian *Anschluss* (1938). Before Canaris's sudden promotion into the forefront of German affairs, there had been, in 1933 alone, the Enabling Law of March, which gave Hitler absolute power in Germany, the abolition of all political parties except that of the National Socialists, and Germany's departure from the League of Nations.

In 1934, after the death of President Hindenburg, Hitler had abolished the Presidency and proclaimed himself Führer, at the same time binding every individual in the Armed Services, whatever his rank, to swear the oath of personal loyalty to himself—the oath which was to prove such an obstacle whenever treasonable activities against Hitler were to be mooted, especially with men highly placed in the Armed Forces.

Canaris's Relations with the S.S.

Partly as the result, no doubt, of Oster's influence, Canaris drew further away from the man to whom he, like all those in uniform, had been forced to take this oath of loyalty. However, his activities during his first three years in office revealed a certain ambivalence of attitude—an ambivalence which can be understood when it is seen in relation to his background and his established interests.

First of all, he renewed his relationship with Heydrich. In 1926 Heydrich had been an officer with every prospect of a sound future in the Navy, but by 1931, after disgracing himself with a girl, he had been cashiered and was ready to turn, in bitterness of spirit, to Himmler to give him a job. He had joined Himmler's S.S. and become head of the S.D.*, the S.S. Intelligence department, and was by 1935 on the way to becoming the most virulent and powerful of Himmler's deputies. The Abwehr under Patzig, it will be remembered, was in dispute with the S.D., the newly-established Intelligence department of Himmler's S.S., and both Heydrich and Canaris wanted to improve relations between their departments. Heydrich appointed a new officer, Werner Best, to act as a liaison with Canaris. As Best put it to us: 'The idea was that my alleged diplomatic skill would provide better relations.' Best also took charge of certain legal and administrative work for the S.S.; he was an intellectual with legal training, and acted as both gentleman and diplomat in his dealings with the senior officers of the Abwehr.

It was evident that an agreement must be reached to preserve at any rate some formal balance between the work of the two departments. Canaris went to live in the Dollestrasse, in Dahlem, a select and comfortable Berlin suburb where the trees gave a touch of opulent privacy to upper middle-class people who fancied living in pleasant, detached seclusion. A little distance down the same road Canaris soon found that he had Heydrich and his family as near neighbours. The musical evenings with Frau Canaris were discreetly reestablished, while the Heydrichs invited the Canaris family back to croquet.

In August 1936 Canaris and his family (there were two daughters) moved west to an even more pleasant part of Berlin, Schlachtensee in the area of the lakes. To help pay for their new home, Erika Canaris sold her most valuable violin. Soon after, the Heydrichs followed them and so became their neighbors once again. As so often in these curious social relations, a kind of invisible, sympathetic bond seemed to link the antagonists, who no doubt preferred to keep an informal eye one each other rather than sever what must often have been an embarrassing relationship. Heydrich, a hard, calculating, ruthless man of action, and an administrator who had no scruples about doing anything which was to his advantage, may even have liked Canaris.

* See List of Service Abbreviations, p. xv.

Meanwhile, the dispute which had led to the resignation of Patzig was soon resolved with suitable face-saving on both sides. Heydrich, a naval cadet in 1922, was now Himmler's deputy and in rank a lieutenant-general of the S.S. Canaris, as we have seen, was a rear-admiral. It was their privilege to patch things up as successful men of the world. But these two very different men had become, in fact, rivals for power in the field of espionage, an activity for which both of them had a pronounced taste. With the arrival of Canaris, a bargaining position between the Abwehr and the S.D. was achieved. The result was an agreement which became known as the "Ten Commandments" through which the appropriate areas of espionage were near-enough defined. Needless to say, neither side felt bound by the formalities of this "gentleman's agreement," but, broadly speaking, Canaris handled all espionage abroad and strictly military espionage at home, where he was supposed to keep clear of all forms of political Intelligence.

Karl Abshagen, Canaris's early biographer, has some interesting comments to make on this strange relationship with Heydrich:

> Canaris was frankly scared to death of Heydrich. Everything about the fellow was sinister and made Canaris uneasy. He was too big for comfort. His cold, penetrating eyes set deeply in his almost mongoloid features had the frozen glint of a snake. Canaris always felt in Heydrich's presence the reality of evil, that his personality had none of the usual human limitations and that he was an evil-doer of the highest order. Yet he was fascinated, virtually mesmerized by the high intelligence of his companion, whom he once called 'the cleverest of the beasts'.

In his diary, says Abshagen, he wrote that Heydrich was a "brutal fanatic with whom it would be difficult to co-operate on a basis of mutual confidence." 'Although he never seemed nervous with Hitler, however difficult the circumstances, a telephone call from Heydrich disturbed him for the whole day. Yet their families were constantly in and out of one another's homes.

Up to 1939 Canaris and Werner Best, of Himmler's and Heydrich's Intelligence department, worked in reasonable harmony. According to Best:

> Canaris was very methodical, very much an organizer building up a vast machinery which, in the end, employed many more civil servants than it did agents or spies. It was not too difficult to segregate the respective spheres of action—such as active military espionage for the Army and criminal investigation for the Police. Much more difficult—in fact, practically impossible—was the division of responsibilities in the field of counterespionage, even though we had agreed in principle that tracing foreign espionage was a matter for the Abwehr (if only because Police Intelligence had insufficient agents for this). In practice, however, friction grew because the Abwehr usually preferred to follow up their own cases rather than hand them over for criminal investigation. There should have been constant collaboration and mutual confidence between the Abwehr and Police Intelligence, but personal rivalries and problems of prestige frequently got the better of us.[7]

In fact, according to Best, while Canaris was intent on building up the staff of the Abwehr, Heydrich was equally set on increasing his own Intelligence department, the S.D. This was later, during the war, to develop into an ambition to absorb the Abwehr itself.

One of the factors of power in Nazi Germany, as elsewhere, was the need for rival concerns to build up dossiers against one another. Canaris opened a secret file on the S.D. leader, which, considering he had been dismissed from the Navy for moral delinquency, soon began to make interesting reading. It was in these papers, apparently, that Canaris discovered information that implied that Heydrich's father, a singer, was a *Mischling,* a part-Jew. True or not, this kind of material could prove most useful.[8] Admiral Patzig remembers a significant conversation he had with Canaris late in 1937. Canaris had invited Patzig to take lunch, but he could not conceal his depression at the way things were going now in Germany. "They're all criminals," said Canaris to Patzig when they were alone together. Patzig suggested that, if Canaris felt as badly as this about it, he should resign. Canaris considered this a moment, and then replied, "No, I can't do that. My successor would be Heydrich."

From 1936 Canaris was able to adopt the peripatetic life which so appealed to his restless nature. Hitler always preferred to appoint his own special ambassadors to undertake missions abroad; again and again, the men near him whom he trusted would be sent abroad to negotiate agreements over the heads of the officials serving in the local embassies. Now Göring, now Himmler, for example, would suddenly appear in some foreign capital—Göring in Warsaw, Himmler in Rome. It was perhaps natural that Canaris, who spoke good Spanish, should be chosen to be Hitler's unofficial envoy to Spain, of all the nations of the Mediterranean the country in which he felt most at ease. It has been said that it was Canaris who finally persuaded Hitler, against the advice of his military experts, to give active support to Franco when the Spanish civil war started in July 1936, and from this time he was frequently in Spain, even during the Second World War. Canaris is said to have first met Franco in Morocco when the future dictator of Spain was in the Spanish Army.

In a long memorandum to us, Best gives an entertaining description of Canaris at this time:

He was obsessed by his work. In spite of his happy family life with his wife and his two young daughters, he had practically no time to spare for private life, and so far as I can recall he never went on holiday during the pre-war years, 1935-9. But he was always travelling in the course of duty, both at home and abroad, and must have been in constant touch with his agents. He organized Intelligence for the Condor Legion in Spain; he was especially friendly with the Japanese ambassador, Oshima, and with the chief of Italian military Intelligence, General Mario Roatta. He kept in touch with Hungary and Rumania, almost acting like a Foreign

49

Office diplomat for the Army.

In spite of his heavy schedule, Canaris maintained his cultural interests. Behind his desk there always stood a table piled with books—usually new works which he would look at between conferences. They included literature. He had the habit of giving his friends and acquaintances books for Christmas. Amongst some of those I received were books about early history, religion and philosophy. I think his reputation as an 'unusual' man was connected with his deeply pessimistic outlook. He always looked serious, even sad. He was always taciturn; only with his friends would he show flashes of his brilliant (and somehow bitter) sense of humor. He had to attend many social functions, but he always left at ten o'clock, even when he was himself the host.

According to Abshagen, Canaris's personal style of living always remained modest. The offices on the Tirpitz Ufer were never modernized, and his own room remained very sparsely furnished, with an old carpet on the floor, and an iron bedstead on which he would rest after lunch, or even spend the night when his work demanded this. On the wall was a portrait of Franco inscribed with a lengthy dedication. On his desk was a marble paperweight with the three familiar bronze monkeys hearing, seeing and speaking no evil. His beloved pair of dachshunds usually accompanied him to the office.

Beck and his Resistance Associates

The fact that Canaris was constantly on the move left Oster virtually in charge in Berlin. Like most of the High Command, Oster was against the rapid rearmament of Germany and the determination ultimately to wage war which Hitler openly revealed as his objective at his military conferences from 1937 onwards. In the forefront of the opposition was General Ludwig Beck, who had become Chief of the Army General Staff in October 1933 at the age of fifty-three. Beck, everyone agreed, was a brilliant student of military affairs rather than a man of action; nevertheless, he was a career officer who had achieved the rank of major during the First World War. His distinction lay in his work as a military historian and instructor, but he was a soldier of the old school, liked and trusted by all. Nevertheless, he was criticized even by his friend Ulrich von Hassell, German ambassador in Rome until 1938 and afterwards prominent in the Resistance, for being an intellectual rather than a strong leader, and a man whose strategy was by no means always well-judged. But no one denied his courage or the nobility of his nature. Beck was thoughtful and hard-working, the kind of man who would always miss his lunch to ensure that some necessary detail of administration was properly completed. He would weigh and ponder every point, worry about the rights and wrongs of any major decision. His authority over his fellow officers and all those who counted among his friends rested solely upon his absolute integrity. But reason was his chief weapon, and reason was ultimately to prove quite useless when virtually every member of the High Command was subject to the domination of Hitler's obsessive will. Beck's attitude to the oath of loyalty, which he, like many other senior officers, felt had been sprung upon him without warning, was that he should never have consented to take it. "This is the blackest day of my life," he said a few hours after he, like the rest, had solemnly sworn to serve the Führer.

From the first Beck raised his voice against any action by Hitler which might lead to war, and conflict developed when the Führer demanded that he replace his plans, which were essentially defensive, with new plans designed for aggression. Beck, however, was, like Canaris and Oster, a man of the right who detested Bolshevism and felt that the ultimate struggle must come, when it did, with the Soviet Union.

Ulrich von Hassell was another gentlemanly member of the old right-wing school who did not approve of the régime and had the courage to dedicate the remainder of his life to the business of its overthrow. Once more 1938

51

proved to be the turning-point. Hassell was a career diplomat and Germany's ambassador in Rome at the time of the formation of the Rome-Berlin axis, an alliance, Hassell was certain, pointed towards war. He was finally retired when Ribbentrop, after serving as Hitler's ambassador in Britain, was appointed Foreign Minister in February 1938. Hassell was recalled to Berlin, and never given an embassy elsewhere.

Hassell was an aristocrat, a member of the Hanoverian nobility married to the daughter of the celebrated Grand-Admiral von Tirpitz. In 1938 he was fifty-seven and, from the period of Munich to his arrest after the attempt on Hitler's life in July 1944, he kept a secret diary which, in spite of its many shortcomings, is one of the sources to which we constantly turn for information about the thinking in the right wing of the resistance. He had great courage, but he remained always the diplomat, not the conspirator. He was a highly cultured man who believed in remaining as calm as possible, making due allowance for all things and all men. During the time he was ambassador in Rome, his wife was far more outspoken than he against the excesses of the Nagi régime, which he served until he was displaced in 1938. This was a blow to his personal ambitions. He hoped, even after 1938, to be given another embassy and then to use this position to modify Hitler's demands in any way he could. His ambitions were never fulfilled, though he retained his diplomatic status and his seat on the Board of the Central European Economic Conference from which he was able to gain much confidential information.

Hassell at this early period was closely linked with Dr Carl Goerdeler, another key man in the growing German opposition of the middle 1930s. Goerdeler represented a further aspect of the right-wing outlook and he belonged to a distinguished Prussian family. His father, a conservative, was a judge who later was elected a member of the Prussian parliament. Goerdeler himself was trained in law and became a municipal administrator with a taste for economics.

Like Canaris, Goerdeler was not at first hostile to the

Nazis. He was, like many of his friends, a nationalist, and disapproved of the Versailles Treaty and the unstable democracy which had taken charge in Germany. When Hitler came to power, Goerdeler was mayor of Leipzig. For a while he even assisted the régime as an economic adviser. It is typical of Goerdeler's intransigence—soon to be turned violently against the Nazis—that he finally resigned as mayor after a heated disagreement with the Party authorities about the removal of a statue of Felix Mendelssohn, the Jewish composer born in Leipzig. He handed in his resignation in April 1937 when the statue had been removed against his express instructions. Disillusioned by this act of political vandalism, he began his campaign for Hitler's overthrow. He became a representative of the firm of Bosch, a post he used for cover, and he was constantly on the move both in Germany and abroad.[9]

Goerdeler, though courageous, was also moody and impatient. His plain-dealing was often indiscreet, while his political ideas, sometimes astute, sometimes absurdly theoretical, were endlessly spilled out to everyone in reach—in conversation, debate and memoranda. Eventually, those who had at first admired him tried to avoid his company, which they felt might lead them into greater dangers than they had really bargained for. But Goerdeler carried on, his ideas constantly changing, and with them his policy for the ideal Germany in which he so fervently believed.

1938: the Fritsch Affair

If any single event served to bring together the hard core of Army men who were opposed to Hitler, it was the occasion of the inquiry into the alleged homosexual misconduct of General Werner von Fritsch. No one who knew Fritsch, a staff officer of the old school who had only recently been appointed Commander-in-Chief of the German Army, believed for one moment in the charges being levelled against him, and the Court of Honor set up early in 1938 to inquire into their validity had been insisted upon

53

against Hitler's will by Beck, as Chief of the Army General Staff.

Like most of the officer caste, Canaris was disgusted by the whole affair, which was nothing but a disreputable trick to get rid of a thoroughly worthy if dull and unimaginative man at the price of his personal honor. Hitler regarded Fritsch as a weak reactionary opposed to his plans for the rapid increase in preparedness for war. Oster, as it happened, was appointed one of the four assessors at the Court of Honor. Another of the assessors, acting for the Ministry of Justice, was a brilliant young lawyer, Dr. Hans von Dohnanyi. So the men who were eventually to form the inner circle of the German resistance to Hitler met now in a common cause: to assist at the inquiry which aimed at clearing Fritsch's name.

Nothing draws people more closely together than a sense of disapproval strongly shared. This disapproval was clearly felt by all four of the assessors, the others being Dr. Karl Sack, Chief of the Army Judiciary, and Rüdiger Count von der Goltz, acting, like Dohnanyi, for the Ministry of Justice. Everyone was acutely aware that Fritsch's former immediate superior, Field-Marshal Werner von Blomberg, Minister of War and Commander-in-Chief of all the Armed Forces, had also been disposed of in circumstances arising out of his private life—the sudden exposure, a few days after his wedding in January 1938, that the young woman he had just married, at the advanced age of sixty, had been a former prostitute. At Blomberg's secret insistence, Göring had expressly permitted this unusual marriage to a girl who was then a secretary, and both Göring and Hitler had acted as witnesses at the wedding. So Blomberg had found himself summarily disgraced, and the man ordered to take the notice of his dismissal to Capri, where Blomberg was on holiday with his bride, was none other than Hans Oster. It was considered that his charm and tact in such a difficult matter could be relied upon. According to Achim Oster, Hans Oster's son, Frau von Blomberg was rather too impressed by his father's good looks, and even began to make eyes at him while her elderly husband went aside to study the papers Oster had bought him from Germany.[10]

All this had happened in January 1938—the marriage, the official "exposure" of the new Frau von Blomberg while on her honeymoon, the confrontation in Hitler's presence of the indignant General Fritsch by Hans Schmidt, a professional blackmailer of homosexuals, the man the Gestapo had produced with a sworn statement that he had been blackmailing Fritsch over a period of several years. By 31 January Beck, speaking for the General Staff, had forced Hitler's hand and established that there should be a full inquiry at an official Court of Honor. So during February, while the Army's investigations were proceeding, Hitler abolished the Ministry of War, conducted a lightning purge involving sixteen of his generals, and made himself Commander-in-Chief of the Armed Forces, consolidating the position he already held as their Supreme Commander. Field-Marshal Walter von Brauchitsch, a tame general, was made Commander-in-Chief of the Army in place of Fritsch, who had meanwhile been suspended.[11]

Canaris learned something of Oster's great integrity during the Fritsch crisis. It was Oster who is claimed to have saved Fritsch's life while he was being interrogated by the Gestapo. The Gestapo's plan had been to murder Fritsch, and then announce that his death was suicide. Oster urged Canaris to arrange through Beck for "unofficial" protection to be given to Fritsch by staging an army exercise in the immediate vicinity of his house. Any attempt to dispose of Fritsch had therefore to be abandoned.

The Court of Honor assembled under the presidency of Göring himself on 10 March; the Army had by now brought together strong evidence that it was the Gestapo, pressed by its chief, Himmler, and by Heydrich, his principal aide, which had conspired to fake the evidence brought against Fritsch. Himmler in fact was known to be anxious about the outcome of the inquiry, as he had need to be. But Göring knew better. He broke up the Court when it became evident that the Austrian *Anschluss,* or takeover, was about to break on 11 March. When the Court was eventually reconvened on 17 March, the prestige of

55

Hitler and of the National Socialist Party was at its height. Göring simply allowed Fritsch to be acquitted with a good-natured casualness, conscious, no doubt, that this would forestall the presentation of the Army's evidence against the Gestapo. It was enough that Schmidt, the Gestapo's witness, was shown to have made a mistake of identity; the man Schmidt had been blackmailing was an officer called *Frisch*. It was all a most unfortunate error. But the damage had been done; Fritsch, his dignity as an officer permanently affronted, deliberately allowed himself to be killed on active service during the Polish campaign the following year.

But the case, resolved with such adroit cynicism, had certain important repercussions. It led directly to the association of the three men who were to plot the Führer's downfall: Canaris, Oster and Dohnanyi. Although it was not until August the following year that Dohnanyi was to be seconded from the Ministry of Justice to join Canaris's inner circle of officers at the head of the department of Military Intelligence, he was to be in the closest touch with Oster later in the year.

The Widening Circle

What was to become an active movement towards conspiracy now developed from the mutual reactions and discussions of a group of men, both military and civilian, who discovered that for various reasons they shared an increasing distaste for Hitler. None of them was a liberal in any modern sense, or opposed to an authoritarian form of nationalist government run along traditional lines. But one by one, sooner or later they arrived at a point where they found Hitler's arbitrary and amoral conduct of affairs roused their common resentment and affronted the traditional principles which were the basis of their lives.

Beck was in as close contact with Goerdeler and Hassell as he was with his military friends. At a meeting in mid-January 1938, Beck told Goerdeler of the plans for war which Hitler had revealed to his senior officers the previous

November. This was the period when Goerdeler first met Gisevius, who was to be very active in the resistance and one of its most colorful historians. After this, Goerdeler went on an extensive European tour which included a visit to Britain in July. He sent back his usual voluminous memoranda—even to Hitler and Göring themselves, as well as to Schacht, Hitler's disillusioned Minister for Economic Affairs from 1934 to 1937. He also wrote to Beck, and to certain relatively disaffected generals, Franz Halder and Georg Thomas, both staff officers, who were opposed to the Führer's aggressive policy but who nevertheless stayed within the army to help him, if only nominally, to carry that policy out. In Britain, though Goerdeler failed to meet Churchill on this occasion (he was to meet him later in May 1939), he did achieve an interview with Sir Robert Vansittart, Chief Diplomatic Adviser to the British Government, but managed only to reach a disagreement with him over the Sudeten question. Vansittart was opposed to the secession of the Sudeten territory to Germany, a change which Goerdeler advocated. As a result, Vansittart found he couldn't approve of Goerdeler, or trust his opposition to Hitler.

Anyone in authority in the High Command who attempted to warn Hitler about the dangers of following the policies his intuition dictated stood in peril of the Führer's displeasure. The ranks of the resistance grew not only from those who were opposed to Hitler's policies from the start, but from his various disillusioned supporters. Of the latter, Hjalmar Schacht, former President of the Reichsbank and Hitler's Minister for Economic Affairs, was perhaps the most spectacular example. In spite of his notable efforts to build Germany's war economy, Schacht found himself edged out of his position by Göring: who in September 1936 became Hitler's Plenipotentiary for the Five-Year Plan, a device to resolve the whole of Germany's economic problems, which was created by Göring to please Hitler although it was opposed by Schacht as economically unsound. Schacht insisted on resigning in August 1937 because he could no longer tolerate Göring's unorthodox methods, and Hitler finally had to let him go the following

December, leaving Göring master of the German economy. As a result, from 1938 Schacht joined forces with Beck and Canaris in secret opposition to Hitler.[12]

Schacht, like Goerdeler, was another strong, egocentric character who could not tolerate any kind of interference with what he regarded as the right policy for Germany. He had first met Hitler through Göring in 1931, when he was introduced to the future Führer as a former President of the Reichsbank. Schacht always liked to insist that he "never laid claim to being a politician." It is typical of Schacht that from the first moment of his initial flirtation with the resistance, he regarded himself as the head of the movement:

> Together with my friends, I began to deliberate how best to overthrow the Hitler régime. Following the Fritsch affair I had approached von Brauchitsch, the new Commander-in-Chief of the Army. I had sought out von Rundstedt, the head of the Wehrmacht detachment in Berlin. I had a long talk with Admiral Raeder. Finally, I went to Gürtner, the Minister of Justice. With all of them I discussed the danger that threatened and implored them to take counter-measures against Hitler from the vantage point of their military and official positions. Everywhere I encountered deaf ears. Not one of these high dignitaries was prepared to take a stand on behalf of right and justice.[13]

At one of the monthly meetings of the Bank for International Settlements which he attended in Basle he attempted in 1938 to make contact with Britain, naturally at the highest level:

> I asked my British colleague, Montagu Norman, whether it would not be possible to bring British policy more into line with my efforts to maintain peace. Hitherto, Britain's policy had appeared to be to leave Hitler a free hand in foreign affairs. When I met Norman again four weeks later he said: 'I discussed your suggestion with Neville Chamberlain.' 'And what was his

reply?' 'His reply was, "Who is Schacht? I have to deal with Hitler." ' This answer caused me considerable astonishment. It seemed to me incomprehensible that the British Prime Minister should set so little store by maintaining a certain contact with those circles which were ranged on the side of peace.

Schacht's main contact with the resistance became Beck:

Beck was a man of absolutely sterling character, highly cultured and possessing a great store of knowledge, not only of his own subject but over a very wide field. As Chief of the General Staff he enjoyed the complete confidence of the Army and was acknowledged moral leader of the Staff. Nevertheless, Beck was more of a scholar than a man of action. His retirement accelerated the moral disintegration of the General Staff. His departure deprived the higher military ranks of their only strong counterelement against Hitler.

Hans Bernd Gisevius was a young man who, as we have seen, survived to comment voluminously upon the resistance movement. As a witness before the International Tribunal at Nuremberg after the war he occupied the stand for a span of three days, making detailed and dramatic revelations. But his colourful recollections of the German resistance movement (particularly in his book, *To the Bitter End*) have not always been as warmly received in Germany as he might wish. He came of a family of civil servants, and he had qualified in law shortly after Hitler's rise to power. He was considered reliable enough initially to be assigned to Göring's political police, the Gestapo. According to his testimony, the moment he discovered the nature of the work the Gestapo was undertaking, he allied himself with Arthur Nebe, a senior officer in the Prussian police who claimed to have given up his support of the Nazis when, in 1934, he was ordered by Göring to arrange for the assassination of Gregor Strasser, the principal opponent of Hitler within the Party, though he was able to sidestep this.[14] For a while Gisevius held an appointment in the Reich Ministry of the Interior. Nebe remained in the police service under the Nazis in the criminal investigation branch, and, according to Gisevius, who maintained a close friendship with him, from then on became an important source of information for the resistance movement because of his contacts with the secret, political police.

Gisevius made it very much his business to know everybody and act in the capacity of chief liaison officer for the movement; therefore he soon came to know Oster. At the Nuremberg Trial Gisevius said:

> I gave him all the material which had accumulated up to that time. We started a collection, which we continued until 20 July [1944], of all documents which we could get hold of; and Oster is the man who from then on, in the Ministry of War, never failed to inform every officer he could contact officially or privately.[15]

Gisevius, who was close to Schacht and Goerdeler, played general post between the various wings of the resistance. After various official jobs, Schacht arranged for him to hold a sinecure attached to a factory in Bremen. This, apparently, left him free to conduct liaison activities as a full-time occupation.

At the time of the Austrian *Anschluss* in 1938, Canaris entered Vienna with the German Army and took over the files of the Austrian Army Intelligence. He also acquired the services of the Chief of Austrian Intelligence, Colonel Erwin Lahousen, a subaltern in Austria's former Imperial Army whom Canaris felt that he could trust.

According to Lahousen when giving evidence after the war before the International Military Tribunal at Nuremberg:

> Canaris was a personality of pure intellect. We relied on his inner, very unique and complicated nature, for this reason. He hated violence and hated and abominated therefore Hitler, his system, and particularly his meth-

ods. Canaris was, in whatever way you may look upon him, a human being.[16]

After the war Lahousen was to become one of the principal sources of information about Canaris, with whom he claimed close friendship. He differentiated between the circle of Abwehr officers who were Canaris's particular confidants (Oster, Hans Grosscurth, Hans Pieckenbrock, Georg Hansen, Wessel von Freytag-Loringhoven, Egbert von Bentivegni) and Oster's own circle, a smaller group "actively concerned with schemes and plans designed to do away by force with Hitler . . . as early as 1938." According to Lahousen, Canaris's group worked with a less defined objective:

It was more of a spiritual organization of people of the same convictions, who were perspicacious and well-informed. Their official functions provided them with the necessary knowledge. These people understood each other and acted jointly, while maintaining their complete individuality. . . . Different demands were made on each individual. Canaris approached at any time the person whose character he knew from his personal knowledge to be the fittest to carry out a certain task.

Canaris very quickly showed his trust in Lahousen:

While I was still in Vienna, before entering service in the O.K.W., I received instructions from Canaris not to admit to his office in Berlin any National Socialists. I was also instructed, whenever possible, not to admit any Party members or officers sympathizing with the Party to high positions in my section.

According to what Lahousen told Ian Colvin, Canaris's English biographer, Lahousen was instructed in Vienna not to admit any Austrian Nazis into the Intelligence staff, and, staring up at him (for Canaris was as short as Lahousen was tall) Canaris added that the Austrians only had themselves to blame for the *Anschluss* because they had not actively opposed the German Army. When Lahousen had first entered Canaris's presence, he had acted very formally, clicking his heels and giving the Hitler salute. Canaris merely smiled; then he reached out and gently drew his visitor's arm down to a more normal position and motioned him to sit. When Lahousen repeated the salute on entering Oster's office, Oster laughed loudly and, unguarded as ever, cried, 'No Hitler salute here, please!' Lahousen soon learned all about "Emil," Oster's favorite name for Hitler.

The general pattern of the inner core of the German resistance was beginning to take shape. By now, in 1938, it was made up of a gradually widening circle of people in different levels of German society whose resentment gathered strength as Hitler himself became more overbearing and self-centered, driving Germany before him in his obsessive pursuit of power. Every political color and every major profession was gradually represented in the resistance counter-movement to prevent Germany's approach to war. The men of the right, officers and gentlemen, were affronted by Hitler's crudity, though they were forced to admit that success attended his "intuitive" decisions and his challenge to the Western powers. But they detested the nature of much that he was doing and the manner in which he did it; this was false to every tradition they believed in, and to the good name of their Fatherland. Their Christian upbringing, whether Catholic or Protestant, was being violated; their professional pride—whether as landed gentlemen, or as officers, diplomats, or men of law, as civil servants, university men, priests or pastors—was being offended by decrees and regulations which left them no sphere in which they could function with good conscience. It was the same with the men of the left, members of political parties long since suppressed or of unions long since disbanded. They too drew together with the same desire to overthrow the régime. For the moment the right and the left were divided. Only much later, when circumstances demanded some kind of active liaison, were they to collaborate in the common need to free their country.

II

Fiasco in 1938

Beck acts against Hitler

The first clear if indecisive steps towards an organized attempt to displace Hitler were to be taken by the Army. As we have seen, after the collapse of the case against Fritsch, the indignation of the officer caste had to some extent been dissipated by the simultaneous, overnight success of the *Anschluss* and the immediate problems of this sudden incorporation of Austria into the Reich. Hitler's popularity in Germany reached new heights, and in any event Hitler was in complete control of the Army—as Führer, as Commander-in-Chief, and as the bearer of the personal oath of loyalty which every officer and serving man had been obliged to take.

Beck and Canaris, both men of the highest intelligence but very different in character and in the nature of their integrity, watched at first hand the growing megalomania of Hitler, for whom 1938 was indeed a year of personal fulfilment. Hitler believed from this time onward that he could proceed by the 'divine' right of his impulse, that neither the High Command at home nor his political opponents abroad need any longer be regarded as major forces to which he must reconcile his will. Beck, a devout Christian who believed in the conduct of public affairs in the light of the Christian ethic and the development of a purely defensive policy in military strategy, and Canaris, more cynic than moralist, realized in their different ways that Hitler's policy, however successful for the moment, could only in the end precipitate Germany into a major conflict for which they knew she was insufficiently prepared. When Beck realized that the men of the High Command were too mesmerized by Hitler's overbearing methods in conference to resist him, his answer was to retire and associate himself with such underground activities as he could. As Gisevius put it at Nuremberg:

> Beck was of the opinion that the General Staff was not only an organization of war technicians; he saw in it the conscience of the German Army, and he trained his staff accordingly. He suffered endlessly during the later years of his life because men whom he had trained in that sense did not follow the dictates of their conscience.[1]

Canaris, while remaining in office, adopted the somewhat ambivalent position of permitting Oster to lead the inner enclave of the Abwehr increasingly in the direction of active resistance, while he himself associated with the Nazi hierarchy and travelled ceaselessly in the apparent pursuit of his many special "missions," including liaison with Franco on behalf of Hitler.

Although there was direct contact between Beck and Canaris, the Admiral tended to leave the details to Oster and his friends, many of whom knew Beck well. Beck's worries had crystallized after reading the minutes of the conference Hitler held on 5 November 1937, attendance at which was restricted to the Minister of War (still, at that time, Blomberg), the Foreign Minister (Konstantin von Neurath) and the three Commanders-in-Chief (Göring, Fritsch and Raeder). At this conference, as is now well known, Hitler outlined quite definitely his policy of winning *"Lebensraum"* for Germany at the expense not only of Austria, but of Czechoslovakia, Poland and even of the Ukraine, and that the sooner this was done the better. 1938, he said, was to be the initial year for action, using "peaceful" means, naturally, if these could be effective, but, if not, paralyzing all opposition by the sudden use of the *blitzkrieg*. Britain and France, he claimed, would succumb to panic inaction just as easily as the territories against which action was to be taken. No one attending the meeting did more than murmur a few tactical reservations, but Neurath suffered a heart attack following the meeting and divulged what had taken place to Beck. All attempts to make representations to the Führer to modify his plans failed, and Hitler himself saw that Blomberg, Fritsch and Neurath were weak-kneed men who would be more hindrance than help. This was why he got rid of them by means analogous to those he was prepared to use against the nations opposing his will.

Before his resignation in August 1938 Beck did everything he could to persuade the new Commander-in-Chief of the Army, Brauchitsch, to reject Hitler's secret preparations to subdue Czechoslovakia under the plan known as "Operation Green." This plan, developed during May, received a temporary setback when it seemed that Czechoslovakia would be actively supported by Britain, France and the Soviet Union in the event of any attack by Germany. But Hitler, all the more angry at this unexpected confrontation, set the deadline for action against the "guilty" country on 1 October, whether it meant war with all four nations or not. Hitler believed it would not.

Beck, however, thought otherwise. During June he canvassed the generals of the High Command, intending to include even Brauchitsch, but the latter disappeared on leave before he could be tackled. As soon as the Commander-in-Chief returned, however, Beck had the courage to propose to him verbally that the generals should assemble in Hitler's presence and submit their combined resignations if he should not withdraw his instructions for war and return to a rule of law in Germany. Brauchitsch, whether he agreed with his Chief of Staff or not, preferred his career to his country; he fended Beck off throughout July, but permitted him to summon, as was his right, a conference of the High Command in August. At this conference Beck voiced his misgivings and found almost unanimous support, though Brauchitsch failed to call for action as Beck had urged him to do, even drafting a speech for him which Brauchitsch did not read. When Hitler, aloof in the Berghof, his mountain retreat in the south, received Beck's memorandum condemning preparations for war, he merely summoned his service chiefs, gave them a further lecture on strategy and trounced them for

65

their lack of spirit. Beck, in despair, tried to make Brauchitsch resign too, but again he failed. So he handed in his own, solitary resignation on 18 August and, after a final address to the General Staff on 27 August, left the War Office to its own devices.

One of the officers present has described Beck's speech of farewell to his fellow officers:

When we entered his office he was standing erect at the side of his desk. He moved slightly to acknowledge the greetings of those coming in. His hands were folded neatly, and the delicately chiselled face seemed worn, almost other-worldly. The gaze from his fine and startlingly beautiful eyes was remote and far from us. Perfectly straight and poised, he delivered a short speech which literally sparkled with the classical elegance of its structure and the wisdom of its content. The sense of it was to make clear to the assembled officers the significance of the struggle for an independent, creative and forceful General Staff. In the prevailing circumstances he could only claim to be partially successful. His appeal to us to preserve our independence in judgment and character was very moving. I am certain that even the small minority among us who felt that Beck's dismissal was necessary and right could not fail to have been deeply stirred by the evident seriousness, dignity and proud sense of moral responsibility of the slender, elegant man, who was to prove to be the last true Chief of the German General Staff.[2]

Beck, it must be faced, was no leader; all he commanded was respect. His nature was too hesitant, too considerate, lacking in the rough impulse which stirs men to action. He was a Brutus in this enterprise, clear-minded and reasonable to a fault. His highly developed form of self-control gave him all the calm and dignity of a statue, or so it seemed to one observer, but there was at least one occasion when he was seen to weep for what he knew to have been lost in Germany.

Beck's place on the General Staff went to General Franz

Halder in September 1938, but no announcement was made of the change until after the Munich agreement in October. Halder was one of Beck's friends and was prepared to keep him informed about Hitler's preparations for war. Precise, sardonic, with pince-nez and closely-cropped hair, Halder seemed to find Hitler as antipathetic as Beck had done, and, initially at least, expressed himself violently on the subject. From the point of view of the conspirators, a great deal was to depend on Halder, at least up to April 1940.

Gisevius described at Nuremberg the situation which faced Beck and Halder in September 1938:

> Beck had assured us at the time of his resignation—by us I mean Goerdeler, Schacht and other politicians—that he would leave to us a successor who was more energetic than himself, and who was firmly determined to precipitate a revolution if Hitler should decide upon war. That man whom Beck trusted, and to whom he introduced us, was General Halder. As a matter of fact, on taking office General Halder immediately took steps to start discussions on the subject with Schacht, Goerdeler, Oster and our entire group. A few days after he took over his office, he sent for Oster and informed him that he considered that we were drifting towards war, and that he would then undertake an overthrow of the government. He asked Oster what he, for his part, intended to do to include the civilians in the plot. . . .
> We were only a small circle at that time, and Oster replied that to the best of his knowledge he only knew two civilians of importance with whom Halder could have preliminary political conversations; one was Goerdeler and the other was Schacht. Halder refused to speak personally to a man as suspect as Goerdeler, because he felt it was too dangerous for him to receive a man whom he did not yet know. While he could find some official reason for a conference with Schacht, Halder asked Oster to act as an intermediary in the matter. Through my agency, Oster approached Schacht. Schacht was prepared. A private meeting was to be arranged,

and I warned Schacht and told him: 'Have Halder come to your apartment so that you are quite sure of the matter.' Halder then visited Schacht personally at the end of July 1938, and informed him that matters had reached a stage where war was imminent, and that he, Halder, would precipitate a *putsch*. He then asked Schacht whether he was prepared to play a leading part in aiding him politically. That is what Schacht told me at the time. . . . I continually acted as an intermediary in these discussions.[3]

It is difficult to see what more Beck, as a staff officer, could have done at this time, when in any case the tide was flowing in Hitler's favour. However, he was in close touch with Oster, Canaris and certain other dissident generals, some of whom had men directly at their comand. With the ceiling date of 1 October kept firmly in mind, the conspirators, for this was what they were fast becoming, took the nature of their plan a stage further.

Instead of a mass walk-out of staff officers from Hitler's presence, there was substituted the more positive action of arresting Hitler and placing him on trial in one of his own People's Courts. Here he would be prosecuted for endangering the safety of Germany. It was intended that part of the case for the prosecution should consist of a medical report on the defendant which proved him to be insane. While Beck and Oster were deeply involved in the plan for Hitler's arrest, Hans von Dohnanyi became one of those detailed to prepare the case for the prosecution, while his father-in-law, Profesor Karl Bonhoeffer, perhaps the most distinguished neurologist in Europe, was asked to endorse the medical evidence demonstrating Hitler's insanity.

A meeting took place with the professor; Dohnanyi, accompanied by his friend Otto John, another civilian member of the conspiracy, went to see him. They produced a report describing every known illness from which Hitler had suffered compiled from reports made by official military doctors. Professor Bonhoeffer studied the papers carefully. All he would say afterwards was, "From this it would

seem very probable that the man is not quite sane."
Dohnanyi and John hoped to persuade the old man to give
them a medical certificate of Hitler's insanity. But this the
professor's sense of correctness prevented him from doing.
Without a thorough examination of the patient, he said,
he was unable to sign any form of certificate concerning
his mental condition.[4]

Hans von Dohnanyi

Dohnanyi's social background, as might be expected,
differed considerably from that of Canaris and Oster. Son
of the celebrated composer, he was born in Vienna in
1902, so that in 1938 he was only thirty-six. He had attended an exclusive co-educational school, the Grunewald
Gymnasium, where he matriculated in 1920. It was at this
school that he first met the brothers Dietrich and Klaus
Bonhoeffer and their sister Christine, his future wife. He
also came to know another pupil, Marion Winter, who was
later to marry Count Peter Yorck von Wartenburg—like
the Bonhoeffers, to become a prominent member of the
resistance.[5]

After reading law at Berlin University, Dohnanyi became an assistant in the Institute for Foreign Policy at the
University of Hamburg, where he finally obtained his
doctorate in law during 1926, a year after his marriage
(in February 1925) to Christine Bonhoeffer. This brought
him into very close association with the Bonhoeffer family.
In 1931, after a brief period as an assistant in the Reich
Ministry of Justice (specializing in administrative measures
which included the laws governing treason) Dohnanyi,
who was by now recognized as a brilliant lawyer, was
appointed State Prosecutor in Hamburg. He was still
under thirty. In January 1933, the month Hitler became
Chancellor, Dohnanyi returned to the Ministry of Justice,
where he became an assistant to Franz Gürtner, Hitler's
newly-appointed Minister of Justice. Gürtner, though Minister of Justice in Bavaria at the time of Hitler's abortive
putsch in Munich in 1923 and one of the Führer's early

supporters, was later to use his position to ease the rigors of Nazism.

Dohnanyi used his personal influence with Gürtner to stay in a position of confidence at the Ministry of Justice for as long as he possibly could. He was able to begin the work of compiling files of evidence against the régime during this time. In 1935 he even refused what must have seemed a very tempting offer of a professorship at Leipzig, ostensibly because Gürtner, who liked him, pressed him to stay in Berlin. In September 1938 he was promoted *Reichgerichtsrat,* a judge in the Supreme Court at Leipzig.

Kleist's Mission to London

Meanwhile, Dohnanyi had been undertaking his secret work with Oster. Beck, free at last of his commitments at the War Ministry, was concentrating on circumventing the drift to war by facing the problem from outside the High Command. It had been decided to send an emissary to London to give warning of the dangers of impending war and to test the reaction of the British government should a *coup d'état* take place in Germany. Canaris and Oster had chosen Major Ewald von Kleist-Schmenzin, a staunch monarchist and a close friend of Canaris, as their envoy. Together with Beck, they briefed him for his mission. It was at this time that Kleist met Ian Colvin, correspondent in Berlin for the London *News Chronicle,* and told him how the situation stood, and of the absolute necessity for Britain to stand firm over Czechoslovakia. Colvin in turn briefed Sir George Ogilvie-Forbes at the British embassy in Berlin, since he had little sympathy for the policy of appeasement pursued by his ambassador, Sir Nevile Henderson. Meanwhile, Colvin's opposite number in London, the German journalist Karl Abshagen (Canaris's future biographer), was sending Oster reports from Britain.

Kleist was sent by Beck and Canaris to London in August, supplied with one of Canaris's special sets of documents of identity and a permit for travel. He arrived on 18 August 1938, returning to Germany on 23 August. During

70

those few days he met Vansittart, Lord Lloyd and Winston Churchill, whom he visited at Chartwell.

Kleist did not, of course, arrive without any prior warning to the British government. A signal was sent by the British embassy in Berlin that "a Herr von Kleist," an emissary of the moderates on the German General Staff and travelling with the approval of the German War Ministry, would be coming by air "to obtain material with which to convince the Chancellor of the strong probability of Great Britain intervening should Germany take violent action against Czechoslovakia;" the ambassador's view, of course, was that "it would be unwise for him to be received in official quarters." It was also known that he wanted to see Vansittart, Lord Lloyd and Churchill. The official view taken by Lord Halifax, the Foreign Secretary, was that "no initiative should be taken in official quarters to see Herr von Kleist, but that, if he asked to be received in such quarters, he should not be rebuffed."

So Vansittart received Kleist privately, but made an official report on the meeting of which the following is a part:[6]

Herr von Kleist at once opened up with the utmost frankness and gravity. He said (and this coincides with a great deal of other information which I have given you from entirely different sources) that war was now a certainty unless we stopped it. I said, 'Do you mean an extreme danger?' He answered: 'No, I do not mean an extreme danger, I mean an absolute certainty.' I said, 'Do you mean to say that the extremists are now carrying Hitler with them?' He said: 'No, I do not mean that. There is only one real extremist and that is Hitler himself. He is the great danger and he is doing this entirely on his own. He receives a great deal of encouragement from Herr von Ribbentrop who keeps telling him that when it comes to the showdown neither France nor England will do anything.' (You will remember that I gave you the same information from an entirely different source this morning as to Ribbentrop's present attitude and influence.)

71

Herr von Kleist continued: 'I do not want to bother to talk about Herr von Ribbentrop. He is nothing but an evil yes-man and although his influence is now cast in the wrong direction by encouraging Hitler he is not of sufficient consequence to matter. Hitler has made up his mind for himself. All the generals in the German Army who are my friends know it and they *alone* know it for a certainty and know the date at which the mine is to be exploded.'

Pressed by Vansittart to tell him this date on which war was so certain to break out unless urgent action was taken to prevent it, Kleist expressed surprise that the British government did not already realize when this period of extreme danger was likely to be, and that it was very naturally linked directly with the time of the Party Rally at Nuremberg during the second week of September, when Hitler was certain to issue a public challenge concerning his claims on Czechoslovakia. Vansittart continued in his report:

> Herr von Kleist appeared still very incredulous that we should not be more exactly informed as to Hitler's timetable, but when I questioned him again he said: 'After the 27th September it will be too late.' (You will remember that in a letter that Lord Lloyd sent to you he mentioned that a friend of his in army circles had told him that the 28th September was the date.)

Kleist insisted that Hitler was sure that no matter what the British and French politicians might so far have said, they would take no positive action over Czechoslovakia. According to Vansittart, Kleist went on:

> 'A great part of the country is sick of the present régime and even a part that is not sick of it is terribly alarmed at the prospect of war, and the conditions to which war will lead them. I have already told you that the army, including Reichenau, is unanimous against it if they can get any support. I wish that one of your

72

leading statesmen would make a speech which would appeal to this element in Germany, emphasizing the horrors of war and the inevitable general catastrophe to which it would lead.'

Kleist went on to declare that there was no prospect of any kind of reasonable policy in Germany while Hitler remained in power. Vansittart describes their final words:

In conclusion he said that his exit from Germany had been facilitated by his friends in the army on whose unanimity he had enlarged earlier and that he had long been on the most intimate terms with them. They had taken the risk and he had taken the risk of coming out of Germany at this crucial moment although he had no illusions as to the fate that awaited him if he failed; but he made it abundantly clear, as I have said earlier, that they alone could do nothing without assistance from outside on the lines he had suggested.

This meeting had taken place on the day of Kleist's arrival in London—18 August. Chamberlain received Vansittart's report on the conversation, and wrote to Lord Halifax the following day:

I take it that von Kleist is violently anti-Hitler and is extremely anxious to stir up his friends in Germany to make an attempt at [the régime's] overthrow. He reminds me of the Jacobites at the Court of France in King William's time and I think we must discount a good deal of what he says. Nevertheless I confess to some feeling of uneasiness and I don't feel sure that we ought not to do something.

However, the only action Chamberlain took was to instruct Halifax to summon Sir Nevile Henderson, the British Ambassador in Berlin, and let it be known that he had been sent for "to consult about the serious position in connection with Czecho."

Meanwhile, on 19 August Kleist had been to see

73

Churchill. A record of the conversation was kept, and Churchill proved more forthcoming than Vansittart:

> C. observed that these generals were correct in their view and that though many people in England were not prepared to say in cold blood that they would march for Czechoslovakia, there would be few who would wish to stand idly by once the fighting started. He pointed out that the successive Nazi coups had hardened public opinion in Britain . . . . He stressed the fact that those who thought as he did were anti-Nazi and anti-war, and not anti-German.

Kleist, however, pressed for some positive action. He thought that some gesture was needed to crystallize the widespread and indeed, universal anti-war sentiment in Germany:

> Particularly was it necessary to do all that was possible to encourage the generals who alone had the power to stop war. He realized the difficulties of action by a democratic government, but enquired whether it was not possible for private members of parliament by letters in the press or by private communications to friends in Germany to stress the dangers of the situation, and to appeal to the peaceful elements in Germany to assert themselves without delay. He was convinced that in the event of the generals deciding to insist on peace, there would be a new system of government within forty-eight hours. Such a government, probably of a monarchist character, could guarantee stability and end the fear of war for ever.

The note on the conversation ends as follows:

> C. told K. that his conversation with V. had been reported to the Foreign Secretary and the Prime Minister and that the former had authorized C. to state that the Prime Minister's declaration in the House of Commons on March 24 still stood. C. undertook to embody this

74

assurance together with his own view in the form of a letter.

Churchill's letter, which Kleist finally received through the British embassy in Berlin after his return to Germany, was dated 19 August 1938, and was intended to give Kleist the form of declaration he needed; though it did not come from a member of the government itself:

My dear Sir,

I have welcomed you here as one who is ready to run risks to preserve the peace of Europe and to achieve a lasting friendship between the British, French and German peoples for their mutual advantage.

I am sure that the crossing of the frontier of Czechoslovakia by German armies or aviation in force will bring about a renewal of the world war. I am as certain as I was at the end of July 1914 that England will march with France and certainly the United States is now strongly anti-Nazi. It is difficult for democracies in advance and in cold blood to make precise declarations, but the spectacle of an armed attack by Germany upon a small neighbor and the bloody fighting that will follow will rouse the whole British Empire and compel the gravest decisions.

Do not, I pray you, be mislead upon this point. Such a war, once started, would be fought out like the last to the bitter end, and one must consider not what might happen in the first few months, but where we should all be at the end of the third or fourth year. It would be a great mistake to imagine that the slaughter of the civil population following upon air-raids would prevent the British Empire from developing its full war power; though, of course, we should suffer more at the beginning that we did last time. But the submarine is practically mastered by scientific methods and we shall have the freedom of the seas and the support of the greater part of the world. The worse the air-slaughter at the beginning, the more inexpiable would be the war. Evidently, all the great nations engaged in the struggle, once started, would fight on for victory or death.

As I felt you should have some definite message to take back to your friends in Germany who wish to see peace preserved and who look forward to a great Europe in which England, France and Germany will be working together for the prosperity of the wage-earning masses, I communicated with Lord Halifax. His Lordship asked me to say on his behalf that the position of His Majesty's Government in relation to Czechoslovakia is defined by the Prime Minister's speech in the House of Commons on March 24, 1938. The speech must be read as a whole, and I have no authority to select any particular sentence out of its context; but I must draw your attention to the final passage on this subject. . . .

> 'Where peace and war are concerned, legal obligations are not alone involved, and, if war broke out, it would be unlikely to be confined to those who have assumed such obligations. It would be quite impossible to say where it would end and what Governments would become involved. The inexorable pressure of facts might well prove more powerful than formal pronouncements, and in that event it would be well within the bounds of probability that other countries, besides those which were parties to the original dispute, would almost immediately become involved. This is especially true in the case of two countries like Great Britain and France, with long associations of friendship, with interests closely interwoven, devoted to the same ideals of democratic liberty, and determined to uphold them.'

May I say that, speaking for myself, I believe that a peaceful and friendly solution of the Czechoslovak problem would pave the way for the true reunion of our countries on the basis of the greatness and the freedom of both.

Following on these meetings, Sir Nevile Henderson, as we have seen, was summoned to London for consultations and sent back with instructions to arrange a meeting between Chamberlain and Hitler. Meanwhile, Canaris was in Hungary frustrating as best he could an attempt by Ribbentrop to involve the Hungarians in territorial claims upon Czechoslovakia. Henderson's visit to London almost coincided with that of another emissary from Germany, sent this time by Halder. This was a businessman who had formerly served in the Army, Colonel Hans Böhm-Tettelbach. Unfortunately, he made little impression, especially on Vansittart, who received him a few days after his talk with Kleist. Yet another representative, Theodor Kordt, a counsellor in the German embassy in London, was prompted by Ernst von Weizsäcker, Senior State Secretary in the German Foreign Ministry (a man who admired Canaris for combining "the cleverness of a snake with the purity of a dove" and who remained carefully, though sympathetically, on the fence as far as outright resistance was concerned) to urge the British government not to give ground to Hitler. On 5 September this diplomatic missioner actually reached the room of Lord Halifax himself. He gave an outright warning about the October deadline for the invasion of Czechoslovakia, and the determination of the conspirators to take action. It is not known what encouragement, if any, he received. It was probably little enough, for Chamberlain had already centered his hopes on a personal meeting with Hitler, who remained carefully concealed in the Berghof, where the conspirators could scarcely reach him. Their plans depended on his presence in Berlin.

The September Conspiracy

It will always be doubtful if this September conspiracy could ever have got beyond being a paper-plot, which would in any case only have been launched had every attendant circumstance fallen precisely as forecast. It is claimed that General Erwin von Witzleben, commander at this time in the Berlin area, Count Wolf Heinrich von Helldorf—president of the Berlin police and a former

Nazi whose army background and training eventually overcame his initial enthusiasm for Hitler—and General Erich Hoepner, who commanded the Third Panzer Division based south of Berlin, were among those poised to take action against Hitler and secure his arrest.

Friedrich Wilhelm Heinz, who had an adventurous career during the First World War and in various nationalist units during the 1920s, had joined the Abwehr in 1936. One evening in September 1938 he found himself in Oster's private residence facing Witzleben. He was ordered to form a trustworthy group of commandos of his own choice—officers, students and workers—whose duty would be to seize the person of the Chancellor. Later, apparently with the knowledge of Oster, Heinz developed the plan in such a way as to lead naturally to Hitler being shot during the action. He held it was tantamount to suicide not to kill Hitler as swiftly as possible since, as he put it to Oster, "Hitler alive has more weight than all the troops at our disposal." Heinz, another monarchist, secretly hoped that this action in which he was to play the principal part, would lead to the proclamation of Prince Wilhelm, the son of the Crown Prince, as Regent.[8]

The tragedy is that there was no one involved at the top of the conspiracy with the ruthless thrust which Colonel Claus von Stauffenberg was to bring six years later in July 1944, when, with Beck still the figurehead of the action, a time-bomb was actually placed under Hitler's table. By now, however, there had been ample discussion about who should take control of the government when Hitler had been arrested. All this would no doubt, have been more than adequate. But Hitler was still in Berchtesgaden when the news came that Chamberlain was indeed to visit Germany.

The news of Chamberlain's flight to Berchtesgaden reached Canaris when he was at dinner with several of his officers, including Lahousen. Lahousen recalls the Admiral's utter consternation: 'What *he*—visit that man!' he kept repeating, leaving his food uneaten, and rising to pace around the room. What was the use of sending missions to London when this was the outcome? Canaris,

78

who had gambled on stirring British intransigence over Czechoslovakia and had tried to persuade the High Command to accept his view, felt that he had been humiliated. There would be no influencing the generals now.[9]

Events suddenly gained momentum; Hitler's blackmailing sense of melodrama supervened. With only days to spare before the Führer's deadline, Chamberlain prepared himself for the confrontation at Berchtesgaden. Far from acting as defender of the Czechs, Chamberlain was determined pressure must be put upon them to come to terms with Hitler and lift the threat of war from Europe. Chamberlain, who was by no means the diplomatic weakling he is commonly made out, believed Hitler had a reasonable case in his claim on the Sudeten territory. Admittedly Benes, a brilliant negotiator, cornered the Sudetens in September by suddenly conceding everything which had formed the basis of their political grievance against his government. But the Nazi leaders made no bones about their attitude to the question. In a speech on 10 September, Göring called the Czechs a "miserable pygmy race" and their country "a petty segment of Europe." Two days later, at the annual Party rally at Nuremberg, Hitler made a brutal attack on Benes and the Czechoslovak people.

On 15 September Chamberlain entered an aircraft for the first time in his life and flew to Munich, from where he drove to Berchtesgaden. He got nothing from his three-hour conversation with the Führer, not even the stenographic record of what they had said. Chamberlain, returning to London the following day to consider Hitler's proposals for the complete secession to Germany of the Sudeten region with its 3-million population of Austro-German descent, gained at this stage a rather favorable opinion of the German leader. 'I got the impression,' said Chamberlain, 'that here was a man who could be relied upon when he had given his word.' During the five memorable days which followed, Britain and France put every pressure they could upon Benes, Czechoslovakia's long-suffering President, to force him to accept that the Sudetenland must go. If he did not yield, he was told, the Allies would renounce the support he had hoped to be given. Benes felt himself "basely betrayed," but Chamberlain returned to Germany on 22 September in good heart to settle the final agreement with Hitler.

This time they met in Godesberg. Hitler, sensing pliancy, demanded an immediate and unopposed military occupation of the Sudetenland by his armies. Chamberlain returned to his hotel, grieved that his diplomatic success with Benes had met with such base ingratitude. So everyone had to wait—the diplomats, the press, the outside world, and not least the anxious group of conspirators whose plans against the Führer had been by-passed by events. Finally, Hitler staged a midnight meeting, and put his ultimatum in Chamberlain's hands. As a sop to the eminent messenger, he changed the date for the threatened military occupation from 26 September to 1 October. Hitler knew how to bluff; it was his method. When he heard that Chamberlain had been unable to persuade Benes to accept this final humiliation of his country, Hitler on 26 September in the Berlin Sportspalast made one of his deliberately wild speeches, full of calculated violence. He claimed the Sudetenland would be his by the beginning of October, though he added that his demands on Czechoslovakia were his last territorial claims in Europe. 'I will smash the Czechs,' he roared repeatedly at Sir Horace Wilson at a meeting in Berlin when Wilson came to see him as Chamberlain's personal representative.

In his testimony at Nuremberg, Gisevius says:

On 27 September it was clear that Hitler wanted to go to the last extremity. In order to make the German people war-minded he ordered a parade of the armies in Berlin, and Witzleben had to carry that order out. The parade had entirely the opposite effect. The population, which assumed that these troops were going to war, showed their open displeasure. The troops, instead of jubilation, saw clenched fists, and Hitler, who was watching the parade from the window of the Reich Chancellery, had an attack of anger. He stepped back from his window and said: 'With such a people I cannot wage war.' Witzleben on his return from the parade, said that

80

he would have liked to have unlimbered the guns outside the Reich Chancellery. . . . The following morning—this was the 28th—we believed that the opportunity had come to start the revolt. On that morning too we discovered that Hitler had rejected the final offer from the British Prime Minister Chamberlain and sent the intermediary, Wilson, back with a negative answer. Witzleben received that letter and took it to Halder. He believed that now the proof for Hitler's desire for war had been established, and Halder agreed. Halder visited von Brauchitsch while Witzleben waited in Halder's room. After a few moments Halder came back and said that Brauchitsch now also realized that the moment for action had arrived and that he merely wanted to go over to the Reich Chancellery to make quite sure that Witzleben and Halder's story was correct. Brauchitsch accordingly went to the Reich Chancellery after Witzleben had told him over the telephone that all was prepared, and it was at midday on 28 September, when suddenly and contrary to our expectation Mussolini intervened and Hitler, impressed by Mussolini's step, agreed to go to Munich. So, at the eleventh hour, the *putsch* was made impossible.[10]

Europe hung now between peace and war. France and Britain were, within the means available to them, mobilizing their forces. Remote, isolated America went no further than to make a verbal protest; had not President Roosevelt, at a press conference on 9 September, already warned journalists not to assume that the United States were associating themselves with France and Britain in opposing Hitler's Germany? Like the British and French, he had been delighted when Chamberlain flew back to Munich; "Good man," he was heard to cry. Prague, on the other hand, bluntly stated they had a million men under arms. Hitler wrote to Chamberlain, and the letter was delivered late at night on 27 September. He reiterated his demands, but ended by leaving the door open, "I leave it to your judgment," he wrote, "whether . . . you consider you should continue your effort." Behind the scenes at the Chancellery

Göring, among certain other close advisers, was trying to calm Hitler and urge the need for a diplomatic solution. Like the High Command, he did not accept that Germany was ready for a major war. Hitler's bluff was being called, not least within his own four walls.

Now, if at any time, was the moment to take action against the Führer, to penetrate the security of the Chancellery and seize the man by force, backed, morally at least, by a sufficient number of generals of the High Command. But everyone both within and outside Germany seemed mesmerized by the dangers of the time; initiative seemed to have passed even from Hitler himself. Tension, and tension only, was supreme. As for Hitler, he retreated into himself.

Mussolini intervened at noon on 28 September, offering to help mediate with the Czechs. The following day, the leaders convened in the Führerhaus on the Königsplatz in Munich—Chamberlain, Daladier, Hitler and Mussolini. Needless to say, there was not a Czech in sight. Mussolini, happy in his new role as an influential mediator, and proud of his modest ability to speak the necessary languages, appeared at first to control the meeting. Indeed, he produced a plan prepared for him, in secret, by Göring and Weizsäcker, State Secretary at the German Foreign Office. So the notorious Munich Agreement was finally concluded in the small hours of 30 September. Czechoslovakia was partitioned, and on 1 October German troops formally occupied the Sudetenland. For Chamberlain, the apparent success of this *rapprochement* with the Führer represented a new hope. "Peace in our time," he called it, in the phrase which became notorious. Within a month, Poland and Hungary had snapped up their desired portions of Czech territory, while Benes had resigned and vanished into exile.

Hitler had won again. Goerdeler, who spent August to October in Switzerland, wrote to a friend about the agreement: "If Britain and France had only taken it upon themselves to risk war, Hitler would never have used force." Later he wrote, "The Munich Agreement is nothing but absolute capitulation by France and Britain to a vainglorious charlatan." Goerdeler consistently overestimated the ability of the Western powers to commit themselves to full-scale war before 1939.

So the opportunity for a *coup d'état* passed. Even so, it will always remain very doubtful whether Germany as a whole would have tolerated the arrest and trial of Hitler when everything appeared to be working in his favor. Had he been assassinated, the situation might well have been much easier. The idea of war itself (as distinct from bloodless seizure of other people's territory) was certainly not popular. The whole Army, in spite of the oath of loyalty, would have had to support any firm stand taken by the High Command against the Führer. But would they have done so? Would the officers with men directly at their command have carried out orders of such a kind originating from men whose only power was on paper? The opportunity, such as it was, came and went within the span of a few days only.

The diplomatic success of Munich behind him, Hitler seemed invincible. With the Sudeten territory in his possession, in less than six months he was able to push his armies into Prague. His plans for this act of naked aggression were put in hand immediately after the Munich settlement. Yet the Allies did nothing about the integrity of the State for which they were the guarantors. As Chamberlain himself argued, the small country of Czechoslovakia was too remote from Britain and Western Europe to be worth the risk of war with Germany. Had he not written to his ambassador in France the previous November that German expansion in Central Europe was to be regarded as "a normal and natural thing?" As Chamberlain saw it, all that mattered to Britain was to forestall any threat of German expansion to the West. So when Czechoslovakia fell to Hitler, it was calmly written off. A small country, and who cared?

III

Anti-War Effort

After Munich: Schlabrendorff joins the Resistance

From the autumn of 1938 onwards we have the advantage of Hassell's comments which, though they are strictly limited to his own circle and range of interest, are of considerable importance in arriving at a proper understanding of the week-by-week shifts and changes of feeling among the right-wing members of the opposition to Hitler. As we have seen, Hassell returned to Berlin from Rome during the summer, and his diary opens on 4 September, when he had a private lunch with Sir Nevile Henderson on the day it was decided Chamberlain should visit Germany. That same evening Hassell met General Wilhelm Keitel, Hitler's new Chief of Staff, High Command, whom he found "uninformed politically" and astonished at England's readiness to march with France in case of conflict. After visiting Schacht, who "called Hitler a swindler," and whom he found completely opposed to the régime, he had an interview with Ernst Weizsäcker at the Foreign Office. Gradually he was renewing the social and political contacts he felt he needed, and using his diary to clarify his judgment of the situation.

On 25 November, for example, two weeks after the violent, nation-wide pogrom organized by Goebbels, he writes "under crushing emotions evoked by the vile persecution of the Jews":

> I am most deeply troubled about the effect on our national life, which is dominated ever more inexorably by a system capable of such things . . . Respectable people were shocked to read names like Gürtner [Minister of Justice] and Schwerin-Krosigk [Minister of Finance] among the authors of the decree prescribing penalties for the Jews. These men cannot see apparently how they are degrading themselves and being used.[1]

84

When, on 25 January 1939, he went to call on Schacht after his dismissal as President of the Reichsbank and Minister of Economic Affairs, he found him "noticeably and deeply upset." He did not think Schacht sincere when he exclaimed, "You have no idea how exuberantly happy I am to be out of all this!" Later, Schacht thundered, "He threw me out!" Schacht seemed caught in some psychological dilemma, as if he wanted at one and the same time the pleasure of hurling his resignation in Hitler's face and the martyrdom of being dismissed.

The atmosphere of uncertainty at this time—it was Hitler's deliberate policy to keep everyone guessing, whether they were his collaborators inside Germany or his opponents outside—is revealed when, on 26 January, Hassell went to see Weizsäcker, his former colleague. Weizsäcker, he wrote in his diary, "thought the barometer indicated peace even in the east, where at the most one might expect action against Poland. On the other hand, Hitler's program still demanded a complete settlement of the Czech issue." A month later, on 25 February, he is writing: "It is becoming more and more evident that England and France are following a tactical procedure, involving a highly accelerated rearmament program . . . by means of which they seek to exert 'peace pressure' on the 'totalitarians.' They seem to believe it will work." After Hitler had moved into Prague on 15 March, Hassell wrote:

This is the first instance of manifest depravity, exceeding all limits, including those of decency, brilliantly executed in its technical aspects, to the utter astonishment of the world, which is looking on aghast. . . . Even if all goes well at first, I cannot believe that this can end in anything but disaster. . . . But since there is no real determination to resist anywhere—and on this fact Hitler is counting—nothing will happen for the moment.

On 28 March he saw Canaris, who was about to leave for Spain. He does not, however, record what they discussed. On 24 May he visited Henderson, who told him that he was suffering from cancer of the mouth, for which he was being treated by radium. "He is naturally very much depressed over the political situation. In England they accuse him of letting Hitler lead him by the nose. It is understandable that he speaks most bitterly about Hitler's breach of faith."

Another prominent member of the resistance who was in Berlin in 1938 was the lawyer Fabian von Schlabrendorff. Born in 1907, Schlabrendorff was a young jurist who from his early twenties, as a student, had been opposed to Nazism. He has been described by the historian and political correspondent Terence Prittie as "a conservative and a Prussian, a man of wit and charm, of considerable courage and absolute integrity," and his opposition to the régime was "founded on respect for the human being as an individual and on solid belief in the Christian ethic." He survived the war, and was to write one of the few personal studies of the resistance movement. After working in the provinces, he returned in 1938 to Berlin, where he had studied law and political economy, and later held an appointment in the Prussian Ministry of the Interior. Like Kleist, he had published papers opposing the régime. He soon met Oster and the Abwehr circle, and learned of the existence of a conscious, organized resistance movement; he noted that

> although Canaris hated Hitler and National Socialism, he himself did not feel capable of leading any decisive action against Hitler. Instead he protected Oster and allowed him to use the opportunities of the Counter-Intelligence, as far as it was under Oster's jurisdiction, to organize, strengthen, and enlarge the German resistance movement.[2]

Schlabrendorff is among those who remain convinced to this day that a stiffer attitude in Britain from 1938 would have materially helped the opposition overcome the lassitude of the generals in Germany; the gamble that Hitler would have fought had he been faced by real Allied determination to stand by Czechoslovakia seems to him to have been a relatively small one. In the end, he believes, too many people both inside and outside Germany behaved supinely, or, like Henderson, were ambivalent in their attitude to the régime and, on the whole, hostile to or suspicious of the resistance.

During the eleven months between the signing of the Munich agreement on 30 September 1938 and the invasion of Poland on 1 September 1939, the opposition in Germany faced grave difficulties. First, there was a general re-alignment of the principal conspirators. Witzleben was posted to a command in Kassel. Dohnanyi was sent to Leipzig; his opposition to National Socialism had been singled out by Roland Freisler, of the Ministry of Justice, who caused Martin Bormann, as Party Secretary, to make an official complaint that, since Dohnanyi continued to avoid joining the Party, he should be removed from the position of influence which he held. Gürtner regretfully complied, and Dohnanyi was transferred to the Leipzig Supreme Court. This was in November 1938.

Brauchitsch, always a doubtful ally, was lost to the movement. He had recently been divorced, and was now married to a woman with whom he was much in love and who was, like only too many women, a dedicated Nazi, and from this time he drew further away from the conspirators. Schacht, dismissed by Hitler, took himself on a tour of India. The pendulum of disaffection swung now in the direction of Oster and his more immediate associates. The High Command of the Armed Forces (O.K.W.) was in the hands of General Wilhelm Keitel (created field-marshal in 1940), General Alfred Jodl, and General Walther Warlimont, all men firmly entrenched behind Hitler.

The inner corps of conspirators were left without any immediate means of staging an action against Hitler. Hassell, however, still felt as late as August 1939 that the opposition could rely on Halder and another disaffected general on the staff of the High Command, Georg Thomas. He wrote on 7 August: "Nothing is to be hoped from the generals. Let's not even talk about Keitel; even Brauchitsch is in the hands of the Party. Only a few have kept clear heads: Halder, Canaris, Thomas." When the Allies swallowed the invasion of Czechoslovakia with little more than a grumble about the inconvenience of conscience such aggression caused them, there seemed little hope of stirring them to take any direct action which might call Hitler's bluff. Hitler, however, had now acquired the last major territorial gain which the Allies were to allow to go unchallenged. There were only five more months of uneasy peace. During this period one spasmodic attempt after another was made to warn the Allied governments of what the future held in store. The warnings were to prove unwelcome, even embarrassing, and were for the most part left unheeded.

Warnings to Britain: Churchill and the Resistance

Gisevius claims that the first of these warnings was given by Goerdeler and Schacht at Ouchy in late March to "a person with considerable influence in London and Paris political circles." [3] Goerdeler's biographer, Gerhard Ritter, identifies this intermediary as a friend of Goerdeler's, Dr. Rudolph Shairer, an educationalist resident in London, who has confirmed that Schacht was present at the meeting before leaving for India, but treated Goerdeler's incessant memoranda on German military weakness with some contempt. He thought that the governments abroad should be warned of Germany's strength. The confused accounts of this warning show at the very least that the Allies were being warned of new moves by Hitler against Poland, Danzig and possibly other territories to the east.

The second warning, given to Ian Colvin, the Berlin correspondent for the London *News Chronicle,* was prompted by Beck and Oster. This was passed on by Colvin on 29 March first to Sir Alexander Cadogan, Permanent Under-Secretary at the Foreign Office, then to Lord Halifax and finally to Chamberlain himself. Colvin, who had penetrated to this high level with the assistance of the British embassy in Berlin and the Foreign Office in London, told the Prime Minister that Hitler intended to invade Poland, whatever the risk might be of starting a war in

Europe. This meeting only confirmed what was already British and French policy; on 31 March the House of Commons heard that the French were prepared, together with the British, to come to the aid of Poland if her independence were threatened by military action. Nevertheless, in April and May Hitler was openly discussing his plans for handling a pan-European war with an ever-widening circle of his staff in the High Command, and at the same time making overtures to Moscow to postpone any likelihood of war on that front while he was conducting aggression against his nearer neighbours to the north and west.

Goerdeler himself joined the relay of messengers to Britain. He met Churchill in May, and told him at some length about the German opposition. Churchill later also received Schlabrendorff, who, with the help of Canaris, visited him in the summer. (The visit was ostensibly to examine the archives at Windsor Castle, since Schlabrendorff's great-grandfather had been Baron Stockmar, Queen Victoria's physician and confidant.) After seeing Lord Loyd (who apparently, and very undiplomatically, "made some scathing remarks about Henderson's abilities and qualifications"), he found himself before someone of more resolute nature when he faced Churchill at Chartwell. Schlabrendorff gives his own account of this meeting:

Churchill's appearance, his way of conducting the conversation, his rapid-fire questions and answers, all made a deep impression on me. I had the feeling that I was in the presence of a statesman of historic stature. Unlike Lord Lloyd, Churchill avoided all personalities; and he also displayed none of Lloyd's doubts about the strength and determination of his country. On the contrary, Churchill seemed confident that the English nation was basically sound and fully capable of putting up a good fight.

Looking at him as he sat, compact and solid, on the sofa beneath the portrait of his famous ancestor, the Duke of Marlborough, he appeared to me the personification of England at the very height of her greatness.

I had no intention of letting any doubts arise about the fact that the men of the German resistance, although anti-Nazi, were unwilling to betray their country. I began the conversation with the sentence: "I am not a Nazi, but I am a good patriot." Churchill promptly retorted: "So am I!" A broad grin spreading over his face showed his delight at this quick rejoinder.

During the course of our conversation, he displayed great interest in the German opposition. Finally he asked whether I could guarantee a successful action by our group. The answer to that question was not easy for me, and I hesitated for a moment before replying in the negative, but I felt that it was most important to remain realistic and not give in to wishful thinking. In view of the difficulties of living under a tyranny, and at the same time working towards its overthrow, it seemed impossible to guarantee a successful *coup d'état*. I believe, by the way, that Churchill fully realized these problems, and that his question was meant to test my reaction.[4]

Schlabrendorff refused a second request from the Abwehr to return to Britain in August. But other went: Erich and Theo Kordt, who saw Vansittart, and a former Rhodes scholar, handsome Adam von Trott zu Solz, who had studied at Oxford 1931-3 and who loved England, as well as Count Helmuth von Moltke, who was half-British and a former member of the English bar. Trott and Moltke met, among others, John W. Wheeler-Bennett, the historian, at Oxford in 1939, and Moltke was also an intimate friend of Lionel Curtis, whom he visited frequently at Oxford. Moltke and Trott were among the "philosophers" of the resistance in Germany, forming the circle which normally met at Kreisau, Moltke's country estate, and endeavoured to keep the spirit of liberal, intellectual discussion alive when academic freedom was lost in Germany.

Hitler's war plans as they were outlined to his generals percolated soon enough to the Abwehr. During the last summer of peace in 1939, the representatives of resistance, as well as those with different motives, moved in force to

England. In June Canaris tried to induce Kleist to return; when he refused on the grounds that it would be useless ("What have we to offer?" he asked), Colonel Bohm-Tettelbach was sent once more in his place and held a secret conference in London with, among others, Sir James Grigg. He came back unconvinced that the British would fight for Poland. Even Weizsäcker sent warnings to Vansittart about the negotiations between Germany and the Soviet Union, which took place during June, July and August.

Throughout August, Hassell, whose official status was, he says, "inactive," was still unofficially very active in discussion. On 14 August he writes:

At ten o'clock I saw Goerdeler in his lodgings on Askanischer Platz. Fresh, clear-headed, active. Perhaps a bit sanguine. One hears generally that he is imprudent and is being closely watched. It is a relief, though, to speak with a man who wants to act rather than grumble. Of course his hands are tied, just like ours, and he is desperate about the losses we have suffered in the Army since February 4, 1938. Nevertheless, he believes there are elements of resistance already growing again throughout the country, even though scattered and without organization. We were agreed that a world war offers no solution, that it would be a terrible catastrophe. Whatever influence we have must be used to prevent it.[5]

That same evening, Hassell dined alone with Beck: "A most cultured, attractive and intelligent man. Unfortunately, he has a very low opinion of the leading people in the Army. For that reason he could see no place there where we could gain a foothold." The following day he visited Schacht, who, following his return from his enjoyable Indian trip, seemed cheered rather than the reverse that things were going so badly in a Germany which had rejected his advice: "Schacht's view is that we can do nothing but keep our eyes open and wait, that things will follow their inevitable courses. I am only worried that while we wait great values will be irretrievably destroyed and one

91

day a complete catastrophe will suddenly confront us." He left Schacht to call on Henderson, who received him with the query: "Madhouse or hospital?" Hassell replied, "Madhouse." Prague, said Henderson, "was the straw that broke the camel's back. Now it was impossible for Chamberlain to fly here again with his umbrella."

Canaris tried without avail in August to warn Keitel that war was imminent because the Abwehr had been asked to provide the S.S. with Polish uniforms for "Operation Himmler." [6] Lahousen has preserved an entry from Canaris's missing diaries; the entry records this interview with Keitel, which took place on 17 August, 1939:

I report to Keitel my conversation with Jost (an S.S. officer). Keitel says that he cannot concern himself with this operation as the Führer has not informed him of it and has only told him to procure Polish uniforms for Heydrich. He agrees that I was right to inform the General Staff. He says that he does not think much of such operations, but that there's nothing else for it, if the Führer orders them. It is not up to me, he says, to ask the Führer how he imagines such an operation is to be carried out. . . . He thinks it would be a good thing if Mussolini told the Führer quite clearly that he would not fight. He, Keitel, believed that Italy would fight all the same. I replied that I considered that this would be out of the question and related to him the full gist of the Ciano-Ribbentrop meeting. Keitel replied that the Führer told him the opposite. I told him also that Count Marogna [Chief of the Abwehr office in Vienna] has learned that the King of Italy has said to King Alfonso of Spain that he will not sign if Mussolini lays a mobilization order before him. Keitel remarks that it was interesting to see that even a nation ruled by a dictatorship could be quite temperamental when it came to war. How much more difficult it must be when it came to democratic countries! He was convinced that the British would not intervene. I try to refute this opinion and say that the British will immediately blockade us and destroy our merchant shipping. Keitel says that this will not be very

92

important as we can get oil from Russia. I reply that this is not the decisive factor and that we cannot withstand a blockade in the long run. The British will fight against us with all means in their power if we use force against Poland and if it comes to bloodshed. I tell him that the British would have behaved in just the same way if there had been bloodshed when we marched into Czechoslovakia. I try to explain to Keitel the effect of economic warfare on Germany and tell him that we have only limited forces with which to fight back. I have just learned that we could only put ten U-boats into the Atlantic. Keitel says that it will be easy to force Rumania to deliver oil to us when Poland is defeated. I inform him of the precautions already taken by the British in the Balkans and tell him that they will have certainly prepared against that eventuality too.[7]

The actual assassination of Hitler was not yet considered by any responsible member of any wing of the resistance movement. His removal would have meant at the worst arrest and trial, a *coup d'état* carried out by patriots who felt that their leader was going too far for the ultimate good of the nation. In the spectrum of opinions within Germany there was everything from the highly ethical, even academic dislike of all that Hitler stood for to those who, while approving of a militant nationalism, the cancellation of the Versailles Treaty and a drastic revision of frontiers in favour of Germany, disliked the increasingly arbitrary way in which Hitler appeared to risk the nation's future. In other words, they approved of his aims, or most of them, but not of his methods, which made them uneasy. The generals, for the most part, belonged to this end of the spectrum of opposition, and so did those elements in the German civilian public who feared a headlong rush into war.[8] The unthinking majority, of course, were all for Hitler, the man with the luck on his side, "right or wrong." In any case, more people had been worried about the gamble of the march into Prague than they were about the gamble of a blitzkrieg in Poland. Everyone claimed that the Polish corridor represented a flagrant injustice to Germany.

Whatever action the different groups and individuals in Germany wanted, they suddenly found themselves faced by a Britain which had issued an unconditional guarantee of support to Poland. This did not seem to worry Hitler or his immediate supporters in his High Command of the Armed Forces, the O.K.W. General Thomas, who tried, as Beck had done one year before, to persuade the O.K.W. through Keitel to avoid the dangers of world war, only received a sharp reproof that he was acting like an alarmist and defeatist. There would be no war, said Keitel, whom the resistance nicknamed *Gummilöwe,* or Rubber-Lion. This was in August 1939.[9]

Last Peace Efforts

Thomas's last attempt to secure a return to reason in the ranks of the High Command was nullified still further by Ribbentrop's *coup* in bringing off the Nazi-Soviet Non-Aggression Pact, which was signed on 22 August. Germany and Russia signed a mutual agreement valid for ten years; should either become involved in war, each agreed to give no help to the enemy of the other, while it was accepted that any differences between them would be settled by arbitration, not force. This was the public pronouncement, but behind it lay a further act of expediency, a secret agreement, in which Eastern Europe was to be divided into acknowledged "spheres of influence," either for political pressure or active subjugation.

Hitler now felt free to conquer Poland. Britain and France, those so-called decadent powers, would never dare to meet their obligations, any more than they had in the case of Czechoslovakia. Last-minute efforts by Schacht and Beck to intervene with the High Command were in Schacht's case violently repulsed by Brauchitsch, and in Beck's case countered by Halder.

The attempt by Schacht, supported by General Thomas and Canaris, to persuade the inner circle of generals in the High Command to back down once Hitler had given the initial order to invade Poland, was described by Gisevius at Nuremberg. According to Gisevius, Halder by this

94

time had "disavowed himself" and refused to see Schacht, who nevertheless went with Gisevius to the War Ministry in the Bendlerstrasse on 25 August to see what he could do.

When we arrived at the O.K.W. and were waiting on a corner in the street, Canaris sent Oster to see us. That was the moment when Hitler, between six and seven, suddenly ordered Halder to withdraw his order to march. The tribunal will no doubt remember that Hitler, influenced by the renewed intervention of Mussolini, suddenly withdrew the order to march which had already been given. Unfortunately, Canaris and Thomas and all our friends were now under the impression that this withdrawal of an order to march was an incredible loss of prestige to Hitler. . . . Canaris told me, "Now the peace of Europe is saved for fifty years, because Hitler has lost the respect of the generals." Unfortunately, in the tension of this psychological change, we all felt that we could look forward to the following days in a quiet frame of mind. So when three days later Hitler gave the decisive order to march, it came as a complete surprise for our group as well. Oster called me to the O.K.W. Schacht accompanied me. We asked Canaris again whether he could not arrange another meeting with Brauchitsch and Halder, but Canaris said to me: "It is too late now." He had tears in his eyes, adding: "That is the end of Germany." [10]

Beck's attempt at intervention took the form of a letter to Brauchitsch, with whom he had broken off all relations. According to Gisevius:

The tone of the letter was such that the normal mind could imagine only two possible reactions to it. Either Brauchitsch would feel that the ideas expressed in this letter were an offense to his loyalty to the Nazi system— in which case he must hand over the letter to the Gestapo—or else he would be struck by the force of the actual arguments and the moral appeal—in which case he must act; but he found a third way out—he said nothing and did nothing.[11]

95

Meanwhile, other further last-minute attempts to stop the war were undertaken by Göring, who played the usual two-faced game of being fully engaged in preparations for conquest while (with Hitler's knowledge) trying on an informal level to secure the non-intervention of Britain. It can fairly be said that Göring did not want a war; he had recently gained all that he wanted in life—a wife, a child, and wealth beyond measure to satisfy his craving for luxurious residences and the founding of a great national art collection.

Finally, Canaris's personal intervention to try to stop hostilities took the form of addressing an appeal to Mussolini through his friend General Roatta, head of Italian Military Intelligence. What influence this intervention had on the Duce cannot be determined. Mussolini, as is well known, pointed out to Hitler that Italy would be unable to take an active part in war beside Germany, and his message was no doubt partly instrumental in persuading Hitler on 25 August to stay his hand for a few days more.

The order for the attack on Poland was finally given—time of commencement 04.45 hours on 1 September 1939. Canaris had been permitted to attend Hitler's staff conference at Berchtesgaden on 22 August, and he had noted what Hitler said. When war finally came, one of Canaris's first acts was, when Henderson delivered Britain's ultimatum to Germany on 2 September, to warn the British military attaché in Berlin, Colonel Denis Daly, that a heavy air-raid was planned for London on the following day, 3 September. The embassy managed to send a coded message to London, and as a result the air-raid alerts sounded in the capital after Chamberlain had spoken at 11.00 in the morning, announcing that Britain was in a state of war with Germany. The air-raid was, in fact, cancelled when Halder persuaded Hitler that an isolated raid of this kind would be useless. Canaris, summoning his confidants to his room at the Tirpitz Ufer, told them that in his view Germany's victory would be a greater catastrophe than her defeat.

PART TWO

I

Treason Becomes Duty

Canaris and the Fall of Poland

As a result of the German strategy of *Blitzkrieg*, Poland's air force was annihilated in a matter of hours and her armies overwhelmed in a matter of days. By 17 September it was all over except for pockets of resistance, in particular around Warsaw. On that day too, the armies of Soviet Russia marched into Poland to claim the territory assigned to Stalin in his secret pact with Hitler. Warsaw did not finally capitulate until 27 September, after a siege lasting almost three weeks.

Canaris, like most of those with a stake in the conspiracy against Hitler, was caught unawares on the morning Poland was invaded. As a measure of the unrealistic thinking current in a nation where only one man took the decisions concerning peace or war, only days before the German army violated the Polish frontier, Oster is reported by Gisevius as saying, "the Führer is finished." This was on 25 August, after Hitler's momentary cancellation of his invasion in an attempt to get what he wanted through a repetition of the bloodless strategy of Munich. Oster's delusion was, as we have seen, shared by Canaris, who is said to have expressed the opinion that Hitler could never survive such arbitrary treatment of his High Command. His wishful thinking was an echo of Chamberlain's reaction after Munich. Goerdeler, on the strength of the seeming relaxation of tension, had actually set off for Sweden. Only Major-General Georg Thomas seems to have kept his head; that is, remained deeply pessimistic. As head of the Economics and Armaments branch of O.K.W., Thomas, who was a brilliant staff officer, continued his normal duties with great proficiency in spite of the fact that he had been

99

a supporter of resistance against Hitler since the Fritsch affair in 1938. He was to be more closely involved with the conspirators now that war was declared.

On the outbreak of hostilities, Canaris had avoided taking any active part in the disgraceful "Operation Gleiwitz" with which the Polish campaign opened. Prisoners had been taken from the concentration camps, put into Polish uniforms and then murdered in order to supply evidence that the Poles themselves had launched an attack in that sector. This was the action to which Lahousen referred when giving evidence before the International Military Tribunal at Nuremberg:

Sometime, I believe it was in the middle of August . . . Abwehr Section I, as well as my section, Abwehr Section II, were charged with the job of providing or keeping in readiness Polish uniforms and equipment, as well as identification cards, and so on, for the undertaking "Himmler." . . . It was, to be sure, an order on which we, the chiefs of the sections concerned, already had some misgivings without knowing what, in the last analysis, it was about. The name Himmler, however, was eloquent enough. . . . We had a very understandable suspicion that something crooked was afoot, particularly because of the name of the undertaking. . . . When the first war bulletin appeared, which spoke of the attack of Polish units on German territory, Pieckenbrock, who had the report in his hand, and read it, observed that now we knew what our uniforms had been needed for. The same day or a few days later, I cannot exactly say, Canaris informed us that people from concentration camps disguised in these uniforms had been ordered to make a military attack on the radio station at Gleiwitz. . . . Although we were greatly interested, particularly General Oster, to learn details of this action . . . I cannot even today say exactly what happened.[1]

Nevertheless, the Abwehr had in fact provided the uniforms. No doubt the Abwehr was regarded as the depart-

100

ment responsible for acquiring and supplying this kind of "irregular" equipment. Canaris was lucky he had not been expected to intervene more directly. He had become responsible on the outbreak of the war for the activities of a unit of commandos known as the Brandenburg division,[2] whose task was to carry out lightning sabotage raids. Canaris resisted Himmler's initial attempts to absorb the commandos into the S.S. so that they might, as Himmler put it, "increase the fear and despondency they were to create." The unit started as a company composed of Poles and Czechs of German parentage who volunteered for the service, and Canaris placed them under the command of Colonel Friedrich Wilhelm Heinz.

On 12 September Canaris, with his aide Lahousen, attended a conference on Hitler's armored train. At Nuremberg, Lahousen told the story of what was said at this meeting; Hitler himself was not present:

Canaris expressed serious scruples regarding the bombardment of Warsaw, stressing the devastating repercussions on foreign policy of such a bombardment. The Chief of the O.K.W. at that time, Keitel, answered that these measures had been laid down directly by the Führer and Göring, and that he, Keitel, had had no influence on these decisions. . . . The Führer and Göring telephoned frequently back and forth; sometimes I heard something of what was said, but not always.

Secondly, Canaris gave an earnest warning against the measures which he knew about, that is, the projected shooting and extermination which were to be directed particularly against the Polish intelligentsia, the nobility, the clergy, as well as all elements that could be regarded as embodying the national resistance movement. Canaris said at that time—I am quoting more or less verbatim—"the world will at some time make the armed forces under whose eyes these events occurred also responsible for these events."[3]

The train, which acted as Hitler's headquarters, was stationed at Gogolin. Canaris saw for the first time what war conducted by Hitler was to mean. So did Halder. According to Hassell, when they finally returned from Poland their nerves were shattered. Goerdeler told Hassell that Canaris "came back from Poland entirely broken" after seeing "the results of our brutal conduct of the war, especially in devastated Warsaw." A broadcast from Britain, which Goerdeler and Beck heard together, mentioned Fritsch's virtual suicide while on active service in Poland. Goerdeler told Hassell that "Beck was overcome."

The Abwehr in Wartime: Dohnanyi joins Canaris

By now Canaris's senior staff formed a hand-picked enclave within the resistance. When Dohnanyi joined the Abwehr in August 1939, it had already been greatly enlarged and reorganized. It had now grown to five departments—the first for espionage abroad, the second for sabotage, the third for counter-espionage, the fourth acting (as before) in liaison with the Service attachés abroad, while the fifth, Department Z, the Central Section, remained the administrative center of the whole organization.[4]

Oster, of course, was chief of Department Z, and Dohnanyi acted as his immediate assistant. At the head of Department I (espionage abroad) was Colonel Hans Pieckenbrock, described by his colleague Lahousen as "a close friend of Canaris." Like most of the leading men in the Abwehr, "Piecki," as he was called by his friends, was a man of pronounced character; he was a Rhinelander, tall, dark, elegant, highly intelligent, with an ironic sense of humor, sophisticated and easy-going in his manner. Later he was succeeded by Colonel Georg Hansen, one of the most loyal members of the resistance and Canaris's successor when the Abwehr was discredited and Canaris himself removed from office.

Department II (responsible for sabotage, and for the initial supervision of the Brandenburg commandos) was controlled up to 1939 by Colonel Hans Grosscurth,[5] later (1939-43) by Lahousen, and subsequently by Colonel

Wessel von Freytag-Loringhoven. Grosscurth was tall, fair, taciturn, and wore spectacles; he was essentially an organizer within the opposition; not only are his diaries of the greatest importance, but his secondment for some months in 1939 to the Army High Command was to make him a direct link between Halder and Canaris. Hansen was to be executed after the attempt on Hitler's life in July 1944; Freytag-Loringhoven committed suicide before the end of the war, and Grosscurth was to disappear while on service at the Eastern Front. Department III (counter-espionage) came until 1939 under Colonel Rudolf Bamler,[6] who was succeeded by Colonel Bentivegni, known as "Benti." Department IV (the foreign department) came under Rear-Admiral Leopold Buerkner. In spite of his name, Bentivegni came from an old-established Prussian military family, and looked like it, with his monocle firmly set in his eye.[7]

It must always be remembered that the normal Intelligence work of the Abwehr continued in spite of the dedication of a few of its members to the work of the resistance. Pieckenbrock, for example, was sent to Copenhagen to negotiate with the Norwegian collaborator Quisling and came back, according to a report quoted during the International Military Tribunal at Nuremberg, with "good results." Canaris himself was frequently occupied with quite normal duties; only Oster and Dohnanyi in Department Z, with Canaris's knowledge and support, devoted their major attention to the work of resistance. But their department held the records, which went back to the period of the First World War, of some 300,000 agents or potential agents who undertook espionage on behalf of Germany, and these records were in constant use for the normal work of military Intelligence.

The movement, which was rapidly growing under Oster's energetic guidance, was in need of a man with legal training and skill in handling the accumulating documents, and Dohnanyi had been brought into the Abwehr to supervise the paperwork for the insurrection which it was hoped would one day take place. Dohnanyi was given the temporary rank of major. The German mind readily gravitates towards the employment of lawyers, the guides, if not the controllers, of any society when its affairs grow too complex for the laymen to administer. The Abwehr in any case was an organization which thrived on paperwork, and the closer the few officers at the top, together with their immediate associates both within and outside the Army, drew towards active conspiracy, the more their activities had to be fully covered by the regular, and wholly "correct" work of the complex Abwehr organization which, as we have seen, had by now grown conveniently large. However, under the influence of Beck, the conspirators continued to build up their collection of documents which recorded every scrap of evidence against the régime and every resolution in every phase of every plan for its overthrow and replacement by a healthy form of government. The documents included Oster's special collection of atrocity evidence.

Since the Fritsch case, Dohnanyi's association with Oster had grown much closer. During the ten-month period Dohnanyi was relegated to Leipzig—that is, from November 1938 to his assignment by Canaris to the Abwehr in August 1939—he had managed to visit Berlin regularly through a weekly commitment to lecture in the capital. Dohnanyi had used these occasions to keep in constant touch with Beck and Oster, through whom Dohnanyi had learned, to his great satisfaction, that if war seriously threatened, Canaris intended to apply for his secondment to the staff of the Abwehr. During his visits to Berlin, Dohnanyi also kept in touch with Goerdeler and Hassell.

Dohnanyi was essentially a quiet, firm, discreet man— the opposite in many respects of Oster; which may help to account for their friendship. He was, perhaps, something of an introvert, and he kept his undoubted warmth of nature very much to himself. Reliability was his strongest point, and he was a man of absolute integrity. In his public life, there were men who found him obstinate, and even accused him of arrogance; the arrival of this stranger in the Abwehr, with his insistence on correctness and his strictness of outlook, was certainly not universally popular.

104

He arrived as a civilian and was immediately promoted to what soon proved to be a very influential position.

According to his wife, "he had no political ties whatsoever." One might, she said, "call him a liberal, with pronounced Christian convictions." Nevertheless, he fitted without any difficulty into the predominantly right-wing atmosphere which prevailed in Canaris's and Oster's circles. His wife admits that he was "an implacable enemy of any kind of political radicalism." In his family circle, Dohnanyi unbent; he was almost always cheerful and enjoyed the company of his children. From his father, the composer and professor of music Ernst von Dohnanyi, he had inherited a great love for music, and he and his wife passed this on to their children. Dohnanyi was also a very good amateur painter and graphic artist.[8]

Canaris's attitude to the members of his staff was very informal. He believed in the use of first names in the office, and when addressing some of his colleagues he used the intimate form *Du*; he was fond of them all, and determined to protect and cover for them, at considerable risk to himself, when they undertook dangerous missions. On the other hand, Canaris was a past-master at the art of camouflage, and kept himself personally quite clear from active participation in any form of conspiracy. Social contacts were always maintained with the Army and the S.S. Werner Best of Himmler's S.D. reports that on 3 September, the day war was declared between Britain and Germany, Canaris and some of his departmental chiefs went to have dinner with Best and his wife. Best declares that he was "deeply disturbed and depressed" by the outbreak of war with Britain and France; he thought the war might last for years. He was surprised, however, to find Canaris's colleagues more optimistic. The war, according at least to the opinions expressed in S.S. company, would be over in a few months. That was what Colonel Bentivegni said. Canaris did not say a word. By 1942, he was, according to Freidrich Wilhelm Heinz, "a broken man."

With the outbreak of the war, the generals of the High Command drew themselves clear from any kind of treasonable taint; any active disloyalty to the man to whom they had taken their oath became increasingly difficult to contemplate. Only General Hammerstein, brought out of retirement and given a command on the Rhine, spoke up: he was, he declared, determined to invite Hitler to his headquarters and arrest him. But Hitler refused to respond; his mind was on Poland.

It became increasingly clear that the civilian wing of the resistance could achieve nothing on its own in wartime Germany. It had no means at its command to depose Hitler. Talk, of course, went on unceasingly, but any hope of action lay with the military, who were by now the only section of the German community with any regular access to the Führer apart from his personal staff. From 1940 to 1943 the core of this action centered on Department Z of the Abwehr, that is, on Oster and Dohnanyi and the men who joined them as their agents and collaborators.

Renewed Activity: Oster and Halder

A whole complex of activity followed the outbreak of war. In consultation with Beck and Dohnanyi, Oster had sketched out in pencil the draft of a plan which came to be known as the Oster Study—a document of only three pages which was later to fall into the hands of the Gestapo and to be destroyed by them before the end of the war.[9] Although Oster disguised what he wrote as if he were drawing up the plan for some kind of hunt, in fact he anticipated the much more elaborate plan for the *coup* of July 1944 by outlining the disposition of the regiments and units needed to seal off the governmental sector of Berlin and seize the means of communication, and detailing how all leading Nazi ministers and officials were to be arrested and put on immediate trial. Peace negotiations were to be initiated, while at the same time Hitler's secret plans for aggression in the West were to be exposed.

The network of conspiracy extended through Hassell from the Army into the Foreign Office, where Weizsäcker, always cautious and self-protecting, was still in favor of some form of *coup d'état*. His link with Halder and with

106

Oster was maintained through a friend of Erich Kordt, Hasso von Etzdorf, who in addition to his position at the Foreign Office was also a reserve cavalry officer. Etzdorf had been appointed to O.K.H. at Zossen in order to act as Army liaison with Weizsäcker at the Foreign Office. He kept in constant personal touch with Halder. Like Grosscurth, who was Canaris's liaison officer at Zossen until his curt dismissal by Brauchitsch on 1 February 1940 on the grounds of "incompatibility," Etzdorf helped to complete the Army-Abwehr-Foreign Office circuit through which the current might pass to ignite the revolt; Erich Kordt and he were responsible for drafting another, more elaborate plan for a *coup d'état* (known as the Etzdorf-Kordt memorandum) which Halder among others examined and, whatever he may have felt at the time, endorsed after the war as a remarkable document.

The idea of a *coup* against Hitler, a revival of the 1938 plan, had never therefore been wholly abandoned, though the difficulty of activating it was greatly increased in wartime. Plans for the arrest of the Führer by a determined section of the High Command were being discussed during the early months of the war not only by Beck, Canaris and Oster but by a number of other men both inside and outside Zossen, including Halder's deputy, Lieutenant-General Karl Heinrich von Stuelpnagel, the future leader of the July 1944 *coup* in Paris, who was by now a resolute advocate of Hitler's overthrow and yet another painful goad to Halder's conscience. According to Grosscurth, Halder was being 'bombarded' daily and was deeply depressed when matters reached a crisis during October and November. It is no wonder, with so many men at headquarters dragging their heels, that Hitler was to bring his fist down on Brauchitsch's head during a conference at the Chancellery on Sunday 5 November and rage at him about the defeatist "spirit of Zossen." Brauchitsch left the presence of the Führer utterly cowed and broken, his pale objections to any immediate invasion of the West disregarded, and the date for action set at 12 November, one week ahead. Even though on 7 November Hitler entered on his cycle of postponements for the invasion, neither Brauchitsch nor Halder were to be of much use to the conspirators again.

Halder, however, had been directly involved in the conspiracy as late as early November, when Oster had been asked "to bring the 1938 plan up to date." Halder had even admitted to Grosscurth in October that he secretly carried a pistol into the Führer's presence with the vague idea of shooting him. It is ironic that Halder, as Beck's successor, while still identified with the opposition even to the point of approving Hitler's assassination, had as Chief of Staff to assist in planning the war he secretly desired to frustrate. However, as Hassell put it later, "Those generals supposed to be plotting Hitler's downfall would seem to be waiting for the Führer's orders to act." The story was told in evidence at the International Military Tribunal at Nuremberg by Gisevius, now a party to every successive phase of the plans for a *coup d'état*:

During November of 1939, General Halder actually had plans for a *putsch,* but these plans came to naught when at the very last minute Hitler called off the Western Offensive. Strengthened by the position of Halder at that time, we believed we should continue discussions at the Vatican. We reached what you might call a gentleman's agreement on the basis of which I believe that I am entitled to state that we could give the generals unequivocal proof, that in the event of the overthrow of the Hitler régime, terms could be made with a decent civil German government. . . . These were oral discussions [at the Vatican] which were then put into a comprehensive report. This report was examined by the Ambassador von Hassell and by Dr. Schacht before it was given to Halder by General Thomas. Halder was so taken with the contents that he gave the report to von Brauchitsch. Brauchitsch was enraged and threatened to arrest the intermediary, General Thomas, and thus this action which had every prospect of success, failed.[10]

The discussions at the Vatican which led to the report to which Gisevius was referring originated with the Abwehr. The negotiations came to be known as Operation X, and the outcome was to be of crucial importance to everyone involved in Department Z. Among the widening circle of Oster's agents was Dr. Josef Müller, a lawyer of forty-one practicing in Munich, one of the most fearless of the Catholic opponents of Nazism, and a man prepared to give unflagging help to those in trouble in his community. He was well known to Pope Pius XII, and his advice was even sought by the Vatican in dealing with regional problems arising from the relations between the Church and the Nazi régime. Müller was (and fortunately still is) famous for his courage and good humor, and his delight in being called *Ochsensepp* (Joe the Ox) a nickname deriving from his schooldays.

Müller had been first introduced to the Abwehr through a friend, Wilhelm Schmidhuber, a businessman who was a captain in the reserve of an artillery regiment; he was also an honorary acting-consul for Portugal.[11] Anxious to be added to the Abwehr strength, and as a result to be promoted major, Schmidhuber had originally been interviewed by the Abwehr's representative in Munich, an officer called Teschenmacher, and it was during this interview that Müller's name was raised and his good relations with officials at the Vatican noted. Müller was invited to Berlin as soon as Oster and Dohnanyi had satisfied themselves as to his worth and reliability, and there was no difficulty in establishing common ground and inspiring mutual trust. Both Müller and Schmidhuber found their way into the Abwehr; like Dohnanyi and, for that matter, Dietrich Bonhoeffer, they were simply 'drafted' as wartime recruits, and they were directed at once to make contact with representatives in Britain through diplomatic channels in the Vatican. Müller's primary links were with one of the Pope's principal advisers, a German Jesuit called Father Robert Leiber, and Monsignor Ludwig Kaas, a former leader of the German Center Party who was

109

resident at this time in Rome and acting as an administrator in the Vatican.

Mü'ler was detailed by Canaris and Oster to bring the British government to the point of acknowledging that it would be prepared to negotiate peace terms with a Germany which had discarded Hitler, and at the same time to induce the Pope to act as an intermediary and guarantee fair dealing. His initial conversations in Rome began to bear fruit during October and November 1939.

Müller was never to meet the British Minister at the Vatican, Sir Francis D'Arcy Osborne (later to become the Duke of Leeds), nor for that matter did he meet the Pope at that time. His appeal to the Pope to act as mediator between the Western Allies and Germany, a country of which he was known to have become exceptionally fond after his residence there from 1920 to 1929 as Papal Nuncio, was presented through Father Leiber and readily answered. Beck, Canaris and Dohnanyi already knew the Pope slightly; according to Müller, all three had on occasion met while exercising on horseback during the period the Pope had been Nuncio in Germany. The Pope, a highly trained diplomat—he had also been Cardinal Secretary of State from 1930 to 1939—saw himself best in this peace-making capacity, and his desire to appear neutral or impartial was to make him behave later with undue restraint in the face of the worst crimes committed in Hitler's name. Until his unfortunate arrest in 1943, Müller, who brought the Pope ample evidence of atrocities committed against churchmen, was to persist in his efforts to achieve a situation in which peace, with the Pope's help, could be negotiated. The inquiries he launched informally on behalf of the resistance reached the attention of D'Arcy Osborne through the Pope.

A memorandum kept by the emissaries of the Abwehr and covering these discussions has survived.[12] Code names are used to conceal the identities of the principals involved; for example, Father Leiber is known as Gregor. The opening date in this memorandum is 6 November 1939; at a meeting during the evening, "Gregor" told Müeller that the Pope was prepared to assist Germany achieve a fair peace "once conditions justify it." The Pope, said "Gregor," was ready to approach Roosevelt to assist in the negotiations provided the United States did not herself enter the war. The continuing neutrality of Italy was then discussed, and "Gregor" reported a little wishful thinking on the part of the French envoy at the Vatican, who apparently believed Italy would be prepared to withdraw from the Axis and achieve closer relations with France. The antipathy the Italians felt towards the war was emphasized throughout the conversations.

The following day they met again. "Gregor" stressed how concerned the Pope was about reports, which he considered irrefutable, describing the atrocities taking place in Poland. No statement had been received from Berlin denying these reports, nor did the Vatican think the Nazi régime wise in pursuing its anti-Catholic policies at such a time. It could only lead to anti-German feeling in Italy. According to notes of Müller's conversations on 8 November, the Pope had actively tried to get some statement from Germany concerning the position in Poland. Among other things discussed, which may seem unrealistic now but recall the climate of opinion at the time, was the possibility that Germany when she was ready to attack in the west, would violate Swiss neutrality in order to surmount the obstacle of the "impregnable" Maginot line. The Dutch, too, "on the strength of recent information from Berlin," were warned about an impending German attack. On the other hand, in the search for a path towards peace, "Gregor" said that the Pope's relations with Edouard Daladier, the French Prime Minister, were good, and that Chamberlain and Halifax had informed the Vatican that, in the event of genuine efforts for peace, the British government would welcome the co-operation of the Pope.

Once again, these attempts to gain some form of assurance from Britain before Hitler had actually been displaced made little impression in London, though D'Arcy Osborne informed the government of Müller's mission.[13] The first outline of the celebrated "X" memorandum or report, which Müller, with the help of Leiber, drafted while in Rome was so-called because Müller's code reference for it was "X." Apparently, the copies prepared both for London and Berlin were written on Vatican notepaper. The memorandum was supposed to outline the kind of conditions to which the Western Allies would be most likely to agree once Hitler was removed; it was drafted with the tacit approval of the Pope, the last person to give support to any proposal which might be thought unfair to Germany. The copy of the report which Müller brought back to Germany early in February had attached to it Father Leiber's personal card with a message written on it that the bearer enjoyed "the full confidence of His Holiness."

The report, as drafted in Rome, was most carefully redrafted in Berlin by Müller and Dohnanyi who, with the knowledge of Canaris, prepared its contents in a final form, the "X Report" proper.[14] It was reworded in a form thought suitable for presentation through Halder to the generals of the High Command. The X Report stated that it was understood in Germany that any peace negotiations with the Allies would depend on Germany ridding herself of the Nazi régime and form of constitution, and setting up in their place a responsible government capable of fulfilling its obligations. Among proposals affecting frontiers, while the Allies would be expected to recognize that the Sudetenland should remain a part of Germany, Austria's future should be determined by plebiscite.

This, then, was the document which reached Halder in April, brought by Thomas, and passed on by Halder the same evening to Brauchitsch. But Brauchitsch was by now convinced that he must help Hitler fulfil his chosen destiny, that he must fight for Germany's survival in Europe, come what may, and no longer even remotely remain party to any form of *coup d'état*. "You should never have shown me this," he told Halder the following day. "This is pure treason against the State." However, a copy of the report was preserved in a safe by Colonel Werner Schrader, a man who could be trusted at the High Command headquarters at Zossen. The copy sent to Britain was, apparently, destroyed at the request of the negotiators at the Vatican.

Hassell was the next man to try to obtain from Britain conditions for the restoration of peace in return for the overthrow of Hitler. Hassell involved himself in a dangerous mission of an extraordinary nature for a man who still regarded himself as a professional diplomat. He was relatively free to travel in connection with his official researches into the European economy, the only employment left to him after his removal from his embassy in Rome. An Old Etonian called J. Lonsdale Bryans, who knew Lord Halifax, had vaguely discussed with Halifax the possibility of initiating wholly unofficial peace-feelers in neutral places. He was not actively discouraged. Quite by chance, he met Hassell's future son-in-law, the Italian Detalmo Pirzio-Biroli, in Rome. The first step was taken by Pirzio-Biroli, who revealed in confidence, for Halifax's ears alone, that Hassell was an important member of the German resistance. He then gave Bryans a written statement concerning the plans of the resistance to pass on to Halifax. As it turned out, Bryans did not manage to see Halifax again until 8 January 1940, and by then the Foreign Minister was very lukewarm about the value of the contact with Hassell or, for that matter, with any German. He only grudgingly agreed to Bryans's plea to be allowed to meet Hassell secretly in Switzerland. In the end, they met in Arosa late in February, Bryans found Hassell "strangely English."

What Hassell was after was some written declaration from the British Government that they would conduct immediate peace negotiations with the responsible leaders of a *coup d'état* in Germany designed to bring about Hitler's removal. The British government was in no mood to give any such assurances; all Bryans was allowed to take back to Switzerland, when he met Hassell for the second and last time in mid-April, were the cold meats of formal gratitude. By the time Bryans arrived in Switzerland, Hitler had invaded Denmark and Norway. "I cannot understand how the English managed to be taken by surprise again," remarked Hassell in his diary, and then added, "Will it finally open the eyes of the generals?"

113

Writing in English, Hassell produced his own version of the kind of terms he hoped could be reached with Britain. In these he voices the views of the right-wing of the resistance, including Beck, Goerdeler, Canaris and Oster. It was, rather naturally, headed "Confidential":

I. All serious-minded people in Germany consider it as of utmost importance to stop this mad war as soon as possible.

II. We consider this because the danger of a complete destruction and particularly a bolshevization of Europe is rapidly growing.

III. Europe does not mean for us a chess-board of political or military action or a base of power but it has 'la valeur d'une patrie' in the frame of which a healthy Germany in sound conditions of life is an indispensable factor.

IV. The purpose of a peace treaty ought to be a permanent pacification and re-establishment of Europe on a solid base and a security against a renewal of warlike tendencies.

V. Condition, necessary for this result, is to leave the union of Austria and the Sudeten with the Reich out of any discussion. In the same way there would be excluded a renewed discussion of accidental frontier-questions of the Reich. On the other hand, the German-Polish frontier will have to be more or less identical with the German frontier of 1914.

VI. The treaty of peace and the reconstruction of Europe ought to be based on certain principles which will have to be universally accepted.

VII. Such principles are the following:

1. The principle of nationality with certain modifications deriving from history. Therefore

2. Re-establishment of an independent Poland and of a Czech Republic.

3. General reductions of armament.

4. Re-establishment of free international economical cooperation.

114

5. Recognition of certain leading ideas by all European states, such as:

    a. The principles of Christian ethics.

    b. Justice and law as fundamental elements of public life.

    c. Social welfare as *leitmotiv*.

    d. Effective control of the executive power of state by the people, adapted to the special character of every nation.

    e. Liberty of thought, conscience, and intellectual activity.[15]

It was mid-March before Hassell learned anything of Müller's negotiations at the Vatican. By then he had told both Goerdeler and Schacht of his efforts in Arosa, which were then in abeyance. Schacht still felt himself important because early in March the envoy of the American President, Sumner Welles, had visited Germany and asked specially to see him, a request Hitler had not found it possible to refuse. As Hassell put it—"Asked whether he thought Sumner Welles's visit would have any result, Schacht said yes, if he, Schacht, were sent to America. But Ribbentrop would not consent." Hassell set it all down with quiet amusement, but his humor was by now too often a foil to his anxiety, for, like his friends, he sensed that an offensive of some sort was being prepared against the West. Goerdeler even managed to talk to the king of the Belgians, who told him peace in Europe was still possible, but only without Hitler. Then, on 16 March, Hassell was told that Beck wanted to see him. Of this meeting Hassell wrote:

I found him alone and discussed the situation with him thoroughly. Oster and Dohnanyi came in later; they read me some extraordinarily interesting documents covering the conversations of a Catholic intermediary with the Pope. Following these conversations the Pope established contact with Halifax through Osborne.

The Pope was apparently prepared to go to surprising lengths in his understanding of German interests.

Halifax, who spoke definitely for the British government, was much more cagey in formulating his statements and touched on points like "decentralization of Germany" and "a referendum in Austria." On the whole, the desire to make a decent peace is quite evident, and the Pope emphasized very strongly to the intermediary that such things as "decentralization" and "plebiscite in Austria" would certainly be no barriers to the peace if there was agreement on other points. The prerequisite for the whole thing, naturally, is a change in the régime and an avowal of Christian morality.

The purpose of this talk with me was: (i) to hear my views on the foreign aspects of the problem; (ii) to ask me to present the matter to Halder, because no other intermediary had much chance of success.[16]

Hassell, therefore, was now involved on both fronts— that of Müeller and that of Bryans. On 19 Barch, as a preliminary to meeting Halder, who was becoming far less willing than formerly to associate with men hostile to Hitler, Hassell went to see Thomas to discuss what would, in decent German eyes, constitute at this stage a "tolerable" peace. Thomas told him that Halder would see him —but only after Easter. Through the agency of Thomas, Halder had met Beck two months earlier, on 16 January.[17] Halder had been prepared then to agree with all Beck's arguments against the outcome of a war which must eventually be fought on two fronts. Halder had put the blame for inaction against Hitler squarely on Brauchitsch, and then added that he did not feel it right to turn against his Commander-in-Chief in time of war. Brauchitsch and Halder had developed a warm personal regard for each other.

Hassell retired to his home in Ebenhausen; the days drifted on, and no appointment for a meeting was offered by Halder. Then, on 2 April, Hassell travelled back to Berlin. He describes the situation in his diary:

Soon after my arrival in Berlin, Goerdeler came to see me and confirmed my suspicion that Halder had got cold feet. He showed me a letter in which Halder refused for the time being (!) to take action for very naïve reasons. (England and France had declared war on us, and one had to see it through. A peace of compromise was senseless. Only in the greatest emergency (come, now!) could one take the action desired by Goerdeler.) Halder, who had begun to weep during the discussion of his responsibility, gave the impression of a weak man with shattered nerves.

Furthermore, it seems too late now for anything, for, according to Goerdeler's information, action against Denmark and Norway is imminent. Goerdeler had the impression that Halder had talked to his chief, Brauchitsch, and that both had agreed to give an unfavorable reply, i.e., to yield to Hitler.

Inevitably the tension grew; everyone was expecting an attack to be launched. The Swedish Minister went to Weizsäcker at the Foreign Office to ask him if this were so. Oster, entertaining Hassell and Dohnanyi at his home, declared the attack would come on 9 April. After this, they studied further notes sent in by Müller from Rome; it was evident that the British would not stir. Neither would Halder, who pointedly refused to see Hassell. Then Hassell moved on to Beck's house, where he also found Goerdeler. "We were not in a happy frame of mind," he writes, "and felt the menace of an inescapable fate."

On the precise date given by Oster, 9 April, Denmark was occupied and the Norwegian harbors invaded. There was nothing for Hassell to do now but go to Switzerland and learn from Bryans how little his own mission had accomplished. Attempts to achieve something on the diplomatic front in Britain and on the military front in Germany had proved equally fruitless. Brauchitsch and Halder were being drawn into the whirlpool of Hitler's strategy, and seemed to have lost all will to escape. Another of Hassell's intimate friends, Professor Johannes von Popitz, a Prussian civil servant in his fifties who, like Goerdeler and Schacht, had originally served the régime (in Popitz's case, as Prussian Minister of State and Finance), possessed a readier access to Brauchitsch than the rest. He found that his appeals, based on saving the honor of the Army in face of the increasing powers of the S.S., met with little response; except for a single moment when Brauchitsch seemed to revive and asked whether peace with honor could, in Popitz's view, be obtained for Germany. But that was all. A further attempt to bring pressure on Halder had also been made by Thomas early in April, with no better outcome than Goerdeler had achieved. Halder had looked at the X Report, and had even seemed to approve its terms; then once more he had fallen back on the state of his conscience and his need to follow the lead of Brauchitsch.

It seemed better now to try the persuasive strength of the X Report on the commanders in the field with the hope that they in turn might be able to make Brauchitsch see reason. The man chosen for this mission was Hans Grosscurth of the Abwehr, but that too came to nothing, as Hassell, himself returning empty-handed from Switzerland, soon discovered when he visited Beck and Thomas late in April.

There is a record of exceptional interest in the German Military Archives in Freiburg concerning a conversation which took place on 1 May 1940 between Count Wolf Heinrich von Helldorf, President of the Berlin Police, and a prominent supporter of Hitler at an earlier period, and Oster, in the presence of Grosscurth.[18] Helldorf expressed his disgust with events in Poland, where his deputy, Canstein, had recently paid a visit of observation. He had found the local S.S. chief in Cracow in a state which, he said, bordered on hysteria because neither he nor his men felt capable of carrying out the orders they had been given unless they made themselves drunk in advance. Helldorf said that in his opinion no one who performed such tasks could come back and live a normal life, though he was aware of the decree which prevented the men concerned from saying a word about their experiences in Poland. When Oster asked Helldorf about morale in Berlin, the Police President reported that only 35 to 40 per cent of the people were in favor of war or even of the

Party, and scepticism seemed to be widespread. Though petty offenses were on the increase, there was little serious crime; people were fearful of the severe penalties imposed. His police force, he said, had only some 6,000 men capable of real action out of the 14,000 enrolled.

Oster's "Treason"

April was Hitler's month in Scandinavia. By the end of it the Allied troops who had been landed in Norway on 16 April had been withdrawn. There was then a pause of a bare ten days before the second wave of invasion began —west this time, into the Netherlands and Belgium. Throughout the period Oster committed what might be regarded as a series of acts of treason, though as he saw it what he did was for the good alike of the German people and the German armed forces. He sought to frustrate or disrupt Hitler's surprise attacks by giving the victims of German aggression as accurate a forecast as he could of the date on which they might expect invasion.

It is uncertain to what extent Canaris was directly involved in Oster's attempts to forestall Hitler's attacks by sending out his desperate warnings. He was probably aware of them. Oster had been deeply upset by the news of Fritsch's suicidal death in Poland; he had admired Fritsch and fully believed that his death had been an act of self-immolation. He was right; Fritsch had in fact sent his friend Count von der Goltz a written message stating: "I go out strictly as a target."[19]

Oster (and, it would seem, Canaris) felt that to send warnings to the countries threatened by Hitler might prevent further escalation of the war. He was convinced that an offensive against the West would lead to the ultimate defeat of Germany, as well as to her moral degradation. Oster therefore did not feel himself to be a traitor to his country, but rather the instrument through which the Fatherland might be saved. When, following a conversation between Grosscurth and Halder's spirited deputy, Lieutenant-General von Stuelpnagel in France on 14

119

November, he became convinced that the invasion was inevitable, he determined to do what he could to ensure that the countries set for invasion were warned in advance. Nevertheless, he foresaw that if in the future his acts were revealed, he might only too easily be branded a traitor. It was with this in mind that he said subsequently: "I am no traitor. I hold myself a far better German patriot than those who chase after Hitler. It is both my hope and my duty to rid Germany, and also the world, of this scourge." Oster's misfortune was that his warnings were not only disregarded, but utterly disbelieved.

The bare facts concerning certain of Oster's acts of "treason" are well established. Among his close friends in Berlin was the Dutch military attaché, Colonel Jacobus Sas, whom he had known well for many years and whom he frequently entertained at his home in Berlin. Oster decided to pass on to Sas whatever information he felt to be justified. According to Sas, Oster's warnings began as early as October 1939, when he told his friend: "Your turn's still to come. They're planning first the invasion of Belgium." Oster added that he would certainly warn Sas as soon as he had any definite information about preparations for invading the Netherlands. Sas left for Holland in order to pass on this initial warning, but it was received with incredulity. Sas felt so badly about the matter that he seriously contemplated resignation; it was as if his own honor were in question, especially as he did not feel it right to reveal the sources of his reports.

He returned to Berlin during the night of 6 November. The following day he received a letter from Oster saying that he wanted to see him immediately. Sas reported what happened:[20]

Oster was in uniform, which was very unusual for him. There was a military staff car in front of his house, which was unusual too. We lunched together, and he told me that the invasion of Holland was to take place on 12 November. He asked me to go back to Holland immediately and to warn the authorities so that the assault would not find us absolutely unprepared. At that

120

time my wife was still in The Hague. We had a form of code by means of which I could warn her even by telephone. She passed it on promptly, and when I arrived back on the morning of Wednesday 8 November, I was taken immediately to see Ministers de Geer, van Kleffens and Dijxhoorn and General Reynders. I was more than a little agitated about this alarming news and reported exactly what Colonel Oster had told me. He had added that he was on his way to the Western Front, which indeed he was, and that he was going to see General von Witzleben and others, in the hope of persuading them to prevent the attack on Holland. But he considered the possibility of success most unlikely. On Wednesday [8 November] I passed this information on to the Dutch Council of Ministers, and that same evening occurred the bomb-attempt in the Bürgerbräukeller—the one, of course, which Hitler escaped. This was immediately after the Venlo incident in which Lieutenant Klop, who had previously been one of my assistants, was murdered.

The strange events referred to by Sas occurred on 7 and 8 November, and were purposefully linked together by Himmler's Intelligence department. After Hitler had made his customary speech at the annual gathering in the beer-cellar in Munich where the notorious *putsch* of 1923 had been planned, he had left in good time to avoid the results of an explosion from a concealed bomb, an incident for which the S.S. may indeed have been responsible with Hitler's own connivance. Someone had to be found to act as political scapegoat for this overt attempt on the Führer's sacred life. Prior to this event, Walther Schellenberg—an ambitious young man, of whom we shall hear a great deal later on and now working his way up in the S.S. Intelligence department—had been detailed to abduct two British Intelligence agents with whom he was in contact. This had been done on 7 November. These men, Captain S. Payne Best and Major R. H. Stevens, were accused of being involved in the "attempt" which, it was now alleged, had been inspired by the Allies.

Though Sas was technically subordinate to the Nether-

121

lands Foreign Office, as a colonel in the Army he gave his warnings to his Supreme Commander, General Reynders, who at once forbade him to pass on any such information either to the Queen or to any Minister. But when Sas realized that nothing appeared to be happening, he set aside this order and gave his information privately to a number of contacts, including a friend, the former Minister Colign, and General van Ooerschot. But they too seemed unimpressed. His attempts to reach the Queen herself were frustrated. In the event, the invasion did not occur, which only served to increase the general disbelief in the warnings Sas received from Oster.

Sas returned to Holland shortly before Christmas, and he had the courage to see General Reynders once more and ask him point-blank whether or not his word was trusted. At this, the General merely grew angry and told him he did not believe in all this time-wasting gossip, and that in any case the dates Sas had passed on had proved to be false alarms. After Christmas, Sas returned to Berlin, since he had been warned by Oster that important decisions might be taken around 26 or 27 December. However, Hitler's designs were further postponed when, on 10 January, the emergency landing of a German aircraft in Belgium carrying two staff officers with the plans for the invasion of that country, led to the discovery of Hitler's intentions and in turn to a further postponement of action. The following month Reynders, who had meanwhile refused to allow Sas to retain his position as military attaché, was himself removed from his command and replaced by General Winkelman. Sas was reinstated, and returned to Berlin in March.

Sas's report continues:

Then came April. On Wednesday afternoon, 3 April, Oster told me about the forthcoming invasion of Denmark and Norway, and added that the invasion in the West would almost certainly start soon after . . . I used the private code arranged with Captain Kruls [adjutant of the Secretary for War], telephoning him to say that

I would gladly dine with him on 9 May, which indicated that the invasion was to be on 9 April. I also informed the Danish Naval Attaché, van Kjolsen, and the Norwegian Attaché, Stang. Kjolsen passed on the information, but Stang did not because, as later came out, he was already acting as a Quisling in the service of Germany.

On this occasion the date was right. At the end of the month Müller was instructed by Beck to go to Rome, ostensibly on an Abwehr mission, and warn the Allies of Hitler's intention to invade westwards on 10 May.

Müller received his instructions through Oster. During the first days of May he was in touch again with Father Leiber in Rome, returning immediately to Germany once he had delivered his message. By 7 May Schmidhuber had reached Rome with further warnings. The Pope then took it upon himself to have the information he had received passed on to his nuncios in Brussels and The Hague and, somewhat later, to the British representative, D'Arcy Osborne, and the representative of France. Leiber's original information also reached the Belgian envoy at the Vatican, who sent lengthy coded messages to Brussels concerning the reliability of the information and its source. Unfortunately, these messages, which were sent by radio, were intercepted by a German monitoring service; the monitors broke the code and so learned that an unnamed German informant at the Vatican had betrayed the dates for the invasion. Immediately both Himmler's Security Service and, ironically, the Abwehr itself were ordered to investigate the leakage. Canaris, with a stroke of genius equalled only by its wit, brought Müller up from Munich and placed the investigation of the leak entirely in his hands. He was dispatched immediately by direct flight to Rome. Here, with the help of Leiber, he produced a satisfactory story with which to cover himself. But unfortunately this did not prove to be the end of the dangerous affair. Another department in the Abwehr had been informed about the leak; they were determined to investigate its source and so gain credit with Canaris for the zeal with which the German traitor was unmasked. This other department duly sent an agent to Rome who came back with a report that suspicion rested mainly upon Müller. The officer in charge of these Abwehr investigations, Colonel Rohleder, dutifully brought this dossier to Oster and Dohnanyi. Filled with anxiety, they accompanied Rohleder when he went to report the matter to Canaris, who finally had to use his authority to close the matter and silence his over-dutiful subordinate.

Further warnings were issued to Switzerland to stand by for possible invasion, and Oster is said to have passed a message to Leopold III through Count Albrecht Bernstorff. According to August Lindt, press attaché at the Swiss Legation after the war, Canaris was to pass a second warning to the Swiss in October 1942, at a time when Ribbentrop was making a new assessment of Switzerland's resources.

Meanwhile, contact was resumed between Oster and Sas, and Sas himself reported after the war:

On Friday, 3 May, Oster informed me once more of the possibility of an imminent invasion of Holland, but he suggested that we should wait until his news was more precise. We agreed to wait a while. As Oster said to me: 'You've had so much trouble in Holland, they will scarcely believe you anyway. So let's wait a little and see what happens.' That was Friday at lunchtime.

On Saturday, a telegram from the Foreign Office in The Hague revealed that a source in the Vatican had given a warning that Holland was about to be invaded . . . I should add that the undestroyed papers found in the aircraft in which General Student crash-landed had revealed an invasion time-table with the date 8 May scribbled in by hand. . . .[21]

On Thursday I had my last contact with Oster. I went to see him at seven o'clock in the evening. I had seen him almost every day. He now informed me that matters had really been set in motion. The orders for the Western invasion were in force, and Hitler had left for the Western Front. But he added: 'There might possibly still be a postponement. After all, we've been through all this three times already. So let's wait a little longer. The

124

critical hour is nine-thirty. Should there be no counter-orders by then, it is final.' Oster and I then went to have dinner in town. It was more or less funereal, and we went over all we had done. He told me that in the affair of the leakage concerning Denmark an investigation had been ordered, since they had discovered the certainty of a leak somewhere. Oddly enough, suspicion had fallen on the Belgian military attaché who was supposed to have contacts with Catholic circles in the High Command. 'Very well,' said Oster, 'we've shuffled our cards all right. So far they haven't cottoned on to us yet.' After dinner, at nine-thirty, I went with him to the O.K.W. and waited outside in the dark. After twenty minutes he came back and said, 'My dear friend, things have already started. The orders have not been counter-manded. That swine's gone to the Western Front, and the invasion's started. Let's only hope we'll meet again after the war.'

I dashed off at once to my embassy, having mean-while asked for the Belgian military attaché to come and meet me there. I told him what I knew and he hurried to his embassy to pass on the news. As for myself, I reached for the phone and asked for the War Office in The Hague. These are the moments you never forget in your life. I was literally sweating while waiting for the call. It came after twenty minutes, and luckily there was an officer I knew well, the naval commander Post Uit-weer. I said, 'Post, you know my voice, don't you. I am Sas in Berlin. I've only one thing to tell you. Tomorrow at dawn—sit tight! You understand me, don't you? Please repeat that.' He repeated it and added, 'Letter 210 received.' This was according to a previous arrange-ment. 200 stood for invasion, and the last two digits for the day of the month. About one and a half hours later, Colonel van Plaasche, Chief of the foreign news depart-ment, telephoned me and said, 'I've bad news about your wife's operation. Have you taken every medical advice?' I was furious at being compromised again on an open line, and shouted back, 'Why the hell do you bother me in the circumstances? Now you know. I've taken all the

125

medical advice available. The operation's got to take place at dawn. It can't be helped now.' Then I banged the receiver down. . . . That was the end of my function in Berlin as military attaché. I had done everything I could. I went back to my hotel, fetched my toothbrush and pyjamas, and went to bed at the embassy, following the ambassador's instructions. At five-thirty he banged on my door and said: 'It's started. I've been sent for by Ribbentrop.' We switched on the radio and heard that the invasion was in full spate.

After the war, when Sas was asked by his commanding officer if he would not agree that Oster was, after all, a despicable traitor, he replied that he considered him to have been the most remarkable man he had ever known, and recklessly courageous in his opposition to Hitler, all the more since he and his friends were surrounded by the Gestapo.[22]

II

The Abwehr Network

Summer 1940: Canaris's Tactics

Now came the period of gravest risk to the conspirators. Western Europe was virtually in Hitler's possession either by right of occupation or through the ties of alliance. Britain seemed on the point of being invaded. Who except some fanatic would want to assassinate a man so obviously destined to make Germany the ruler of Europe, perhaps of the world? As Gisevius put it at the International Tribunal at Nuremberg:

After the fall of Paris, our group had no influence for months. Hitler's success deluded everyone, and it took much effort on our part through all the channels open

126

to us to try at least to prevent the bombardment of England. Here again the group made united efforts and we tried, through General Thomas and Admiral Canaris and others, to prevent this disaster.[1]

The period from autumn 1940 to the collapse of the German Sixth Army at Stalingrad in January 1943 was therefore the most difficult of all for those opposed to Hitler. Though Hitler conveniently diverted his attention away from the conquest of Britain (Operation Sea-Lion) after the failure of Göring's Luftwaffe to blitz the country into a state of prostration, Germany's "greatness" was manifested once more in the success of the invasion of the Balkans and of Russia during 1941 and in her merciless will in the secret decision taken early the following year to destroy the Jewish peoples in Europe. Hitler's casual declaration of war against the United States of America on 11 December 1941 is typical of the euphoria of the period. Only towards the end of 1942 and the beginning of 1943 could it be said that Germany was beginning to meet with serious reverses—in North Africa and at Stalingrad. The powerful waves of conquest were stayed or reversed, and Britain's shining defiance of the Führer was at last confirmed by victories in the field of battle.

Canaris's despondency really began with the fall of France. He invited his predecessor of the First World War, the celebrated Colonel Nicolai, then living in retirement, to accompany him and Oster on a tour of inspection of occupied France. Colonel Heinz went with them, and was therefore in a good position to observe Canaris at the period; he records what Canaris said in his presence during this tour:

'It may take a hundred years for people to realize our luckless state. Should Hitler win, this will certainly be the end of us, and also the end of the Germany as we love it and desire it to be. And if Hitler loses, this will also be the end of Germany, and of ourselves too for having failed to get rid of him—if indeed we do fail. Even if we are successful in our political struggle against Hitler,

127

it will be not only his downfall we compass, but our own too, for our opponents outside Germany won't believe us. Our opponents, whether serving under General de Gaulle or Tito, in Norway or in occupied Russia, will regard the end of the struggle underground as equal to a national victory. Whatever we do inevitably leads to national self-destruction. The average general can never be expected to grasp this, which means that even before our defeat of Hitler we ourselves will die, abandoned by all the world.'[2]

As usual, Canaris sought consolation by leaving France for Spain. According to Abshagen, he had a nephew in Madrid who had just become engaged and who sought his uncle's advice as to when it might be proper for a German to get married. He asked if Canaris thought he should wait for "the final victory." The admiral, his face filled with sorrow, told the boy to marry at once and enjoy life while he could. In his view, the future held only catastrophe for Germany.

In spite of the great increase in his staff of agents overseas and his own specialized knowledge of the Mediterranean, Canaris failed to warn the High Command of the Allied invasion of North Africa from behind Rommel's lines. The buildup of Allied shipping, according to Canaris, was for the relief either of Malta or of Alexandria. He was to be found constantly in Algeciras, where he was in consultation with the agents whose responsibility it was to report on all activities connected with Allied ships and supplies; according to Abshagen, on the eve of the New Year of 1942 he even cooked dinner for his staff, wearing a chef's cap and apron. He delighted in cooking. Colvin relates that there was at one time a British plot to capture him while he was in Algeciras, but that this was eventually put aside because "he was more valuable where he was." Whether or not this doubtful compliment was ever paid, there is no doubt that Canaris's Intelligence service kept silent about any knowledge it may have had concerning the possibilities of the Allied landings in Tunisia. According to Colonel Heinz, the information was deliberately withheld.

Gisevius commented at Nuremberg on the problems of trying to filter information to Hitler through Keitel, who seemed determined only to present Hitler with the kind of reports he wanted to receive:

Keitel decided what documents were to be transmitted to Hitler. It was not possible for Admiral Canaris or one of the other gentlemen I mentioned to submit an urgent report to Hitler of his own accord. Keitel took it over, and what he did not like he did not transmit, or he gave these men the official order to abstain from making their report. Also, Keitel repeatedly threatened these men telling them that they were to limit themselves exclusively to their own specialized sectors; and that he would not protect them with respect to any political utterance which criticized the Party and the Gestapo, with regard to persecution of the Jews, the murders in Russia, or the anti-church campaign; and, he said later, he would not hesitate to dismiss these gentlemen from the Armed Forces and turn them over to the Gestapo. I have read the notes of General Oster in the same connection from the command conferences in the O.K.W. . . . . He put these men under pressure, and they considered that as a special insult. . . .

MR JUSTICE JACKSON (Chief-Counsel for the USA, cross-examining): In other words, whatever Hitler's own inclinations may have been, these men in this dock formed a ring round him which kept out information from your group as to what was going on unless they wanted Hitler to hear it, isn't that a fact?

GISEVIUS: Yes. I believe that I should cite two more examples which I consider especially significant. First of all, every means was tried to incite Keitel to warn Hitler against the invasion of Belgium and Holland, and to tell him, that is Hitler, that the information which had been submitted to him, regarding the alleged violation of neutrality by the Dutch and Belgians was wrong. The counter-intelligence was to produce these reports which would incriminate the Dutch and the Belgians. Admiral Canaris at that time refused to sign these reports . . .

129

JACKSON: Did others participate with you in the preparation of these reports?

GISEVIUS: Yes, it was the work of a group. We gathered reports about plans and preparations of the Gestapo, and we gathered material about the first infamous acts, so that the courageous men at the front, officers of the General Staff and of the Army, went to the scene, prepared reports, and made photographs, and this material came then to both Canaris and Oster. Then the problem arose, how we could bring this material to Keitel. It was generally known that officers, evenly highly placed officers like Canaris and Thomas, were forbidden to report on political matters. The difficulty was, therefore, to avoid Canaris and the others coming under suspicion that they were dealing with politics. We therefore employed the round-about method of preparing so-called counterintelligence agents' reports from foreign countries or from occupied countries; and with the pretext that different agents from all countries were here reporting about these outrages, or that agents travelling through or in foreign countries had found photographs of those infamous acts. We then submitted these reports to Field-Marshal Keitel.

JACKSON: Did Canaris and Oster participate in submitting these reports to Keitel?

GISEVIUS: Yes. Without Canaris and Oster the working out and the gathering of this material would have been inconceivable. . . . From the first Jewish pogroms in 1938 onwards, Keitel was minutely informed of each new action against the Jews, particularly about the establishment of the first mass graves in the East, up to the erection of the murder factories later.

JACKSON: Did these reports mention the atrocities that were committed in Poland against the Poles?

GISEVIUS: Yes, indeed, here I would say again that the atrocities in Poland, too, started with isolated murders which were so horrible that we were still able to report on single cases, and could add the names of the responsible S.S. leaders. Here, too, Keitel was spared nothing of the terrible truth.[3]

According to Lahousen's evidence at Nuremberg, it was Keitel who put pressure on Canaris late in 1940 to assassinate Field-Marshal Weygand, Chief of the French General Staff:

Canaris told us that for a considerable time Keitel had put pressure on him to execute an action leading to the elimination of the French Marshal Weygand; and that I —that is to say, my section—would be charged with the execution of this task, as a matter of course.

COLONEL JOHN HARLAN AMEN (U.S. Associate Trial Counsel): When you say 'elimination', what do you mean?

LAHOUSEN: Killing.

AMEN: What was Weygand doing at this time?

LAHOUSEN: Weygand was, so far as I recall, at that time in North Africa.

AMEN: What was the reason given for attempting to kill Weygand?

LAHOUSEN: The reason given was the fear that the unbeaten part of the French Army in North Africa might find in Weygand a point for crystallization for resistance. That, of course, is only the main outline of what I still remember today. It may be that there were other contributing factors.

AMEN: After you were so informed by Canaris, what else was said at this meeting?

LAHOUSEN: This request, which was put to the military Abwehr openly and without restraint by a representative of the Armed Forces, was repudiated strongly and indignantly by all those present. I myself as the person most involved, since my department was charged with the action, stated before all present that I had no intention of executing this order. My section and my officers are fighters but they are not a murderers' organization or murderers.

AMEN: What did Canaris say then?

LAHOUSEN: Canaris said, 'Calm down. We'll talk it over later on.'

AMEN: Did you talk it over with Canaris, then?

LAHOUSEN: After the other gentlemen had left the room,

131

I spoke alone with Canaris. Canaris told me immediately, 'It is obvious that this order will not only not be carried out, but it will not even be communicated any further;' and so it happened.

AMEN: Were you questioned subsequently as to whether you had carried out this order?

LAHOUSEN: At an audience that Canaris had with Keitel, at which I was present, I was addressed by the then Chief of the O.K.W., Keitel, on this subject. He asked me what had happened or what had been undertaken so far with regard to this matter. The date of this event is recorded in my notes, with Canaris's knowledge and with his approval.

AMEN: What reply did you make to Keitel?

LAHOUSEN: Naturally I cannot recall the precise words I spoke, but one thing is certain; I certainly did not answer that I had no intention of carrying out this order. I could not do this, and did not do it; otherwise, I would not be sitting here today. Probably, as in many similar cases, I gave the answer that it was very difficult but whatever was possible would be done, or something of that sort. Naturally, I cannot recall my precise words.[4]

Royalist Interests

From the point of view of the conspirators, Hitler's activities were those of a man leading his country to ruin. The generals of the High Command were little more than complacent or subservient aides to a leader who must ultimately overreach himself however successful he might appear during the first phases of aggression. Meanwhile, there seemed much that might be done to mitigate the situation, as well as the completion of the plan for the new constitution which must come into force the moment Hitler was struck down. The conspirators, men of the left as well as the right, seemed agreed that a restoration of the monarchy might be the soundest way to restore a new order to Germany. This objective lay behind the thinking of men as different as Canaris, Beck, Goerdeler, Hassell and Julius Leber, one of the socialists in the resistance, though they were not always agreed as to which member of the former Kaiser's family might be the most suitable one with whom to re-establish the throne.[5]

The death of Prince Wilhelm on 20 May 1940 as a result of war injuries was followed by that of his grandfather, the Kaiser himself, on 4 June 1941. The choice then turned in the direction of Prince Louis-Ferdinand of Prussia, the oldest surviving son of the Crown Prince. He had the advantage of youth, of being a "democrat" who had worked both in the Ford plant at Detroit and with Lufthansa, and, above all, of being a friend of such prominent conspirators as Otto John and Dietrich Bonhoeffer. Prince Louis-Ferdinand, aged only thirty-three, also appealed to the younger monarchists in the resistance—men such as Dohnanyi and Schlabrendorff. With his charm and good sense, the Prince was in himself a considerable addition to their ranks. Hitler's suspicion of the potential popularity of the monarchy was confirmed when a crowd estimated at 50,000 attended the funeral of Prince Wilhelm. To prevent the recurrence of such an unwelcome form of patriotism, Hitler forbade any members of the royal family to serve in future in the armed forces, even though, as early as 1933, he had for a while considered making use of Prince August Wilhelm's son Alexander as a nationalist figurehead.[6]

Discussion concerning details of the nature of the future constitution, the length of time before the initial, authoritarian military government should be replaced by one elected democratically and the degree of authority to be vested in the monarchy occupied in particular the minds of such men as Hassell, Goerdeler and Popitz. Indeed, it largely preserved them from despair at a time when the extension of the war into Russia seemed inevitable. From late 1940 the High Command was engaged on Operation Barbarossa—Hitler's plan for the invasion of Russia during 1941—a war which, as Hitler put it bluntly to his generals, must be conducted with "merciless and unrelenting harshness." Hitler was determined to compromise Germany and involve her armies directly in his acts of

133

ideological and racial extermination. When, in August 1941, Roosevelt and Churchill published the text of their Atlantic Charter, it became apparent that the future Allied leaders drew no moral distinction between Hitler and the "traditional" German Army. Only the complete subjection of a Germany conceived as totally militarist was acceptable to the West. This was the situation before Hitler's onrushing armies were eventually brought to a halt during the winter of 1941-2.

Russia and the Expanding Front: Canaris East and West

On the Russian front, the opposition centred on Major-General Henning von Tresckow and his A.D.C., Fabian von Schlabrendorff, whose wife was Tresckow's cousin. Tresckow, who came from the landed gentry of Pomerania, was a handsome, sensitive and profoundly humane man. He was a staff officer of forty at the start of the Russian campaign. He was to become, with the help of his close friend Schlabrendorff, one of the most courageous and idealistic men of action within the resistance.[7] He and Schlabrendorff, the distinguished young lawyer drafted into the Army, had met before the war—they were distantly related—and each knew the other's conviction that Hitler must somehow be removed. They were visited during the height of the preparation for the campaign by Canaris, who was, as usual, occupying himself by keeping frequently on the move, preferably in the Mediterranean. Schlabrendorff testified to the admiral's capacity to out-drink his friends in the Army, and he made ironic comments on the propaganda issued to the armed forces that the Russians were as good as defeated. "No one has ever succeeded in defeating and conquering Russia," he declared.

It is interesting to note that at this stage Field-Marshal von Kluge was sufficiently interested, late in September 1941, to send Schlabrendorff to see Hassell during one of his periodic visits to Berlin. Kluge was the most striking example of an officer of senior rank who continually vacillated, now for and now against a *coup d'état*. In

1941 he was in his sixtieth year; in 1938 he had been among the generals relieved of their commands after the Blomberg and Fritsch affairs. He had been returned to active service on the outbreak of the war, and had been rewarded by being promoted field-marshal in July 1940. He was, therefore, among those officers who had felt both the Führer's favor and displeasure, and he was well aware, through Schacht and others, that an organized resistance group existed. However, Hitler made him one of the seven initial commanders in charge of the Army Groups involved in the invasion of Russia.

Of the meeting with Schlabrendorff Hassell wrote:

A few days ago Fabian von Schlabrendorff, a reserve lieutenant and a lawyer by profession, turned up. He had been sent by [sic] Kluge in order to find out whether opposition was crystallizing at home, and to assure opposition groups that 'one' was ready to act. He came to me through Guttenberg to get some information on foreign affairs. A very sensible man, but his comments revealed with what naïveté the generals approached this problem. Among other things he asked whether there was any guarantee that England would make peace soon after a change of régime was effected. I told him there were no such guarantees and that there could be none. Were it otherwise any shoemaker's apprentice could overthrow the régime. But I could guarantee him something else:

(i) that unless England and America were completely knocked out Hitler could get no peace.
(ii) That a respectable Germany, on the other hand, would always have a very considerable chance to get peace, and an acceptable peace at that. However, a change in régime was our own affair—a question which we alone could decide, not our opponents.

He seemed to think that we would have to make peace immediately after the change. I had to explain to him

135

that although peace was, of course, our goal, we would have to proclaim our preparedness to continue war, at the same time emphasizing our readiness to conclude an acceptable peace. What else had to be done was another question. We agreed that immediately after the end of the impending offensive in Russia his general should send a suitable high-ranking man here for further discussion.

The whole incident is gratifying because, for the first time, some kind of initiative comes from that source. But I had to make clear to Schlabrendorff there was no way to avoid the nasty reality that there would be a period in which the disillusioned public might declare that Hitler had been robbed of the victory within his grasp and the new rulers couldn't get peace either. It is the old dilemma. If we wait until the impossibility of victory becomes clear to the whole world we shall have lost the chance for a passable peace. But we must not wait. Whatever the outcome, our inheritance will be a bad one.[8]

Kluge's columns were involved in the terrible November offensive along the approach to Moscow. They were within twenty-two miles of the city before they finally became bogged down in the winter mud and snow. Almost within sight of the Kremlin, Kluge was forced to give the order to withdraw. It was not easy to do this in face of the Führer's brutal insistence on advance, and morale was at its lowest in December 1941. This was the period, for example, when General Graf Sponeck was sentenced to death for insubordination, and General Hoepner, later to become an active conspirator, degraded and cashiered. Von Brauchitsch, Hitler's subservient commander-in-chief of the Army, suffered a heart attack and asked to be relieved of his responsibilities. In December Hitler took command himself.

Thus, at the turn of the year 1941-2, the situation once more appeared to favor the conspirators. Field-Marshal von Witzleben, commander-in-chief in the west, seemed to give them at least his tacit support. He was, unfortunately, in poor health and soon to go into retirement. He was in his early sixties and suffering from hemorrhoids. On the Eastern Front, however, Kluge, now placed in full command of the Center Army Group, still seemed the man most likely to be helpful to the conspirators.

By now, the idea of assassination had to be considered, at least by some of the conspirators. But it is often forgotten how difficult Hitler became to kill, especially after 1939. He was never precisely where he was expected to be on any predetermined date, and he never travelled by any pre-announced route. No one was allowed in his presence armed, and he was surrounded by loyalists or men quite incapable of joining any plan for taking his life. In any case, the majority of those conspiring against him favored only his arrest and trial, and this of necessity required the action of a body of determined men who would force themselves into his presence and capture him in spite of his bodyguards. The only person who could have any possibility of success in removing Hitler became, after 1939, the solitary assassin prepared, if necessary, to kill himself together with the man he had set out to kill. He would have to possess sufficient status to get near enough to Hitler to kill him with some hidden weapon. Several attempts on Hitler's life were to be planned by brave men who were also prepared to make the personal sacrifice of their own lives. The civilians, in the end, could do little in this matter but talk themselves into a state of prolonged wish-fulfilment—though this in itself required courage enough in the face of the secret and often invisible eyes of the Gestapo, who were always ready to bide their time until a man who thought himself immune from discovery had wrapped himself up sufficiently in the winding sheet of incrimination to satisfy their needs. Then they came and knocked on his door. However, at this stage the idea of an actual attempt at the assassination of Hitler, rather than his mere arrest and trial, was in the minds of very few of the conspirators, though urged by Tresckow and Schlabrendorff. The older men, such as Hassell and Canaris, were not yet quite ready to entertain the idea of themselves, and some of them were never to approve of it.

137

Meanwhile, Canaris continued his policy of diminishing the effects of Hitler's war as far as possible. According to Colvin it would appear that Canaris had leaked information concerning the abortive Operation Sea-Lion at an early stage of its preparation by sending Müller to Rome with such details as were known. He delighted in reading the monitored reports of Churchill's defiant speeches to his wife at home, and he used to declare his pride in having the same initials (*Wilhelm Canaris*) as the British leader. Abwehr reports tended to exaggerate the preparedness of Britain for defense—whether deliberately or through faulty Intelligence is not known.

Canaris's principal personal contribution was to help keep Spain out of the war. Perhaps this was due as much to his love for that country as to his desire to rob Hitler of an active ally. Canaris, as we have seen, knew Franco personally, and made it his business to dissuade him from letting his forces enter the battlefield, even in the case of Gibraltar. He sent the Caudillo a message through Müller in Rome to the effect that Spain would only be joining a losing campaign and that in spite of the current run of success which Germany was enjoying, Hitler could not hope to win ultimate victory. He also affirmed that Hitler was in no position to "occupy" Spain by force. Lahousen claims that Canaris was not invited to accompany Hitler to meet Franco at Hendaye in October 1940 because he was not at one with the Führer and Ribbentrop over the problem Spain represented. Nevertheless, it was Canaris who was sent ostensibly to try to persuade Franco to join forces with Hitler and at the same time to permit German troops to enter Spain and march south to take Gibraltar from the rear. That he signally failed in this mission no doubt appealed to his sense of humor, while the situation of everyone watching everyone else in neutral Spain appealed to his innate sense of guile. However, pro-Nazi sources in Spain passed messages to the Gestapo officer, Walther Huppenkothen, that Canaris was dissuading Franco from entering the war. Be that as it may, Canaris was very frequently in Spain between 1940 and 1943. Colvin believes that he tried to act in a similar way in the Balkans, dissuading King Boris of Bulgaria, with whom he had personal contacts, to refrain from joining the Axis for as long as he could. In this case, he failed; Boris allied himself with Hitler on 1 March 1941.

Canaris, it must always be understood, was skilled in leaving just the right measure of doubt in other people's minds. Naturally, he could never appear to be against his Führer. But a great deal could be achieved, whether inside or outside Germany, in the form of confidences shared over a bottle or two of wine. Canaris knew how to drop a hint—don't be precipitate here, he might suggest, be cautious there, don't cross your bridges, don't burn your boats. He was an engaging companion at dinner, an intellectual who knew precisely the right moment to make a generalization, or lift the discussion of an immediate problem into a matter of philosophical or historical speculation. In this way, he could suggest a warning without stating it precisely, or reinforce an already existing desire not to be directly involved in the war without going on record as having actually advised it. Canaris seldom addressed himself directly to the conscience of an outsider. Only with the men of his own inner circle did he trust himself to speak his mind openly.

In April 1941 Hitler's bombing of Belgrade was preceded by a warning said by Abshagen to have originated once more with Oster. Canaris was among the high-ranking German officers who visited Yugoslavia after Hitler's devastating air-raids on Belgrade. He endured this horrifying experience for a single day only, and then promptly left for Spain. For as long as he remained at the head of the Abwehr, he was to travel constantly—in France, Italy, Turkey, Switzerland, North Africa, Bulgaria, Hungary, Scandinavia, Spain and Portugal, as if by this continual movement he could exorcise his depression. Werner Best, among many others, has testified to this. Best, whom he twice visited in Paris and more frequently in Copenhagen, confirms that he always seemed "worried and critical, and deeply pessimistic about the war." So he travelled. Needing no permit to go where he liked—since his department was one authorized to issue such permits to others—

whenever his depression overcame him he would disappear in the direction of the Mediterranean. In 1941 he even visited Rommel at his headquarters in North Africa and took the opportunity to inform him about the atrocities committed by the S.S. in Europe. The Army, he claimed, must in the end be held responsible. But all Rommel cared about at that time was the conduct of his own campaigns in the deserts of Africa.

Canaris Recruits the Anti-Nazis; Relations with the S.S.

Canaris's methods of staffing the Abwehr in wartime were often unorthodox. It was laid down that all recruits should be approved by the Gestapo and the S.D., its Intelligence service. But Canaris avoided this when it suited him to do so. He even managed (by the use of false papers) to introduce Jews into the Abwehr, men such as Colonels Simon and Bloch.[9] The fact that his department could create whatever documents, passports and visas that it pleased made it almost impossible for the Gestapo to take effective action as the numbers of Abwehr officers and secret agents grew during the war years. Even known anti-Nazis like Bonhoeffer, Bethge and Werner Schrader were introduced into the Abwehr. Many, in any case, were either recruited abroad or posted there. Typical, perhaps, is the case of Gisevius himself, which he described to the International Military Tribunal:

> On the day of the outbreak of the war I was called into the Abwehr by General Oster with a forged order. However, since it was a regulation that all officers or other members of the Abwehr had to be examined by the Gestapo, and since I would never have received permission to be a member of the Abwehr, they simply gave me a forged mobilization order. Then I was at the disposal of Oster and Canaris without doing any direct service.[10]

Later, his position changed:

> After the fall of Paris I stated to Canaris and Oster that I would have to ask them now to release me from that

somewhat complicated situation. At that time Canaris's position was so strong that he was able to place me in an intelligence post with the Consulate General in Zurich. There I received the title of a Vice Consul, and I stayed there as an 'intelligence' man, without belonging to the Abwehr formally, until 20 July [1944]. After 20 July I was dismissed from all posts.

According to Colonel Heinz, Canaris wanted to establish his own military police in order to circumvent the S.D., who spied on his men or the men he sought to cover and sent in their own independent reports about them. Canaris was never able officially to free himself or his agents from the surveillance of Himmler's departments, and this was one of his main reasons for finding it politic to keep in constant touch, both socially and officially, with the men who at any moment could prove to be his deadliest enemies.

In conversation with Colvin, Leverkuehn described Canaris during his mid-war period as "very bright, animated and talkative, like a little old lady." He added that his chief had "an extraordinary disregard for military conventions" and, because he trusted Leverkuehn, he frequently asked his advice on the appointment of men of more senior rank. Although Leverkuehn was fond of Canaris, he found him "the most difficult chief in the world" and he was often irritated by the admiral's habit of breaking off in the middle of an important conversation to talk to his dachshunds. On the other hand, although Leverkuehn claimed that Canaris at no time even hinted at the subject of discovering some way of initiating peace discussions with the Allies, he was sure the admiral was quite certain about his objectives. "He saw quite clearly what he was doing and why he was doing it," he told Colvin. "Maybe the British expected more action of him; but violence was not in his nature." In this most dangerous field of secret moves for peace, Canaris worked with the greatest circumspection.

When he was in Berlin Canaris maintained his connection with Heydrich and the head of Heydrich's Intelligence section. Walther Schellenberg. In his memoirs Schellenberg claims a form of friendship with Canaris whom, he says, he "could not help liking." He found Canaris "a highly intelligent and sensitive man." Then he adds:

> He was very good company on the many trips we made together, and his attitude to me was always kind and paternal. Whether in Spain, Portugal, Hungary, Poland, Finland or Scandinavia, Canaris always had a fund of knowledge about the peculiarities of the countries, and especially about their cooking and their wines. In the South he always made sure—in spite of the great heat—that I wore a woollen stomacher! And he would ply me with all sorts of medicaments and with pills which he himself constantly took. He often asked me to attend the various meetings of his organization, and I was thus able to acquaint myself with the weaknesses of the Military Intelligence Service. In this huge over-inflated organization, Canaris's methods were far too humane. His subordinates were able to twist him round their little fingers, and when he was eventually forced to take strong measures, he would always try to make up for his severity afterwards.[11]

Heydrich maintained his friendship with Canaris for the purpose of spying on him and his department. He looked with great disfavor on the enormous growth of the Abwehr, and the file on Canaris began to grow; in order, says Schellenberg, to 'bring about his downfall at any moment'. At the end of May 1940, Schellenberg states that Heydrich summoned him, together with the chief of the Gestapo, Heinrich Müller; he demanded a closer investigation into the activities of Josef Müller and Dohnanyi in their dealings with the Vatican, and into any connection they might have with the leakage of the news of invasion to the Dutch government. It was decided that Schellenberg should raise the matter with Canaris, who was not himself suspected. Canaris knew how to fence when dangerous matters were broached, and he did his best, successfully for a while, to cover Josef Müller's activities. Schellenberg gives something of the atmosphere of his curious social contacts with Canaris:

As well as on visits between our families, and on our morning rides, Canaris and I used to meet in Heydrich's house, and I was usually present at the talks between him and Canaris. Indeed, they not only tolerated me but seemed glad of my presence. If ever I failed to attend of my own accord, one or the other of them would be sure to call me in. It was curious to see how they would both ply me with questions afterwards, though I was far younger than either of them. 'What should I have understood by that?' 'What do you think was behind this?' 'Did I say the right thing?' 'Was I too aggressive?' I was a sort of go-between—a *postillion d'amour* for them, whom they both trusted. Heydrich always had the greatest respect for Canaris. . . . Though he liked to assert his superiority over his former chief, he always maintained an outward respect for him; and for a man like Heydrich this meant a great deal. Shortly before his death, Heydrich spoke to me about the continual differences and frictions between him and Canaris. He was no longer willing to give in to Canaris, whatever might be the outcome. 'You should not let yourself be lulled to sleep by him,' Heydrich warned me. He suggested that I should assert myself more ruthlessly. 'Seeing the two of you together, one would take you for bosom friends. You won't get anywhere by handling him with kid gloves.' Canaris was fatalistic, said Heydrich, and only firmness would be effective with him. 'And you have to be even tougher with his followers—a bunch of talkative highbrows; they interpret courtesy as a sign of weakness.'[12]

The complications involved through the overlapping of the Intelligence sections of different departments did not stop with the Abwehr's most serious competitor, the S.D. Goebbels at the Propaganda Ministry and Ribbentrop at the Foreign Office had their recognized Intelligence services, while Göring had developed a small organization for telephone-tapping long before the War. The Nazi régime would scarcely by its very nature avoid a multiplicity of spy networks of very varying efficiency. Canaris did what he could to withstand the constant pressures from outside to curtail his rights and powers, but he was not always successful. During the period prior to the invasion of France, Canaris was initially responsible for having leaflets shot into the French lines; the message they carried was designed to persuade the French that it would be unnatural to start any hostilities against the Germans, with whom they had so many cultural and other ties. Goebbels complained that this kind of activity belonged entirely to the Ministry of Propaganda, and he obtained an order from Hitler to this effect.

The surviving fragments of Goebbels's diaries reveal how Canaris managed to retain a reasonably good name with the Nazi leaders. On 25 January 1942 Goebbels noted that Canaris had a long talk with him about the 'defeatism' shown by certain staff officers owing to the widespread granting of permits to listen to foreign broadcasts, or to receive the Seehaus service, which was a daily monitor-bulletin taken from the broadcasts. Goebbels, in fact, liked Canaris in much the same way as Schellenberg did, and was rather flattered than otherwise that the admiral had taken the trouble to report the matter to him.

However much one speculates about the curious tensions in the relationship between the Abwehr and the S.D., Schellenberg's rise to full charge of the S.S. Intelligence service after the death of Heydrich was not in the long run to help Canaris.[13] Schellenberg, aged at this period only thirty-one, was a quick-witted and ambitious young man with the tortuous intelligence of the typical secret agent; he had studied law at Bonn and was over twenty years younger than Canaris. Also, he had nothing of Canaris's respect for Service tradition, and loved above all to play the spy who outwits men larger and more highly placed than himself, including even Himmler, his own commander-in-chief. Nevertheless, it was part of Schellenberg's policy to display only charm and intelligence to friends and opponents alike, and with the death of Heydrich, whom he had feared, Schellenberg was determined to extend his sphere of influence under Himmler. It was his ultimate objective to take over all the Intelligence services, includ-

ing the Abwehr and the Intelligence department attached
to Ribbentrop's Foreign Office.

The idea had originally been put in his mind by Heydrich
himself. Heydrich, Schellenberg wrote in his memoirs,

> was very critical of Canaris's work. . . . He felt certain,
> in fact, that Canaris had betrayed the date of the attack
> in the West . . . but nevertheless he did not want to
> proceed against him yet. He would wait and gather more
> evidence. The day would come, however, when Canaris
> would be punished for all the damage he had caused to
> the régime.[14]

According to Schellenberg (whose memoirs, compiled
after the war and subsequently much cut and edited for
publication, must be taken with a dose, rather than a pinch,
of salt), Heydrich was always complaining about Canaris's
devious nature, but, intent on his new work in Prague,
he left Schellenberg to fence with the admiral. So the two
went riding together and discussed their mutual problems.
What, for example, should they do if certain of their
agents were discovered abroad and arrested? According to
Schellenberg, Canaris suggested it would cause useful confusion if, in the event of capture, Abwehr agents pretended
to belong to the S.S., while any S.S. agents who were caught
pretended to be men of the Abwehr. Schellenberg, no
doubt searching for the failings in Canaris which he wanted
to find, thought this suggestion, to say the least, "extremely
curious." He then went on to observe the weaknesses in
his older rival:

> I noticed now for the first time signs of an inner weari-
> ness in Canaris. He was worn out by the continual inter-
> necine conflict. Heydrich's ice-cold tactics of the last
> months were beginning to show their effect. He felt
> insecure and restless, and, or so I thought, something
> like a physical fear of Heydrich. And his pessimism about
> the war situation was increasing. Repeatedly he said to
> me, 'Haven't we said again and again that things in
> Russia would not go the way the Führer and his ad-

visers imagine? But they won't even listen to the truth any longer. I know I'm much older than you, but please let us stick together. If those at the top notice that we both hold the same opinions, perhaps they'll take some notice. I insist on returning to a workable relationship with Heydrich, though. Things can't go on this way much longer.'

Canaris, said Schellenberg, 'gave way all along the line' when, in May 1942, a meeting took place in Prague to reformulate the "Ten Commandments." After the adjustments had been made, Schellenberg claims that Canaris admitted that Heydrich's intrigues had upset him, and that he was convinced Heydrich would "attack again."

Within a matter of days Heydrich was on his deathbed. Shortly after two o'clock on the afternoon of 27 May he had left by open car for the airport. Unlike most of the Nazi leaders, Heydrich was frequently careless of his personal safety. As his driver slowed down to negotiate a sharp bend in the road, which was blocked by two tram-cars passing each other, a grenade was hurled at the staff car. Two free Czechs, agents sent from Britain, one with a Sten-gun and the other with a grenade, had been waiting at the corner to make the attempt on Heydrich's life. When the first agent's Sten-gun jammed, the other flung the grenade. Then both of them fled, dodging between the tram-cars.

Heydrich seemed for the moment to be quite uninjured. He jumped out of the staff car, his pistol drawn. He took a few steps after his assailants, firing as he ran. Then he staggered and collapsed. When he was hurried to a hospital, it was discovered that he had sustained internal injuries at the base of his spine, and he died a lingering death a week later. A reward of one million crowns was offered for information leading to the arrest of his killers. They were finally traced, and died resisting arrest the following month. Walther Huppenkothen claims that Canaris openly wept at Heydrich's funeral in Berlin. He told Huppenkothen that he had lost a real friend; but his emotion might well have been due more to relief than sorrow.

Shortly after, the Abwehr was to become involved in yet another order to murder a French general in an operation to which Keitel gave the code name "Gustav." Canaris was adroit enough to use the assassination of Heydrich to avoid this second attempt to involve the Abwehr in political murder. This was revealed by Lahousen during his evidence before the International Military Tribunal, where he was questioned by Colonel Amen, one of the Associate Trial Counsels appointed by the United States:

AMEN: Will you tell the Tribunal what was the meaning of 'Gustav?'

LAHOUSEN: 'Gustav' was the expression used by the Chief of the O.K.W. as a cover name to be used in conversation on the question of General Giraud . . . The Chief of the O.K.W., Keitel, gave an order of this kind to Canaris, not in writing, but an oral order. . . . The essential part of this order was to eliminate Giraud in the same way as Weygand. . . . that is, he was to be killed.

AMEN: Do you recall the approximate date when this order was given by Keitel to Canaris?

LAHOUSEN: This order was given to Canaris repeatedly. I cannot for certain say when it was given for the first time as I was not present. It was probably after the flight of Giraud from Koenigstein and it was probably given for the first time prior to the attempt on the life of Heydrich, in Prague. According to my notes, this subject was discussed with me by Keitel in July of the same year [1942]. Canaris also being present. . . . According to my recollection, this question was discussed once more in August. . . . Canaris telephoned me in my private apartment one evening, and said impatiently that Keitel was urging him again about Giraud, and the Section Chiefs were to meet the next day on this question. . . . Canaris repeated to his larger circle what he had said to me over the phone the night before, that he was being continually pressed by Keitel that something must at last be done in this matter. Our attitude was the same as in the matter of Weygand. . . . We

147

mentioned our decision to Canaris, who was also of the same opinion, and Canaris thereupon went down to Keitel in order to induce him to leave the Military Abwehr out of all such matters and to request that, as agreed prior to this, such matters should be left to the S.D. . . . After a short time, Canaris came back and said. . . . he had convinced Keitel that we, the Military Abwehr, were to be left out of such matters. . . . Canaris said the execution must be prevented. . . . He would take care of that. . . . A little later, it must have been September. . . . Keitel rang me up in my private apartment. He asked me what was happening with 'Gustav'. . . . I answered, 'I have no information on the subject. Canaris has reserved this matter to himself, and Canaris is not here, he is in Paris.' . . . Then came the order from Keitel to ask Heinrich Müller [Chief of the Gestapo] immediately how the whole matter was progressing. 'I must know it immediately,' he said. I said, 'Yes.' I went at once to. . . . General Oster and informed him of what had happened, and asked for his advice as to what was to be done by Canaris and me in this extremely critical and difficult matter. I told him what (as Oster knew nothing yet of what it was expected to do) Canaris had told the S.D. so far concerning the murder of Giraud. General Oster advised me to fly to Paris immediately and to inform Canaris and warn him. I flew the next day to Paris, and met Canaris at an hotel at dinner in a small circle, which included Admiral Bürkner, and told Canaris what had happened. Canaris was horrified and amazed, and for a moment he saw no way out.

During dinner Canaris asked me in the presence of Bürkner. . . . as to the date when Giraud had fled from Koenigstein, and when Abwehr III had been in Prague, and at what time the assassination of Heydrich had taken place. . . . When he had the three dates, he was instantly relieved, and his face, which had been very clouded, relaxed. . . . Canaris then based his whole plan on these three dates. His plan was to attempt to show that Heydrich, during the conference, had passed on the

148

order to carry out the action. That is to say, his plan was to use the death of Heydrich in May 1942 to wreck the whole proposition. The next day we flew to Berlin, and Canaris reported to Keitel that the matter was taking its course, and that Canaris had given Heydrich the necessary instructions at the three days' conference in Prague, and Heydrich had prepared everything, that is, a special purpose action had been started in order to have Giraud murdered, and that the matter was completed and all mapped out. . . . Nothing more happened. Giraud fled to North Africa.[15]

Nothing could be more revealing than this story of the tightrope the chiefs of the Abwehr walked and of the astuteness shown by Canaris in extricating himself and his staff from difficulty.

After the death of Heydrich, Canaris gained some breathing space. But, in Schellenberg's biased opinion, Canaris's pessimistic acceptance of inevitable defeat had become by now part of his nature:

Canaris felt all this, but with an almost oriental fatalism made no attempt to resist. He believed in his preordained fate and let himself and his organization drift with the stream. Inflated with false hopes, he neglected his own duties and travelled restlessly from one country to another and from one sector of the front to another. From time to time he made real attempts at a far-reaching conspiracy, but drew back at the decisive moment. He was bedevilled by his anxiety about the outcome of the war and the muddle of his own plans.

The whole situation was complicated by Schellenberg's own relationship with Himmler. With Heydrich gone, Schellenberg set out to become the *éminence grise* in Himmler's life, urging him to take the intiative out of Hitler's hands and bring about peace negotiations on his own behalf. Himmler, always worried and irresolute, had just enough willpower to be obstinate and refuse to be pushed in a direction as dangerous as this. Like the

149

generals, he always balked at the point when he was finally pressed to commit himself. Whatever was suspect in Canaris's own behavior or that of his staff, it was still of sufficient interest to Himmler and the S.S. to prevent any sudden arrests being made. On the other hand Canaris was as adept at keeping his files clear as was Heydrich. He told Schellenberg after Heydrich's assassination that he held proof of the latter's Jewish ancestry.[16] You never knew when information of this kind might not prove invaluable during an argument between departments. Meanwhile, the morning rides on horseback with Schellenberg continued; according to Schellenberg, on at least two or three mornings a week from 1941. During their conversations Schellenberg gathered how deeply concerned Canaris was about the Russian campaign and the underestimation of the strength of the Soviet Union of which the High Command was guilty through Hitler's influence. Keitel had even reprimanded him for the incessant warnings which, as head of military Intelligence, he thought it his duty to give. "When Canaris repeated such remarks," Schellenberg recalled, "he would usually rein in his horse, look at me with wide eyes and say quite seriously, 'Wouldn't you find all this quite funny—if it weren't so desperately serious?' "

The discussions often continued at Horcher's, the celebrated restaurant serving black market food and French wines. Heydrich and Canaris had lunched there regularly when they happened to be in Berlin. In June 1941, a year or so before Heydrich's death, when the campaign against Russia was imminent, Canaris, Heydrich and Schellenberg were lunching one day at Horcher's; Schellenberg remembered Canaris's vain attempts to win over Heydrich to his point of view that Russia was invincible and the campaign a fatal mistake. According to Colvin, the admiral twice sent warnings to the British that the invasion of Russia was to take place; once through Müller at the Vatican, and again in Moscow itself through one of his personal Abwehr agents, Nicholas von Halem. Halem travelled as a German businessman, of whom there were many in Moscow before the attack was launched, and made contact in his hotel with an English resident with whom he had been acquainted. Canaris, however, was not prepared to warn the Russians himself.

Part of the routine work of Intelligence also involved committing acts of sabotage. With a large department and staff of secret agents working for him, Canaris could scarcely circumvent every act of violent sabotage. Lahousen, speaking to Colvin, has admitted that this was the case. "Canaris was not always able to prevent acts of terrorism," said Lahousen, "sometimes it was technically impossible. Sometimes it was a question of personality. That he was always opposed to it is without question." Keitel, for example, gave a direct order for the New York-Lisbon plane to be destroyed in flight; Canaris, visiting Portugal, ordered that the bomb his officers had smuggled on board the plane, which had been delayed by bad weather, must be removed. According to Baron Hoinigen-Huene, the German ambassador in Portugal, Canaris had agreed that no acts of sabotage to Allied shipping should be undertaken in Portuguese harbors. Keitel also passed on an order that an attempt to assassinate Churchill should be made through Arab agents in Casablanca; naturally, this came to nothing. But when Churchill was known to be returning to Britain from North Africa on 1 June 1943, the regular B.O.A.C. airliner flying between Lisbon and London was shot down by the Luftwaffe because, it would seem, there was a passenger on board with a slight resemblance to Churchill. This was how Leslie Howard, the film actor, met his death, together with all the other passengers and crew in the aircraft. Canaris's agents in Portugal kept in touch with the Polish legation representing the Polish government in exile. Colvin believes that on one occasion Canaris himself, using an alias, met the head of the Polish mission in Lisbon.

Goerdeler was almost as indefatigable in his travels as Canaris. He had shared the appalling shock which the fall of the countries north and west of Germany had administered to every member of the resistance. He poured out his revulsion in a memorandum ostensibly addressed to the generals, claiming the aggression had been committed

151

because Hitler was at his "wit's end," and only this unnecessary violence could cover the bankruptcy of the régime. However much of the world he might conquer, wrote Goerdeler, "Hitler is quite incapable of ruling that vast area in such a way as to preserve the honor and freedom of the nations living in it, and that is the indispensable condition of achievement. . . . A tyrant can never create anything but a tyranny." Goerdeler foresaw the mass destruction and the collapse of all values in Europe which Hitler's conquests implied.

He realized, like his friend Hassell, that the only hope lay in the Army taking effective action against Hitler. The number of younger officers favoring the resistance was growing, but members were thinning in the ranks of their seniors, who had failed to muster the strength to deal with Hitler when he was on the crest of his fortune. After the fall of France, some of these had assembled at General Stuelpnagel's headquarters in Paris and openly discussed the possibilities of a *coup d'état*. Among them were Tresckow, later to be posted to the Russian front, and also Generals Eduard Wagner and Erich Fellgiebel (both to be involved, like Stuelpnagel, in active resistance work), and the young staff officer Count von Stauffenberg who was to be the hero of the attempt in July 1944.

Halder was also present, but he tried to persuade them to do nothing. It was not, he said, the right moment to stage a *coup d'état*. Meanwhile Goerdeler continued writing, bombarding now this person, now that, with his wordy but eloquent memoranda on the economic, political and ideological collapse of Germany. Even to his friends he became known as the "preacher" and he was resolute that Germany must expiate her wrongdoing, bringing every Nazi criminal to justice in German courts of law. He took grave risks in sending these secret statements to men he felt should be sympathetic to his views. No one betrayed him until the end, and if any individual had done so at this time, it is anyway doubtful whether the Gestapo would have thought the moment ripe to take direct action. In their view, Goerdeler's form of disaffection was relatively harmless, if not academic; they were far more interested in discovering his many contacts than in stopping his literary activities.

In his schemes for the future, Goerdeler tried to allow for the proper representation of the labor movement in the social and economic development of Germany. Not all his more right-wing associates were ready to agree with him, nor with his pattern for the new Europe, which he modelled on the British Commonwealth, a free association of nations both politically and economically, opposed only to Fascism and Communism. It was a deep blow to Goerdeler when, following the German invasion of Russia, Britain and the Soviet Union signed a treaty binding them not to make a separate peace, while America joined in the Atlantic Charter which foresaw a Germany disarmed and subjected by the Allies.

Goerdeler was never to be convinced that the assassination of Hitler, which certain of the conspirators were beginning to entertain as the only course of action, was the right one after all. The idea was offensive to his keen moral sense; he continued to favor the idea of Hitler's arrest and trial. The years 1941 and 1942, the years dominated by the great movements and frustrations on the Russian front, also saw the prolonged secret discussions of the *coup d'état* which never came to a head. Response to the efforts of the conspirators to win support among the generals naturally reflected the situation on the front. While the campaign had been succeeding with a dramatic precipitation—within the first twenty-four days the German armies had reached Smolensk, some 200 miles from Moscow—no one had had the time, let alone the inclination, to listen to a bunch of scattered malcontents who wanted to overthrow the Führer. But with the arrival of winter, the Russian campaign began to fall into the doldrums, bogged down in the freezing cold for which no one had been prepared. Then the generals with an ear left open for the sound of insurrection proved a little more approachable. Hitler had rejected his High Command's desire to attempt an immediate, decisive victory over the Russian armies by concentrating their strength on the Moscow front, and had deliberately weakened the initial impact of

153

his attack by driving into the Ukraine, the resources of which he had for so long been anxious to acquire.

At first the only high-placed general who seemed whole-heartedly for resistance against Hitler was Field-Marshal Witzleben. All other attempts to stir those at the head or near the head of the Army seemed doomed to failure; from generals plied with arguments by Goerdeler (who lost a son in the war during the spring of 1942), by Thomas, or by Beck, the response was always the same: "The time is still not ripe." Then another important member of the military wing of the resistance joined them: General Friedrich Olbricht, head of the Supply Section of the Reserve Army in Berlin. Like Goerdeler, he had recently lost a son on the fighting front. And then gradually the situation seemed to crystallize round Tresckow and Schlabrendorff at the central Army Group in Russia, with Kluge as their commanding officer from December 1941. Kluge, essentially weak of character, became increasingly subject to Tresckow, his General Staff Officer; his moral position, however, was seriously compromised when he accepted a personal present from Hitler of 250,000 marks. Such presents became a part of Hitler's policy in order to bind the generals to him, but Witzleben, for example, had refused to be bribed in this way.

It is against the background of the progress of the war —the successful drive of the German Army into the Caucasus during the summer, followed by the shock of the German defeat at Stalingrad and the landing of American and British troops in northwest Africa during November —that the extraordinary events of the next twelve months May 1942 to April 1943 must be understood. These events were almost entirely the result of activity by the men of the resistance working either inside the Abwehr or in direct association with Oster and Dohnanyi.

It was during May 1942 that Pastor Dietrich Bonhoeffer, provided with suitable papers by the Abwehr, went on a visit to Stockholm, the visit timed to coincide with that of George Bell, Bishop of Chichester. Bonhoeffer, one of the most remarkable of the Abwehr's secret agents, was, as we have seen, Dohnanyi's brother-in-law, and as soon

154

as it became known through the Swedish press that Bell was to be in Stockholm, an excuse was found to send Bonhoeffer to Sweden.[17]

Bonhoeffer had much in common with Bell, whom he had come to know during the period of almost two years when, as a young chaplain in his late twenties, he had served the German Congregation in Forest Hill, London. Both Bonhoeffer and Bell were deeply interested in politics. Neither was a conventional member of his respective church; Bonhoeffer had become, even as a young man, a distinguished if unorthodox theologian closely identified with the Confessional Church, the body in which all those German Protestants who were opposed to Hitler congregated.

Bonhoeffer, carrying the papers given him by Oster and Dohnanyi, flew to Sweden on 30 May. He met Bell in Sigtuna, some thirty miles north of Stockholm. During the Whitsun weekend Bonhoeffer, delighted to be with his friends once again in these strange and unforeseen circumstances, gave Bell a detailed account of the resistance which was building up in Germany against the régime. Bell realized with emotion how deeply Bonhoeffer's conscience was affected by the crimes his nation was committing. He warned him that it was very late in the day to expect much by way of response from the British government unless positive action was actually taken in Germany against Hitler. Nevertheless, they discussed the possibilities of keeping in touch, even to the extent of meeting again in Sigtuna. This idea was abandoned, however, for fear of compromising the neutrality of Sweden. Among the messages which Bonhoeffer asked Bell to deliver in England was one to his brother-in-law, Dr. Leibholz; it informed him that Hans Dohnanyi "was active in the good cause." Bonhoeffer's visit was naturally kept a closely-guarded secret; Josef Müller, who knew of it, could not persuade Dohnanyi to give him any details of what had transpired in Sweden. On his return Bell did his utmost to persuade Anthony Eden to give open encouragement to the German resistance, but failed.

As if in confirmation of all that Bell and Bonhoeffer

155

were trying to bring about, earlier in 1942 the group in Berlin had renewed their efforts to bring pressure on the various commanders-in-chief to take action against Hitler. At field-marshal level, Erwin von Witzleben, now commander-in-chief in the West, was (as we have seen) closest to the conspirators; he was approached with the suggestion that he might take what was called an "isolated action"— that is, lead an open insurrection against Hitler's command or arrest him without the preliminary of agreeing concerted action with the other supreme Army commanders.

Hassell had visited Witzleben's headquarters in mid-January, ostensibly to give a lecture to the staff. He took the opportunity to have what he called a "thorough discussion" with him; subsequently, he had a further discussion with another of the sympathetic commanders, the aristocrat General von Falkenhausen, military governor of Belgium, to whom he had been introduced during 1941 by Oster and Dohnanyi. Falkenhausen, a dedicated opponent of Hitler, had for a while been sent on a mission to China to advise on the training of Chiang Kai-shek's troops. Hassell has described the preparation for these discussions:

Before my trip I had numerous discussions with Popitz, Goerdeler, Beck. . . . as well as with Oster and Dohnanyi, about the general situation, the tactics to be adopted, and particularly about the line to be followed in my talks with Falkenhausen and Witzleben. Astonishing optimism, especially on the part of Beck and Goerdeler with respect to the possibilities of both generals. Goerdeler composed a document to be used, and we went over it.[18]

As for the evening itself, it went as well as might be expected:

I spent the evening in St Germain. . . . with Witzleben in his villa. I had met him only once before, at a banquet Hitler gave for Mussolini in 1937. He didn't feel very

156

well this evening and looked older than his age. He was somewhat dull, especially at the stiff and boring gathering following my lecture. Nevertheless, I had a good feeling about him—a man of clear purpose and good perception.

A second meeting was arranged; at this Witzleben seemed "more lively," though he thought Beck and Goerdeler "Utopian" in their idea of an "isolated action."

But again, the conspirators were unlucky. Witzleben, suffering from hemorrhoids, had arranged to be operated upon in March. By the time he emerged from hospital he found himself among those whom Hitler, as usual without either warning or explanation, announced as retired from their commands. To be fair to the conspirators, who are normally criticized for their inaction, it must be emphasized that they were helpless without the support of senior officers, like Witzleben, who had direct authority over troops. No administrator, however elevated, could carry out a *coup d'état* sitting at his desk. He had to have the support of commanders in a position to deploy armed forces the moment the authority of Hitler was removed. Yet whenever the conspirators had brought a man who was sympathetic to their cause to the point of considering action, they were not only in danger that he would ultimately fail them, they were also subject to the chance that he would, like Witzleben, be suddenly removed from his command or transferred to another sector.

However, it was at this stage that Schlabrendorff invited Goerdeler to visit Kluge in Smolensk and add the pressure of his arguments to those of Tresckow. Still covered by the bogus papers given him by Oster, Goerdeler set out during the winter of 1942 on the difficult journey to Group headquarters in Smolensk; it took him eight days, and involved him in some considerable risk. Kluge, urged by Tresckow, met Goerdeler at a secret place in the forests. Goerdeler's powerful personality impressed Kluge, and his eloquence filled both Tresckow and Schlabrendorff with admiration. "A political mind of the first order," wrote Schlabrendorff. But Kluge still vacillated:

Each time Tresckow believed that he had finally got Kluge where he wanted him, he had to realize the very next day that the Commander-in-Chief had again started to waver. But Tresckow was untiring in his efforts, and in the long run Kluge succumbed to his influence—but to his influence alone. In jest, I used to call Tresckow the watchmaker who wound Kluge every morning and made him run all day.[19]

Initial Plans for the Coup d'État: *Co-ordinating the Resistance*

The first seeds of the plot which was later to lead to the most fully developed of the many attempts to assassinate Hitler, that of 20 July 1944, were sown during the autumn of 1942. Beck, Goerdeler, Olbricht and Tresckow met in Berlin during November, and the plan took shape for the outright assassination of Hitler followed by an immediate *coup d'état* by the Reserve Army—that is, the army based in Germany itself and commanded by General Fritz Fromm, on whose administrative staff Olbricht served as supply officer. Although Fromm was one of the more time-serving generals whom the conspirators could least afford to trust, Olbricht was a sufficiently senior staff officer to influence the placing of men regarded as reliable in key places throughout the command. By now it was becoming clear that the reverses in North Africa and on the Russian front in the Stalingrad salient were the first major setbacks to Hitler's triumphal progress. The conspirators hoped to bring General (later Field-Marshal) Friedrich Paulus, the German commander of the Sixth Army at Stalingrad, to the point of refusing to accept the orders from Hitler which must lead to the total annihilation of his forces. But neither Paulus nor his supreme commander, Field-Marshal von Manstein, were men capable of making a public demonstration against Hitler. Paulus, in an impossible situation, was forced to surrender to the Russians, but did so without any dramatic denunciation of Hitler. The conspirators in Berlin were deeply disappointed. They had hoped for some great gesture, some stirring appeal from the Stalingrad inferno, which would have acted as the signal for the deposition of Hitler. What von Manstein said when he subsequently gave evidence before the International Military Tribunal at Nuremberg shows, on the one hand, how insecure was the position of almost all the commanders who served Hitler, and on the other hand how they turned what was in effect a blind eye towards anything which might directly implicate them in action against the Führer. What he felt, they all felt:

> Of seventeen field marshals who were members of the Army, ten were sent home during the war and three lost their lives as a result of 20 July. Only one field marshal managed to get through the war and keep his position as field marshal. Of thirty-six colonel generals, eighteen were sent home and five died as a result of 20 July, or were dishonorably discharged. Only three colonel-generals survived the war in their positions. . . . It was always my point of view, however, that the removal or the assassination of Hitler during the war would lead to chaos. . . . I had never made a promise to anyone to participate in such affairs.[20]

The story, seen from the conspirators' point of view, was presented at Nuremberg by Gisevius:

> Since the outbreak of war, General Beck tried to contact one field marshal after another. He wrote letters and he sent messengers to them. I particularly remember the correspondence with Field Marshal von Manstein, and I saw with my own eyes von Manstein's answer of the year 1942. To Beck's strictly military statement that the war had been lost, von Manstein would reply, "A war is not lost until one considers it lost." . . . At the time of the Stalingrad *putsch,* contrary to all expectations, Field Marshal Paulus capitulated. This, we know, was the first mass capitulation of the generals; where as we had expected that Paulus and his generals, before the capitulation, would issue a proclamation to the Eastern Front

159

and to the German people, in which the strategy of Hitler and the sacrifice of the Stalingrad army would be branded in suitable words. This was to have been the clue for Kluge to declare that in future he would take no further military orders from Hitler. We hoped with this plan to circumvent the problem of the military oath which kept troubling us more and more, in that one field marshal after another would refuse military obedience to Hitler, whereupon Beck was to take over supreme military command in Berlin.[21]

With the failure of this rebellion, Beck found himself at the head of a group of men who were either retired from their commands or merely serving in the Army in an administrative capacity. So from 1943 Tresckow had to ensure even more energetically his task of "winding up" Kluge. Another attempt to win over a field-marshal was made by Thomas, who suggested to Field-Marshal Wilhelm List that he should permit Goerdeler to visit him; but this arrangement, even had Goerdeler been successful, would have been frustrated because List, like so many of his rank approached by the conspirators, was removed from his command before he could be tested. Beck, Thomas and Olbricht continued to approach every commanding officer they knew, and were as constantly turned down, or otherwise disappointed. In August, Goerdeler, who had no right to visit any battlefront but went there on the strength of the papers provided by the Abwehr, visited Königsberg to sound Field-Marshal Georg von Kuechler, who commanded the Army Group North. But this journey, too, was in vain.

Hassell, like Beck, provided a focal point for the conspiracy, but he is often critical of his associates. Beck, for example, he found "very theoretical. . . . a man of tactics but little willpower." On the other hand, Goerdeler "has much willpower but no tactics." He wrote in September of that year:

We were rather concerned about Goerdeler, who is much too optimistic and too "reactionary." He has visited me often during these days and always refreshed me by his liveliness and enterprising spirit; but I was disturbed by his facile prophecies of an early breakdown of the régime. He also worries me with his somewhat childishly contrived plans.[22]

He also maintained contact with Schacht, of whom he was equally critical: "Schacht sees things very clearly, but his judgment is always affected by his boundless personal ambition and his unreliable character." It was at this time, too, that Hassell learned through Canaris and Dohnanyi that they had gathered from army officers in Italy that Mussolini would be overthrown by the military during the course of the winter.

Hassell thought it necessary to have closer relations with the younger men among those opposed to Hitler: "I was always afraid that we had too little contact with younger circles." These younger men, however, whom he began to cultivate at the turn of the year, presented him with some difficulties. Adam Trott zu Solz for example, although a monarchist, was against the militarist "image" which was settled now upon the conspiracy; Peter Yorck said the same, and then introduced Hassell into the heart of the so-called Kreisau circle of intellectuals headed by Moltke. He met Moltke in the company of Trott and Yorck. Soon he found himself sandwiched between the "reactionaries," Goerdeler and Beck, and the "intellectuals," who seemed to favour Pastor Niemöller, and not Beck, as the new head of State. It was a dilemma. As Hassell put it:

We must keep in mind that we may be used only to clean up and will then be replaced by others, or that we may fail altogether. The task is to manage this as well as is humanly possible. Moreover, we shall have to fashion a government that is as free as possible of the odor of reaction, militarism, etc. Action, however, is now the main thing![23]

The action Hassell was considering personally was "making one or more speeches at a psychological moment to

161

serve as a signal." He did not, however, make them. Returning to Berlin early in February 1942 after his visit to Witzleben in Paris, he was told by Oster and Dohnanyi that the Gestapo were not only watching them but watching him and Popitz also. Everybody is rather intimidated," writes Hassell. "It seems that at the moment nothing can be done about Hitler."

Meanwhile, the struggle for power-to-be intrigued as much as it concerned Hassell, another of whose contacts was Carl Langbehn, a lawyer who wanted to bring Himmler, whom he knew socially, into the resistance! Hassell writes:

I spent an interesting evening recently with Langbehn. He still suspects all sorts of things are being planned around Himmler. A person in that corner is in a better position to act than one in Beck's entourage, where things are going to pieces, especially since the last disappointment with Witzleben. The incident has been rather satisfactorily patched up, but, for all that, some remnants of suspicion still linger on; Popitz against Oster, the younger group against Popitz, *et al.* I am trying to smooth things out. For instance, today I shall go with Oster to see Beck, who is at the center, and who must hold all the strings.[24]

In April, Hassell left for a tour of Vienna, Budapest, Sofia and Bucharest. In Sofia, he met King Boris ("who seemed to have very little respect for Italian politicians except Mussolini"), and in Bucharest Queen Helen. On his return once more to Berlin, he visited Weizsäcker and his wife and was received in a fashion which shocked him:

He carefully closed the windows and doors, and announced with some emphasis that he had a very serious matter to discuss with me. He brusquely waved aside my joking rejoinder. For the time being he had to ask me to spare him the embarrassment of my presence. When I started to remonstrate he interrupted me harshly. . . . Every time I asked for enlightenment he cut me short. . . . He then proceeded to heap reproaches on me as

162

he paced excitedly up and down. I had been unbeliev-
ably indiscreet, quite unheard of; as a matter of fact,
'with all due deference', so had my wife. This was all
known in certain places (the Gestapo), and they claimed
even to have documents. He must demand, most em-
phatically, that I correct his behavior. . . . He paid no
attention to my objection that he seemed to associate
himself with these unsubstantiated accusations. . . . I
had no idea, he said, how people were after me (the
Gestapo). Every step I took was observed. I should
certainly burn everything I had in the way of notes
which covered conversations in which one or another
had said this or that. Apparently he meant himself. He
opposed my efforts to get at the facts behind all this;
this concerned my future behavior, not the past. Finally
he said, 'Now, *auf Wiedersehen,* but please not too
soon!'[25]

The following day Trott, who was on the German
Foreign Office staff, told Hassell that he had been warned
officially about him. By now Hassell was sufficiently
alarmed and shocked to discontinue writing his diary for
several weeks. When he eventually resumed it in August,
he wrote: "The memory of my conversation with Weizsäcker torments me." He was having trouble, now, in getting
visas for his various travels. He linked the new suspicion
surrounding him to a certain extent with the assassination
of Heydrich in Prague the previous May. Although free to
travel inside Germany to lecture, he was forced to give up
certain of his remaining professional duties and keep a far
more careful watch on his resistance activities. "I would
perhaps do well to keep out of sight," he writes. However,
he managed to maintain some contact with such men as
Peter Yorck and Trott, as well as with Oster and Dohnanyi.
He was also aware of Langbehn's tentative peace discussions undertaken very secretly on behalf of Himmler.

The Communist "Red Band" Exposed

Slowly, but inevitably, the Gestapo was closing in on its

suspects, both those who stood on the left politically and those who stood on the right. It is perhaps ironic that the first major conspiracy to be exposed had nothing whatsoever to do with any of the conspirators with whom we are concerned. The German Communists had had to endure a *volte-face* when the pact was signed between Nazi Germany and Communist Russia in 1939. Suddenly the direst enemy had become the newest friend. It had meant, in effect, a cessation of all Communist "cell" activity in Germany until the disparate ideologies recovered their natural antagonism when Hitler invaded the Soviet Union. Once more the underground cells began to function. They developed afresh, and had virtually no contact with the right wing or even the socialist resistance movements. Their objectives, after all, were totally different. While the right-wing resistance workers wanted to establish a new national government and even hoped for a return of the monarchy, the Communist resistance desired only the victory of the Red Army and the future of Germany as a Communist State directly associated with the Soviet Union. They had no plans to assassinate Hitler.

It was recognized that the Communist resistance in Germany took all its directives from Moscow. This meant that contact had to be established and maintained, and this was done partly through the neutral countries and partly direct, by means of radio transmissions. The Communists were well organized and strong enough to print and distribute their own leaflets and journals. Throughout 1942 the Gestapo concentrated on uncovering these Communist cells, silencing the underground radio-transmitters and receivers, and breaking up the publishing centers. The cells frequently operated in the war factories and even inside the ministries themselves. It was in the spring of 1942 that one of the strongest of these Communist resistance organizations was caught. It was known both to Schellenberg and to Canaris as the Red Band or Orchestra, the *Rote Kapelle,* and its cells were spread in many parts of the country, and in particular in Berlin. It existed primarily to supply the Red Army with Intelligence reports, but it was also concerned with wider political issues inside

164

Germany. It maintained its own journal, *Innere Front,* and was thought to operate in the occupied countries. According to Schellenberg, its short-wave transmitters extended from Norway to the Pyrenees, from the Atlantic to the Oder, from the North Sea to the Mediterranean.

The Nazi government had a particular fear of the Russian Intelligence service, which was known to be the best organized in Europe. According to Schellenberg, it was superior even to that of the British, which was especially admired in Germany for its thoroughness. After the death of Heydrich the search for the agents of the *Rote Kapelle,* with their mobile transmitters and printing plant, was intensified by Himmler, and with the collaboration of Canaris. The decoding of the signals sent out from Belgium had been completed after the arrest of a group of Russian agents in Brussels late in 1941, and as a result it had become clear that the information exchanged originated from circles within the German government itself. A Russian agent who had been parachuted into Germany was also caught, and further valuable information was obtained following his arrest.

In 1942 further decoding of monitored messages led to the uncovering of addresses in Berlin where Communist agents were to be found. Working in close collaboration, Schellenberg, Canaris and Bentivegni, chief of military counter-intelligence at the Abwehr, arrested one of these agents, Becker, a colonel of the Engineers, who had access to technical information concerning Germany's fighters and bombers. Following his arrest, it became known that a number of men on the general staff of the Luftwaffe must also be Communist agents. More arrests were made, and the whole *Rote Kapelle* organization was to a considerable extent uprooted. It was revealed to be a strange political enterprise composed not only of Communists, but also of intellectuals, bohemians, socialites and others.

At the head of this subversive group in the heart of the Luftwaffe administration was Harro Schulze-Boysen, a flamboyant character whose father was an admiral and whose great-uncle was the celebrated Grand Admiral von Tirpitz. He was a noted bohemian with a great shock of blond hair, and normally attired in a huge black sweater. In spite of his Communist activities, he had been given a staff appointment in Göring's Luftwaffe—probably because his mother knew Göring socially and because his wife's grandmother, the Princess Eulenburg, was also well established with the Nazis. Schulze-Boysen's somewhat unstable character combined recklessness with much sincerity and courage. He is described by Schlabrendorff as "intelligent and capable, but uncontrolled and devoid of scruples, a fanatic and a born revolutionary." He built up around him an organization for Intelligence work and the promotion of political propaganda which to a considerable extent threatened the Nazi war machine. Among his associates was Arvid Harnack, whose wife, Mildred Fish, was an American Jewess, and who was responsible for planning the allocation of raw materials in the Ministry of Economics, Frau Schumacher of the Ministry of Labor, Dolf von Scheliha, an impoverished Prussian aristocrat who was a first secretary at the Foreign Office. Horst Heilmann in the Foreign Broadcasts Monitoring service, and the Countess Erika von Brockdorff. Other left-wing intellectuals and civil servants who belonged to this group— the "Communist aristocracy," as Gerhard Ritter calls them —included Luftwaffe Colonel Gehrts, a Dr. Krauss, professor of Latin, and the author Adam Kuckhoff. According to Schlabrendorff, and other sources, the organization was initiated during the period of the Russian-German entente by the trade attaché at the Soviet embassy, known as "Erdmann." "While 'Erdmann' managed to win over Schulze-Boysen and Harnack on the basis of friendship,"

he put Kuckhoff under obligation by giving him money. By the time 'Erdmann' left Germany—a few days before the start of the hostilities with Russia—he had won the cooperation of Schulze-Boysen, Harnack, and several others for the Soviet Secret Service. Also the methods of the proposed collaboration during the war with Russia had been determined. 'Erdmann' left several radio transmitters for the use of the group as well as the code and code key and 10,000 marks. The functions

166

which were to be performed by each member had been decided upon while 'Erdmann' was still in Berlin. Schulze-Boysen accepted the responsibility for gathering information, Harnack was assigned the job of transferring the messages into code, and a third collaborator was picked for the handling of the transmitter.[26]

An extremely able and ruthless investigator, Dr. Manfred Roeder, a legal officer of the judge advocate's department, was placed in charge of the interrogations which followed the arrests. In spite of the severity of the treatment, even Roeder testified later to the courage and fanaticism of Schulze-Boysen; his wife Libertas, however, lacked the stamina to face the form of interrogation she was given. She broke down under torture, as she had warned the others she might. Roeder was working under great pressure; he was sent for by Göring and told the trial must be speeded up. The first of the two trials began almost immediately in August, followed by a second trial in November. It would appear that over a hundred prisoners were finally executed.

There is no doubt that the inner core of the *Rote Kapelle* was Communist or "fellow-travelling," and that the leading figures, Schulze-Boysen, Arvid Harnack and Adam Kuckhoff, had been left-wing opponents of Hitler since long before the war. When the war was over a statement made by Greta Kuckhoff, Adam's wife, at the time of the legal interrogation of Roeder, gave some background to this movement:[27]

I first met Harro Schulze-Boysen in 1938. I had come to know the Harnacks ten years earlier, in 1928. I did not know then about Harnack's socialist or Communist tendencies; he appeared to be a kind of nationalist, and did scientific work for the Rockefeller Foundation. When I returned from America I found that Harnack had married an American girl, Mildred Fish. I met them both again in 1930, and they asked me to join them in their work, but in 1930 I went to Zurich and was away

167

for three years. My work there was for the Communist Party, though I concealed this.

In 1933 I was in London. Then I returned to Germany. It was then that I made the acquaintance of Adam Kuckhoff and met the Harnacks once again. Independently of one another, they tried to involve me in anti-Nazi work. We took part in evening sessions telling young people about the background to the situation, though our meetings were mostly camouflaged as lectures on American literature, or we had talks about philosophy, National Socialism and so forth. . . .

In 1937 Kuckhoff and I were married. By then, we, Harnack and others were working very intensely. Our contact at the Russian embassy in Berlin was Alexander Erdberg. . . .

I also did a certain amount of courier service. . . . It was about this time that we met Harro and Libertas Schulze-Boysen and started meeting with them regularly. Schulze-Boysen was very keen on his activities and had excellent sources of information. It was Kuckhoff who introduced him to Harnack. When war first broke out we forwarded much useful information through the Russian Embassy, usually through Alexander Erdberg, and a week or so before the war with Russia actually began we received our first transmitter.

We kept the transmitter for a few days, moving it around in a small trunk. The first news about the preparation for the war against Russia came to us from Harro. He knew exactly which cities would be first attacked. . . . We used to make our transmissions from the house of Erika von Brockdorff. . . . The transmitter was not very good, and after some time we got a better one brought in by a parachutist. We were also given money for our work. It was distributed over various households —items such as 3,000 Marks, or perhaps 1,600 which we passed on for someone else.

After the arrest, both Harnack and Kuckhoff managed to pass off their acquaintance with Schulze-Boysen as being of no significance. At first the Gestapo seemed to believe them. Unfortunately, the Gestapo got hold of information later connecting Kuckhoff with the Harnacks. Even then, the Gestapo extracted nothing from either Kuckhoff or Harnack, though they were tortured on 11 October. They remained in good heart, believing that everything depended on being able to gain time. Gertrud Viehmeyer was sent out to warn our friends. ... Kuckhoff and Harnack thought they must be given at least four weeks to manage their escape, but they did not get away.

Once the four weeks were up, Kuckhoff mentioned some names to stop the daily tortures. . . . I was arrested on 13 October. I was aghast when I heard that Adam Kuckhoff had mentioned names, and very angry with him at first. But later he told me quietly that the people involved had had time enough to get away. He felt no guilt at all. It was stupid of them not to have gone. This reassured me. In jail and facing the Gestapo, both Harnack and Kuckhoff behaved in an entirely heroic way. . . .

Only when the war with Russia began did we feel the need for action. Before that, we had not done much active work for the Party.

The significance of the *Rote Kapelle*—apart from the important fact that the investigations initiated by the Gestapo and the Abwehr were conducted by Roeder, who was to be responsible later for the investigation of Dohnanyi and his colleagues—was the extraordinary diversity of the men and women involved. They came from every stratum of German society and intellectual life. This widespread Intelligence network was in the end uncovered, as it were, by accident—which is how underground movements usually are unearthed, as the resistance workers in the Abwehr were soon to realize to their cost.

The Schmidhuber Affair

Roeder Probes the Abwehr

Though Himmler's policy favored watching and waiting rather than arresting suspected persons, ambitious officials in the lower levels of the secret police were always anxious to be the first to uncover treachery against the State. It became a question of who would be the first to go too far and make arrest inevitable. The man who went too far and led to the initial exposure of resistance in the Abwehr was Dr. Wilhelm Schmidhuber.

Schmidhuber, it will be remembered, was the Portuguese acting-consul in Munich, and had been responsible for introducing Josef Müller to the Abwehr at the beginning of the war. It was he who had been sent to Rome by Müller with information about the Western offensive in May 1940. The following year he was much in favor and was promoted a major in the Luftwaffe, but he remained on the staff of the Abwehr in Munich under Lieutenant-Colonel Ficht.

During the summer of 1942, however, Schmidhuber was in trouble. He was under suspicion for serious currency offenses and faced prosecution, and his case was in the hands not of the Abwehr but of the S.D.; in other words, of Schellenberg. According to Karl Bartz, who was apparently engaged to write his well-known book on the Abwehr in an attempt to clear Schmidhuber after the war, Canaris was alarmed at the dangers the case represented, and even proposed that Schmidhuber should be assassinated. Dohnanyi and Bonhoeffer, who are represented by Bartz as being drawn into this discussion, are shown to have been strongly opposed to such an utterly uncharacteristic proposal by Canaris. Schmidhuber undoubtedly encouraged Bartz to make the allegation.

Bartz then gives the details of what happened as they were given him by Schmidhuber, all of which are most carefully angled in his informant's favor. The Portuguese consul is discovered sitting with a companion in the lounge of an hotel in Zurich. It is September 1942. His companion, who is not named, urges him not to return to Germany. He also passes on the thanks of certain Jewish refugees who owe their escape to Lisbon from Germany to Schmidhuber's good offices. He had used his position as consul to give them illicit passports and to arrange for the transfer of foreign currency. It was this transference of currency for the refugees, and ostensibly not for Schmidhuber's own profit, which was the cause of the trouble, says Bartz; he was a wealthy and good-natured man who put himself in jeopardy for others. In fact, he rendered these services for what he could get out of them financially.

According to Bartz, a man was arrested in the act of leaving Germany with a quantity of American dollars which he claimed he was carrying on behalf of Schmidhuber.[1] It was this arrest which led to the inquiries which, says Bartz, Schmidhuber did not take seriously enough, believing he would be protected by the Abwehr. As a result, he took the risk of returning to Munich, where he was once more warned of his danger by Müller himself and told to leave immediately, taking his wife with him to Italy. He accepted this advice, says Bartz, and received every courtesy from the Portuguese ambassador in Rome. The Italian authorities accepted the ambassador's recommendation that Schmidhuber should be given permission to reside in Italy indefinitely without danger of extradition.

Müller had promised to come and see Schmidhuber at the Park Hotel in Merano. September passed, and he failed to come. Eventually, on 7 October, Schmidhuber received a call from Müller summoning him to Bolzano in the Tyrol. He went, and immediately, according to Bartz's account, discovered Müller's manner to have changed. He had come, he said, to order Schmidhuber's immediate return to Munich to present himself before Lieutenant-Colonel Ficht. The orders, said Müller, came from Berlin, and implied that Schmidhuber was due for military service and would

171

be prosecuted for desertion if he failed to appear. In addition, there were still the currency offenses to be faced. And, Müller is said to have added without any further explanation, his life was at stake. Schmidhuber then lost his temper and, without noticing whether anyone might be listening, said he would only return to Munich as British High Commissioner and that it was his intention now to go to England via Lisbon and offer his services to the Allies.

Had Schmidhuber not been ready to return voluntarily to Germany, Canaris would have had to ask Roatta, head of Military Intelligence in Rome, to arrange for his arrest and deportation from Italy. But Bartz, no doubt speaking for Schmidhuber, insists that Canaris was plotting Schmidhuber's death. There is no truth in this allegation. Schmidhuber claims that he was spied upon by the hotel staff in Merano. Eventually he learned that Müller was in Rome, and he attempted without success to contact him by telephone. Then, without any warning, he was arrested by the Italian police and in spite of his protests and claim of diplomatic immunity taken on 2 November to Bolzano. He was handed over to the German police on the Brenner frontier.[2]

They took him straight to Munich, and his interrogations began. The remark he had made about returning only as British High Commissioner was raised. This was, he now realized, a very serious matter, making his case far worse than it would have been had his only offense been connected with currency. The Gestapo were mainly concerned with political charges, such as that single stupid remark invited. Alarmed by now, Schmidhuber was to prove extremely cooperative under interrogation and the Gestapo, satisfied, it would seem, with what they managed to find out about men more senior than their present prisoner, disclaimed further interest in the matter, and handed Schmidhuber back to the Wehrmacht. He was lodged in the Tegel military prison in Berlin, and the next stage in his interrogation was placed in the practised hands of Dr. Manfred Roeder, representing the Luftwaffe division of the Army judiciary and fresh from his triumph over the *Rote Kapelle*.

172

This is the version of the story as set down by Bartz; a version deliberately slanted in favor of Schmidhuber, except that nothing is said about the revelations concerning his colleagues which he made under interrogation. Quite another picture of Schmidhuber comes to light following a study of the Roeder files and discussion of the matter with Josef Müller and others with first-hand knowledge of what actually happened. Schmidhuber was a man of some means and he had considerable charm, but once he came under pressure he was unable to put up any resistance. He survived his interrogation and imprisonment largely by turning "State's evidence," no doubt under skillful questioning and the threat of torture. Whether by actual design or as the result of panic, he gave confused and divergent information concerning his currency offenses and his relations with the Abwehr. The most favorable comment on him is perhaps that of Frau Dohnanyi, who had every reason to detest him; in a statement she made after the war, she said:

Schmidhuber was a businessman who travelled a great deal and who worked as a so-called V-man (*Vertrauensmann,* i.e. confidant) for the Abwehr. My husband had come to know him through Dr. Müller of Munich, and he rather liked Schmidhuber who was an amusing companion though a weak sort of man. There was no doubt about his being anti-Nazi, yet my husband was very careful not to take him into his confidence where really important matters were concerned. Schmidhuber definitely tried to be helpful when we were worried about my brother, Pastor Bonhoeffer, who after being exempt temporarily from Army service owing to certain administrative work he was doing for the Church, was once more threatened with conscription. For a year or more Schmidhuber came to see us quite frequently. As a matter of fact, when staying in Berlin for a day or two he even lodged with us, and occasionally, following his many trips abroad, he would bring back some small gift, though never anything of value. A little later Schmidhuber became involved in a rather unpleasant affair; he was accused of currency irregularities, and the Gestapo tried very hard to involve my husband in this as well. Under pressure Schmidhuber told a good many lies, but when Müller was interrogated it was easy enough for him to disprove them. As for my husband, though he was not directly injured by this, he was put under suspicion. It was only much later, in 1944, that Schmidhuber's lies were admitted.[3]

The worst that can be said of Schmidhuber is that he misappropriated money and that he was a liar, weak enough to be of the greatest danger to the Abwehr; there was never any question, however, of Canaris or anyone else planning his assassination. This was pure invention on his part which he passed on to Bartz. After the war, he prospered in the black market and he died a wealthy man in 1961. Müller, who had it in his power to contest many of the statements against Canaris and Oster which appeared in Bartz's book, did not wish once the war was over to become involved in attacking him. When facing execution at Flossenbürg, Müller had resolved to forgive his enemies, and he has not deviated from this position.[4]

These probes into the activities of Schmidhuber and Müller put Canaris and Oster on a bed of nails. Roeder has himself described how Oster approached him late in December or early in January urging him to let them know at the Abwehr if any trials were contemplated. According to Roeder:

> I found out by telephone while Colonel Oster was still with me that no trial was contemplated in connection with this affair before a Berlin court, and I promised to keep him informed about any further developments. After a day or two Oster telephoned me and said that the matter was still being dealt with by the Luftwaffe judiciary in Munich, and would I kindly see that it was speeded up, since the admiral was very concerned about the matter. I promise to do so, telephoned Munich and was told that they wanted to hand the files over to Berlin. Then I heard nothing more until the second week

174

in February 1943, when the files actually arrived, amounting to about sixty-five or seventy pages of type-script. I glanced through them and then handed them to the then acting head of the Luftwaffe judiciary, since it was for him to decide who was going to deal with the case. So far as I can remember, the files dealt with currency offenses and admissions on the part of both Schmidhuber and Ickrath. Furthermore, there were most incriminating statements against Admiral Canaris, implying that he had been planning a *putsch* against the government during 1939-40, and that he was supposed to be interested in the formation of a break-away state of southern Germany, including Bavaria, Austria and Galicia. Anyway, for Canaris, the whole statement was very incriminating and I can remember how very relieved I felt when it was decided that this was scarcely a matter for the Luftwaffe judiciary in Berlin; I would probably have nothing to do with it. . . . Before 4 April I had nothing more to do with this matter other than what I have described in this statement.[5]

It was fortunate that Canaris knew nothing about these threats to his safety following the accusations so readily devised by Schmidhuber during his interrogations in Munich.

In a further statement made after the war, Josef Müller claimed that Roeder became directly involved in the Schmidhuber case rather earlier than he had implied in his affidavit:

I am quite sure that Roeder's name was mentioned immediately after Schmidhuber's arrest. I do not remember who mentioned it for the first time. . . . [This] is by no means surprising, because at the time Roeder was already head of certain courts in the Luftwaffe judiciary. . . . When his name was mentioned for the first time, either Ficht or myself immediately contacted Berlin. I remember clearly how anxious Dohnanyi was and how he told me about Roeder's bad reputation. He used such words as *Bluthund* (bloodhound) and *Blutrichter* (blood-judge). Whether or not Roeder initiated the prosecution of Schmidhuber and Ickrath I do not know. . . . After Schmidhuber had been arrested in Merano and taken back to Munich, I was interrogated myself. Schmidhuber had left his briefcase with me before his departure. In it were a variety of meticulous but often erroneous notes about presents he claimed to have given to many people. Dohnanyi was mentioned repeatedly. As for myself, he mentioned 50,000 Slovenian crowns which he alleged he had given me to purchase stamps with. In fact, the sum was 5,000, which was repaid later by the Abwehr office in Munich; Colonel Ficht had wanted me to give these stamps to certain contacts in Rome who were proving useful to us. When challenged on this, Schmidhuber immediately admitted that it was a matter of 5,000 rather than 50,000 crowns, and that in any case he had not made a present of the sum. Schmidhuber appeared anxious at this time, and once, when we were alone, he asked me in a whisper whether he had not better shoot himself. I shook my head, but frankly I never thought he meant it seriously. Once when Schmidhuber was being interrogated in the next room and was speaking rather loudly, I heard him make observations of a political nature. He mentioned Dohnanyi as well as Bonhoeffer, and I am quite sure he mentioned Dohnanyi more than once. After my interrogation, Admiral Canaris immediately flew to Munich to see about these matters. At that time he was well aware that Schmidhuber could incriminate our resistance group, particularly me, and, in the same connection, Dohnanyi and Oster.[6]

Another member of the resistance in Munich, Karl Süss, has stated that he tried to protect his friends before the officials from the Judiciary arrived:

In our files there was proof of certain political activities by Admiral Canaris, as well as of support given to certain Jews escaping abroad—in particular, the help they received in getting money out. I tried my best to 'purge'

176

the files of anything incriminating our friends, but I soon realized that through lack of sufficient knowledge of the complex background, I could not do this on my own. So I arranged for Dr. Müller to look into the files in my office and. . . . 'purge' them as best he could. At that time we knew the matter was already in the hands of the War Office Judiciary in Berlin, and very soon officials arrived to start interrogation.[7]

This was the position during the winter of 1942-3. But more was due to happen which led to an intensification in the activities both of the resistance and of the Gestapo.

The Independent Resistance: Hans and Sophie Scholl

The next act of open resistance came from a section of the German youth, among whom disaffection was for the most part individual and spasmodic rather than organized. Often it passed unmarked by the public in the form of hidden acts of heroism followed by a martyrdom as savage as it was secret. But the case of the Scholl family became celebrated even at the time it occurred. Hans and Sophie Scholl, whose parents lived in Ulm and were opposed to Hitler, were the eldest of a family of five. After the usual Nazi education, they had become students at Munich during the early period of the war. Both became Catholic and were dedicated anti-Nazis; Hans became the center of a small, subversive group in the university which adopted the romantic name of the White Rose.[8] During 1942 they began to publish and distribute leaflets, and at the same time come under the influence of a member of the university staff, the Professor Kurt Huber. He began to take part in the composition of the society's leaflets, which now appeared monthly; these publications openly proclaimed the decadence of the Nazi government and gave examples of atrocities committed in Poland and of crimes against the Jews. Students were urged to sabotage the war effort. In August 1942, Hans was sent to the Russian front as a medical orderly, and he dared to reveal

177

there his open revulsion at Nazi brutality to the Jews. Meanwhile, his father was suffering imprisonment for his opposition to Hitler.

On his return to Germany at the end of 1942, Hans, now aged twenty-five, and his associates, including his twenty-two-year-old sister Sophie, began to publish their second series of leaflets, which they distributed even more widely than their previous publications. The notorious address to the students at Munich given by Paul Giesler, the Nazi *Gauleiter* for Bavaria, in which he advised the girls to bear a son each year for the Führer and offered the services of his adjutants to help them, caused an open revolt, and the Scholls rushed into defiant protest. On the morning of 18 February they scattered case-loads of their broadsheet openly throughout the university buildings. Their sister, Inge Scholl, believes that they did this because they thought it would inspire a mass rising among the students. Unhappily, it merely led to their own arrest, together with several other members of the group. The Gestapo, as usual, had been watching them over a period of months.

The Scholls readily admitted their guilt; their sole concern was to spare the others by trying to take the blame upon themselves. On 22 February they were put before the notorious judge Roland Freisler in the People's Court. (Freisler was later to preside over the court which tried those accused of complicity in the attempt on Hitler's life in July 1944.) The Scholls were accused by Freisler, rather than tried, and immediately condemned to death and executed, together with a member of their group, Christoph Probst. The rest of the Scholl family were imprisoned with sentences of varying harshness. Nearly a hundred arrests followed, with a further trial in April. Huber was among those executed later in that year.

The importance of the White Rose movement was that it became widely known throughout Germany. Hassell's comment, for example, shows the extent of his feeling for what had happened. Writing on 25 March, a month after the execution of the Scholls, he said, following a visit to Munich:

178

Munich is still much agitated by the discovery of a conspiracy among the students. . . . The Party is trying to make them out as communists. I have read the simple, splendid, deeply ethical national appeal which brought them to their death. Himmler apparently did not want any martyrs and ordered a stay of execution, but it came several hours too late. It is important for the future that such an appeal should have seen the light of day. It seems that Professor Huber, also arrested in the meanwhile, was the author. The brave Scholls died on the gallows, courageous and upright martyrs.[9]

The Situation in 1943

Hassell analyzes the situation at the beginning of 1943 in these terms:

If the generals had it in mind to withhold their intervention until it was absolutely clear that the corporal is leading us into disaster, they have had their dream fulfilled. The worst about it is, however, that our definite prophecy has also been fulfilled; that is, that it would then be too late and any new régime could be nothing more than a liquidation commission. I suppose we cannot say for sure that the war is lost, but it is certain that it cannot be won and that the prospects for persuading the other side to make an acceptable peace are very small indeed. . . . The evil of the situation is revealed in the fact that at this time there come reports from the 'enemy's' side which give rise to ever-increasing doubts as to whether they are now holding out for complete destruction of Germany. . . . The word 'occupation', that is, the occupation of Germany as a condition for negotiations, has often been advanced in this connection. . . . In our inner circle there are strong differences of opinion, fostered by Beck's all-too-lenient leadership. There are serious doubts in different quarters about Goerdeler, at least as a political leader. Also

about Popitz, who is reproached for his earlier ques-
tionable attitude under Göring as well as for serious
mistakes in financial policy, and for his all-too-long co-
operation with the régime. . . . I personally hold myself
as aloof as possible from disputes about personalities
and try to stiffen Beck's backbone. Futhermore, I maintain that the number of usable people is too small and
the good qualities of those mentioned too great for
such squabbling. Gisevius works hard for Schacht. The
newest version, and one toward which Beck seems to
lean, is that before a real cabinet is formed and along-
side a later cabinet there should be a small directorate:
Beck, Schacht, Goerdeler, myself, a general. I have
nothing against this. Leadership by Goerdeler I also
consider hazardous.

Hassell went on with his meetings; he was constantly in
touch with Beck, Goerdeler, Popitz and Oster. He was
encouraged by the warmth of his reception by the men
he called "the youngsters," whom he met by special arrangement at the house of Peter Yorck:

The youngsters, who in contrast to the older men are
presenting a united front toward the outside, were led
by the witty Helmuth Moltke, with his Anglo-Saxon and
pacifist inclinations. I was again favorably impressed
by Gerstenmaier, with whom Popitz and I had a talk
before the meeting. Beck presided. He was rather weak
and reserved. There was a sharp contrast, particularly
in the realm of social policy, between the younger group
and Goerdeler, which the latter tried to conceal. Goerdeler is really something of a reactionary. . . . I am glad
the youngsters have enough confidence to talk over their
doubts with me.

By the beginning of March, his despondency had grown:

Sad to say the serious crisis mentioned at the beginning
of my last notes did not precipitate the cleansing storm,
the bitterly necessary, intensely longed for change of

régime. That alone could still afford us at least the chance of a tolerable peace, an inner healing, and the recovery of Europe. Vain are all our efforts to pour iron into the bloodstream of the people, who are supporting a half-insane, half-criminal policy with all their might. The military events alone, the irresponsible leadership of this megalomaniac and irresponsible corporal, should have induced them to act if the inner rot were not enough. At the moment the acute crisis has dissolved into a more subtle lingering one. A remark by that opportunist, Fromm, to Olbricht is illustrative of this: In view of the improved situation on the southern part of the eastern front the change was now no longer necessary. Olbricht, however, will do nothing without Fromm, and the leaders in the East continue to vacillate.

If the leaders in the East vacillated, Tresckow, Schlabrendorff and their friends in Berlin did not. By the turn of the year, Beck had come to accept the need for Hitler to be assassinated. It was not an easy decision for a man so firmly grounded in Christian principles. Schlabrendorff, himself a man with the strongest ethical sense, lived with the problem in his heart. They thought, he said, of the endless train of death in the concentration camps as well as in the armies engaged in Hitler's war. "His death," he writes, "and his death only, would signal the end of this senseless slaughter. It was Hitler's life against the lives of hundreds of thousands of human beings. If ever in history an assassination was justifiable on moral and ethical grounds, this was one." Schlabrendorff refers to a clause in the Prussian Code of Military Law which asserted that orders "of criminal content" were not to be obeyed, and that the soldier who did obey them was liable to be punished. According to the conspirators, the unconditional obedience demanded by Hitler was, in the light of military law, not only illegal but criminal.[10]

Schlabrendorff, in regular contact with Beck and Oster, reports that during the winter Oster joined with Olbricht to prepare a plan for the military control of central Berlin

181

and its government departments following a *coup d'état*. The inclusion of General Olbricht, Chief of Supplies for the Reserve Army commanded by Fromm, is of great importance, since Olbricht was to be the principal organizer of the July plot of 1944.[11] Olbricht had his headquarters inside the War Office in the Bendlerstrasse in Berlin. The collaboration between Oster and Olbricht therefore established a firm link between the Abwehr, with their somewhat irregular forces, and a man in a strong position inside the War Office itself. With the plan for the occupation of Berlin in the combined hands of Oster and Olbricht, all that was needed was an officer with sufficient resolution to undertake the assassination itself, and occupying a staff position which would enable him to get near to Hitler. Two men were to occupy this key position—the first was Henning von Tresckow in 1943, and the second Colonel Count von Stauffenberg in 1944.

The link between Oster and Tresckow was Schlabrendorff. It is one of the curiosities of this story that Tresckow, who had personal contact with Olbricht, was never to meet Oster. Instead Schlabrendorff acted as both messenger and adviser to the Abwehr wing of the conspiracy during his frequent visits to Berlin. He was a staff officer who remained always more lawyer than soldier, and an idealist with the particular calm of mind that enabled him to undertake acts of courage the generals of the High Command did not dare to contemplate. Schlabrendorff describes the atmosphere of secrecy which had to govern these meetings in Berlin:

We avoided all meetings and discussions which were not absolutely necessary and took great care to draw as little attention as possible to those involved in the plot. Even among the closest allies, only those names essential to the understanding of developments were mentioned, thus reducing the danger of accidentally arousing the suspicion of the ever-present Gestapo spies. It hardly has to be stressed that our precautions, necessary though they were, slowed down and hampered the pace of our preparations.[12]

Schlabrendorff speaks of the need constantly to guard against spies, to sense every sign which might indicate that the Gestapo were noting their movements, their meetings, or recording their telephone conversations. It was, he says, "a paralyzing burden which every member of the resistance had to bear day after day, month after month, without a moment's relaxation or relief."

When the plans in Berlin were completed (the first form of the future Operation Valkyrie which was later to be revised by Olbricht, Tresckow and Stauffenberg in Berlin before the July plot in 1944), a secret meeting took place in Smolensk at the headquarters of the Center Army Group. Canaris undertook to provide a cover for this by organizing a conference for his Intelligence officers on the Eastern Front during the latter part of February; he himself led a considerable delegation from Berlin for the purpose. Among the men accompanying him to Russia was Dohnanyi, who met Tresckow and Schlabrendorff late at night. Canaris told Schlabrendorff over drinks after their secret meeting and the open conference were over that he was off at once to Hitler's headquarters at Rastenburg in East Prussia to confer with Himmler. Although Canaris did not reveal the nature of his business, Schlabrendorff guessed it had to do with the protection of his agents. One of the burdens Canaris had to bear was the constant invective of men who should have been his friends because they could not accept that he had to associate with "swine" like Himmler.

Although no date for this meeting is recorded by Schlabrendorff, it would have taken place early in 1943. Tresckow immediately set about creating the circumstances for an assassination attempt, which meant that he had to devise a visit by Hitler to Kluge's headquarters in the forest area near Smolensk. It was eventually established that Hitler would come on a brief visit to Kluge on 13 March.

Now, once more, everything turned on Kluge's direct collaboration. A cavalry officer, Colonel Baron George von Boeselager, volunteered to lead a group which would undertake to surround and then assassinate Hitler while he was with Kluge. The only person who failed them was

Kluge himself, who produced every argument he could in favor of postponing the attempt. His attitude made it impossible for the action to be taken with his authority. Tresckow then decided to act on his own, though still in close association with the conspirators in Berlin. They fell back on an alternative plan for the attempt, which involved only Tresckow and Schlabrendorff, and, if successful, would force Kluge's hand. There seemed little doubt that, once Hitler was dead, Kluge would give his immediate support to the *coup d'état*.

Bomb Plot 1943

The plan now took the form of smuggling a bomb into Hitler's aircraft. If the plane blew up during the flight back to Rastenburg Hitler's death could the more easily be attributed to accident. Care obviously had to be taken in the choice of the right kind of bomb, and here the Abwehr itself collaborated. It was one of the Intelligence duties of Department II to capture and examine examples of enemy weapons and explosives of the kind dropped by parachute for use in acts of sabotage by the resistance forces in German-occupied territories. Specimens of a British malleable plastic bomb activated by a time fuse which was completely silent were already in the hands of the Abwehr. The fuse was started by breaking a simple capsule filled with acid; the acid disintegrated a length of wire holding back the striking-pin which set off the detonator, igniting the explosive. The timing was controlled by the thickness of the wire through which the acid had to eat; three different fuses were provided for delays of ten minutes, half an hour and two hours. By arrangement with Oster, Lahousen provided for a number of these bombs, with their variant time-fuses, to be brought to Smolensk for the Intelligence officers' conference in February.

Tresckow and Schlabrendorff, neither of whom had much technical knowledge of explosives, organized tests for these bombs, which they found remarkably powerful, although the fuse-timing proved unreliable. The reason for this, they discovered, was that the intense cold of the Russian winter could easily slow down the action of the acid on the wire. This would not be the case in the summer or if the bombs were exploded indoors.

For the first attempt, Tresckow packed two of the bombs together in a parcel which he represented as containing a pair of square Cointreau bottles. This deadly package Schlabrendorff hid away in his quarters early in the morning of 13 March. Hitler arrived by air with his staff—Schlabrendorff noted that he brought with him his own chef and his medical adviser, the so-called Professor Morell, even for this single day's visit.

The staff conference took place before lunch, during which Hitler ate the vegetarian meal prepared by his cook and drank non-alcoholic liquors. It was during this lunch interval that Tresckow asked one of Hitler's junior staff officers, Colonel Heinz Brandt, to take a couple of bottles of Cointreau as a present to General Helmuth Stieff at Rastenburg. Stieff, a senior administrative officer, was later to be closely involved himself in the conspiracy.[13]

Meanwhile, Schlabrendorff had sent word to Dohnanyi in Berlin to warn him of what was to happen. The code word was "Flash." This meant that Oster and his fellow conspirators should stand by to take control in the capital. When lunch was over, Hitler drove to the airport, where his aircraft waited to take him back to Rastenburg, a flight of some two hours. Schlabrendorff set off for the airport after collecting the bombs from his quarters. As Hitler stood talking on the runway with the senior officers of the Group before boarding his armoured plane, Schlabrendorff exchanged glances with Tresckow and then, using a key, pressed down on the fuse of the bomb through the covering of the package. He then handed the innocent-looking parcel to Brandt as he boarded the plane after Hitler. The Führer's aircraft took off acompanied by an escort of fighters. Schlabrendorff hastened to telephone Berlin, giving them the signal for the second stage in the operation.

With Berlin fully alerted, all that could be done now was to wait. Perhaps one of the fighter escort would radio the news of the destruction of Hitler's plane in the air. The "accident" was timed to take place somewhere over Minsk. But the minutes passed and no signal came through. After two hours, Tresckow thought it best to contact Rastenburg in case any news had reached headquarters. All he learned was that Hitler's aircraft had landed safely. Berlin had to be notified at once that Operation Flash had failed.

Tresckow and Schlabrendorff were stunned by the collapse of their attempt. There was also the pressing problem that the dangerous package was presumably on its way to Stieff's quarters where it might be opened by anyone. Tresckow, disguising the anxiety he felt, telephoned Brandt, and discovered to his relief that he had not yet delivered the package to Stieff. He asked him as casually as he could not to do so as a mistake had been made and the wrong parcel handed over. Schlabrendorff devised a reason for taking the regular courier plane to Rastenburg the following day and substituting two bottles of Cointreau for the two plastic bombs. He travelled that night by train to Berlin, carrying the parcel which, as far as he knew, was in a condition that might cause an explosion at any time. Brandt had turned his blood cold by juggling with the parcel of explosive in his amusement at the mistake that had been made. After all, the package did not contain any bottles. Once in the privacy of his sleeping compartment, Schlabrendorff undid the parcel and removed the fuse from the bombs. He then discovered that the failure had been due to a minor fault in the time-fuse mechanism; the detonator had not ignited when the firing-pin struck forward. On 15 March, in Berlin, Schlabrendorff showed the faulty fuse to Oster and Dohnanyi.

The conspirators wasted no time. Now that they had the silent bombs, they believed other opportunities would occur to plant them. Another chance did in fact seem likely to occur within a matter of days. Hitler was due to attend an exhibition of captured Russian war material in Berlin. One of the members of the resistance, Baron Rudolf von Gersdorff, was ordered to be on duty, and he offered to undertake a suicide mission, leaping at Hitler at the moment of denotating a bomb carried in his winter greatcoat pocket. Tresckow alerted Schlabrendorff to give Gersdorff one of the bombs, and, meeting at the Hotel Eden, the two men devised a time-fuse which would take the minimum time. However, Hitler's visit proved so short that there was no opportunity for Gersdorff to take action. Olbricht, meanwhile, had discovered something of the very real difficulties of organizing a take-over of control in Berlin. The conspirators realized that this aspect of the plan would have to be drastically revised and improved. Tresckow feigned the need for sick leave and obtained a period of some months' respite in Berlin which enabled him to give the whole of his attention during the summer of 1943 to this vitally important aspect of the *coup d'état*. These were the preparations which preceded what was finally to develop into the second collective attempt on Hitler's life, that of July 1944 .

Roeder's Pressure on the Abwehr

It was probably during March that Roeder began to investigate the affairs of the Abwehr in some depth. It was evident to him that Schmidhuber, the voluble witness lodged in Tegel military prison, was only a minor agent in some activitiy which involved men of much greater significance and nearer the top. According to Christine von Dohnanyi:

> While under considerable pressure, Schmidhuber made quite irresponsible statements about my husband as well as other officers in Department Z. Also about us women. One of his statements implied that Müller and my husband had had 'dark business' in the Vatican . . . As a result of the Schmidhuber affair the prosecution of the persons connected with Department Z really got under way. It became a political affair.[14]

Among the witnesses Roeder summoned was Gisevius, who came to Berlin from Switzerland and spent two days being cross-questioned. Gisevius claims that he only obeyed the summons because had he refused to do so he might have

187

placed Oster in jeopardy. Gisevius also claims that he finally refused to testify further, saying that Keitel had forbidden him to give more evidence. Having warned his friends, he left again for Switzerland.

Canaris needed little warning. S.S. General Ernst Kaltenbrunner, the successor to Heydrich as head of Reich Security under Himmler and Canaris's most deadly opponent since he wanted to destroy the Abwehr, had already asked to see the admiral in February. Canaris found himself face to face with the tall, ill-mannered, heavily-built and sour-faced Austrian whom Himmler had chosen for this high office. Kaltenbrunner fenced around the subject of the unreliability of certain of the Abwehr's senior men; he instanced Canaris's chief of Intelligence in Vienna, Count Marogna-Redwitz, who, it seemed, was in touch with pro-British elements in Hungary. Canaris, alert and quick-witted, countered. His Intelligence men, he said, had to be in contact with everyone in order to carry out their duties. At the same time, when he returned to his office, he told Oster to take great care of the incriminating files and to destroy everything which could be spared. There had been warnings not only from Gisevius, but from Arthur Nebe, a senior police officer and close friend of Gisevius.[15] Dohnanyi, however, knew that Beck was against the destruction of any documents which could prove useful after the *coup d'état*, and no one, not even Canaris, ever expected the offices of the Abwehr to be invaded by the Gestapo.

In any event, the bulk of the most important and incriminating documents, the mass of evidence against the régime which Beck had from the first insisted on collecting, was kept in a safe not at the Abwehr offices, but at High Command headquarters at Zossen. Dohnanyi was a circumspect man and, like Schlabrendorff, well aware that he stood in danger of discovery at every moment of his life. His wife, Christine, testified to this after the war:

In the spring of 1942 my husband was warned by Dr. Langbehn and Herr Gehre who told him that his mail, his telephone calls as well as he himself were being watched by the Gestapo. According to Langbehn, this

188

had been ordered either by Heydrich or by Bormann, and according to Gehre it had been ordered by a man called Sommer who used to be in Hess's ministry. After this my husband avoided going anywhere near his safe at the Zossen headquarters. So far as I remember, Oster went out there with Guttenberg and Delbrück. Anyway, my husband's safe at the O.K.W. was 'purged' and important documents which were to be kept for use after the war were put in a safer place. So far as I can recall, and according to what my husband told me, the safe was in a particularly deep cellar. Colonel Grosscurth had provided this particular safe for the more incriminating documents at the time when Zossen was still the headquarters. . . . A few days before my husband's arrest Canaris had let him know he need not worry, certainly not in the immediate future, since the Gestapo was preoccupied with other matters. He would, said Canaris, be safe for at least a few days. But it was not so.[16]

According to Christine von Dohnanyi, a case against her husband had been developing ever since the period when he had seemed to fail the National Socialist cause while working for the Ministry of Justice. In the Abwehr, too, he was having his difficulties, since there were officers in the service who had no connection with the resistance and who resented the sudden intrusion of this "civilian" into a place of apparent power in the hierarchy of the service. Frau von Dohnanyi describes his position:

After my husband had left the Ministry of Justice and Heydrich learned that he had been working in the Abwehr since 1939, he is supposed to have said to 'Gestapo-Müller': 'We'll have to keep a closer watch on him now than ever.' My husband had been worried about the situation for a long time, a great deal of his trouble arising from the fact that working with the military was rather different from working in the Ministry of Justice, where he only had to deal with civilians. . . . Many people in the Abwehr intrigued against my husband because they were envious of the position of trust he had in the intimate circle around Admiral Canaris and General Oster; their own ambitions were frustrated. . . . Whenever such intriguers went to Canaris it did not do them much good. He would tell them that he alone decided what was to take place in the office, and it was none of their business if he gave my husband certain things to do. Even if it might, strictly speaking, interfere with someone else's department. In the circumstances, my husband tended to be more careful than ever. He did not keep a diary, and he was most cautious in what he said to others, particularly in relation to politics. . . .

At that time my husband was particularly concerned with certain Jewish families for whom he, and indeed Admiral Canaris too, felt particular responsibility. . . . These efforts went back to the early years of the régime, when Gürtner, the Minister of Justice, my husband's chief, did all he could to help Jewish lawyers. . . . When in the year 1942 things got even more difficult and dangerous for these victimized Jewish families, my husband took the matter up with Canaris, who was most sympathetic, and promised any help he could give. The only help possible was to find some sort of Abwehr employment for these people and arrange for them to be sent abroad quite officially and with the consent of the Gestapo. Canaris agreed at once, and in fact added some other Jewish families with whom he was friendly to this particular undertaking. The operation was called *Unternehmen 7* [Operation 7], and simply indicated that there were some seven persons involved. Later there were quite a few more. . . .

My husband negotiated this matter with 'Gestapo Müller' and a General of the S.S., and it was indeed achieved; these families reached Switzerland and took out some of their money too . . . How the Gestapo got wind of the real nature of this affair I cannot be quite certain. . . . Since my husband was in the Army and therefore could not be arrested by the Gestapo without Keitel's permission, they tried unsuccessfully to imply

190

in connection with *Unternehmen 7* that my husband had enriched himself in the process of assisting the emigration of these Jewish lawyers and their families. . . . They just could not understand how anyone could do a charitable act for the sake of decency and not for any financial advantage.[17]

The First Arrests

When Roeder had completed his dossier against Schmidhuber, he submitted the case to the Reich military court. The evidence he had amassed was such that the arrest of both Dohnanyi and Bonhoeffer was ordered. On 5 April Roeder, accompanied by an officer of the Gestapo, Franz Xaver Sonderegger, arrived without warning at the Abwehr offices on the Tirpitz Ufer. They asked to see Canaris, and told him they had come to see Dohnanyi. Roeder carried a warrant permitting him to search Dohnanyi's desk and safe.

Canaris, though shocked by this invasion into the very heart of his organization, managed to keep calm and, as Roeder put it, "gentlemanlike." In any event, he believed that Oster and Dohnanyi would have been circumspect after the warnings he had given. Canaris, told he might be present during the period of search, led Roeder and Sonderegger to Dohnanyi's room. Since they first had to pass through Oster's office, Oster also accompanied them.

Dohnanyi rose to receive him. Roeder stated formally that he had the right to search Dohnanyi's offices. He was asked to open the drawers in his desk and the door of his safe. He hesitated, pretending to search for his keys, which he finally produced from his trouser pocket. With Sonderegger standing guard, Roeder began the task of looking through the papers and files in the desk and safe. It was Sonderegger who noticed that Dohnanyi was trying to attract Oster's attention with a wink and glances which indicated a particular sheet of paper on the desk. As a result, Oster tried to spirit away the document rather clumsily. Sonderegger only too easily saw what he was doing

191

and cried out a warning. There was nothing Oster could do but allow the paper to be confiscated. It outlined suggestions for the shape of Germany after Hitler's removal, and it was marked with a "O" in colored pencil. Roeder immediately confiscated the collection of pencils on Oster's desk. The search of Dohnanyi's office, which took Roeder some two hours, produced sufficient documentation to permit the immediate arrest of Dohnanyi. He was taken to the Tegel military prison.[18]

In spite of his care, Roeder, according to Christine von Dohnanyi, passed over what could have been the most important find in Dohnanyi's office:

> As it happened, the key to the Zossen safe was still in my husband's safe at the Abwehr headquarters. For reasons of camouflage, he always kept this key tied to a folder which contained various strips of paper indicating harmless routine files, as well as various codes for secret official documents. Among these was a coded list of the contents of the safe at Zossen. Roeder and Sonderegger (the officials who arrested my husband) searched his safe in his presence, looking for incriminating documents. As for the folder with the key tied to it, they simply threw it back into the safe considering it a routine folder. My husband definitely saw this, and as soon as he had been taken away by the two officials, Oster took possession of the key himself.[19]

However, what had been found was of a sufficiently incriminating nature to lead to the arrests on the same day of Christine von Dohnanyi, Dietrich Bonhoeffer, Josef Müller and Müller's wife. Bonhoeffer first realized he was in extreme danger when he telephoned his sister, Christine von Dohnanyi, and an unknown voice answered. He replaced the receiver and, speaking quite calmly, told his father and mother, from whose house he had telephoned, "Now they will come for me." He removed at once every sign of evidence which might tell against him and went then next door to his elder sister's house. At three o'clock in the afternoon the Gestapo came and took him away.

192

PART THREE

I

The Desperate Years

In Prison

The interrogations began.

The Abwehr investigations passed through three distinct phases. During the first months, from April to August 1943, they were conducted jointly by Roeder, representing the military Judiciary, and by Franz Sonderegger representing the Gestapo. Roeder was given the task because of his special experience in the case of the *Rote Kapelle,* though strictly speaking his place in the Luftwaffe division of the Judiciary did not entitle him to examine the men of the Abwehr. The code name for the investigation of Dohnanyi and the others was *Depositenkasse* (literally: branch office of a bank), but Roeder preferred to call the case the *Schwarze Kapelle* (Black Band). The first phase lasted until August, when Roeder had completed his investigations and was almost entirely withdrawn from the case to undertake other duties. From August 1943 to 20 July 1944, the second phase, the interrogations continued with comparatively little interference from the Gestapo. After the attempt on Hitler's life on 20 July, the prisoners were placed immediately and absolutely in the hands of the Gestapo, and the third and most virulent phase of the investigations set in.

Christine von Dohnanyi has described her arrest:

I was taken first to the women's prison at the Kaiserdamm, and later on to the prison on Alexanderplatz. Since this was infested with bugs, I was taken on to the women's prison in the Kanstrasse. I was interrogated about ten times, and some of the interrogations were led by Sonderegger. I was not tortured or otherwise physically maltreated.[1]

Christine von Dohnanyi was released on 30 April because, as she put it, "they thought that I did not know anything." She had been confined for over three weeks.

While he was in prison, Dohnanyi kept a diary—a few words of record and comment for almost each day, some pages of which survive. The remarks are sometimes cryptic, but his initial despairing reaction to his imprisonment and interrogation is apparent through these poignant, fragmentary entries:

5-6.4	Alone.
7-9.4	If only there were not the commandant.
11.4	Parcel from parents. Afternoon commandant.
12.4	First interrogation. Christel [his name for his wife Christine] arrested!
13.4	Second interrogation.
14.4	Evidently Oster lets me down [*Oster versagt offenbar*].
15.4	Roeder with Canaris.
16.4	Saw Cristel! Third Interrogation. Dietrich arrested!
17.4	Went for a walk.
18.4	Went for a walk.
19.4	Fourth interrogation. Letter from Christel. Christel evidently hostage. Saw Dietrich.
20.4	Letter to Roeder.
21.4	Fifth interrogation. He won't let Christel go. Flimsy pretexts. Bribery! ! ! ! Crazy ! ! !
23.4	Good Friday.
24.4	No interrogation. Not allowed to see Christel.
25.4	Easter Sunday.
26.4	Easter Monday. (Chr. relatively well. Information by commandant through parents.)
27.4	Still no further interrogation. New cell.
28.4	Again no interrogation.
29.4	Letter from Christel. No interrogation.

30.4	Still no interrogation. Am slowly going crazy [*Ich drehe allmählich durch*].
1.5	Wonderful weather. Chr. a prisoner! In utter despair—Chr. free! ! Parcel from her, brought by Mama. What a change. Almost happy.
2.5	Marvellous weather. 4 weeks ago I was still enjoying chamber music with the children.
4.5	6th interrogation. Threats to hand me to Gestapo if I don't tell all. Not a chance of getting to see Christel. Currency offenses! ! Am nearly at the end of my tether.
5.5	7th interrogation. 'The Führer will stand no nonsense.'
6.5	Dix seems to do something.
7.5	Mama seems to be optimistic.
8.5	Bärbel brings spring flowers.
10.5	(Six weeks!)
11.5	Letter from Klaus.
12.5	Food parcel from parents. Dietrich ? ? ?
13.5	8th interrogation. Dietrich suspected. Again the Führer threat. Ten days ban on smoking, writing, reading. Roeder confiscates my notes.
14.5	Altogether horrible day. Full of despair.
15.5	Bärbel brings flowers and books. Also painting things.
17.5	7 weeks!
18.5	Food parcel from home.
19.5	Letter from Christel and Bärbel.
22.5	Flowers from Bärbel. Wonderful food.
24.5	8th week.
25.5	Parcel from Mama. *Dies ater* [Black day].
26.5	Still excited about yesterday's letter from Chr.
27.5	Letter from Bärbel.
9.6	9th interrogation (re Canaris).
10.6	Whitsun all alone.
14.5	Children bring flowers. 11th week!
17.6	10th interrogation '*Innerpolitischer Nachrichtendienst*' [Dissemination of news]. Alleged to have been admitted by Oster. ! ? ! Did not sign agenda. Was dictated in my absence.[2]

Müller, his wife Maria and his secretary at that time, Anny Haaser, most fortunately survived the Nazi régime, and the affidavits they made in 1948 in connection with the investigation into Roeder's activities give a vivid account of what confinement and interrogation in Nazi-controlled prisons could involve. It is interesting that Sonderegger of the Gestapo appears as a more humane investigator than Roeder of the Luftwaffe:

Müller: I was arrested on 5 April 1943 in the Abwehr office in Munich, and in the presence of the Abwehr Chief, Lieutenant-Colonel Ficht. I learned that my wife was being arrested in our flat at the same time, and I delayed transfer to prison by asking Colonel Ficht immediately to telephone Admiral Canaris, and to tell him that the Gestapo had arrested me. I emphasized that being an officer of the Army I could not be arrested by the Gestapo and had the right to demand military justice. That way I hoped to avoid getting into a Gestapo prison, and I was indeed transferred to the military prison in the Ludwigstrasse, where I was at first treated very correctly. The treatment changed, however, after a few days. One morning I heard a great deal of noise outside, and a voice shouting and screaming. Later, when I met Roeder, I remember clearly identifying this as Roeder's own voice. I was then repeatedly disturbed by warders coming into my cell and almost blinding me with a glaring light, like a headlamp used on cars.

I was not interrogated while in Munich, but a week later, on 12 April, I was told to get ready for immediate transport. I was taken to Berlin in a specially reserved railway compartment, my companions being an officer of the Luftwaffe, I think a captain, and a military judge, who I believe was a major. They kept close guard on me; even when I used the lavatory one of them stood with his foot in the door. In Berlin, I was at first taken to the Tegel prison, and one of the military judges thought he could frighten me by telling an officer that they should see to it the gallows were ready because they would soon be needed. My first interrogation with Roeder was fairly short; he merely wanted to know about my office in Munich, my work, and so forth. In addition, he wanted information about Dohnanyi.

Altogether, over the weeks, I was interrogated for over 160 hours, and Roeder was invariably bluffing, blustering and shouting, whereas Sonderegger behaved better. He not only treated me more humanely, but he also helped me by the extraordinarily long time he took in his interrogations, so giving me a chance to collect my thoughts. On one occasion he even gave me the opportunity to spirit away a document which would have been most incriminating for me. On another occasion, Sonderegger almost apologized for the harsh behaviour of his superior, Roeder, explaining that he was very anxious to obtain the names which I was refusing to give, and also that he was angry on account of my flat denial of the existence of the so-called military opposition, the 'clique' of generals who were in fact working against Hitler.

There was an occasion, too, when Roeder tried to trap me. This was when I was led into a room where General Oster was sitting; since he was not carrying arms, I was for a moment led to assume that he too was under arrest—which of course was not so at that time. Quite clearly, Roeder wanted to observe how we reacted to one another. I don't think he learned much, and he simply let me be taken away. The only thing I did admit was that though I had while on repeated visits to Rome put out feelers, there was no possibility of an organized peace negotiation. I tried to explain that talking about peace with important foreigners and sounding their opinions was part of my duties as an officer in the Abwehr. Roeder never missed a chance of lashing out against the Abwehr, and particularly against Admiral Canaris. Also, of course, against Oster. Once Roeder screamed at me. 'A trial for treason is more than due; there's no one left to cover up for you. As for General Oster, I've settled his future.' At the time I could only counter by saying that the very fact that Admiral Ca-

199

naris was still in office was ample proof that all this talk about alleged peace negotiations and an alleged plot by generals was nonsense.

No less cruel in his methods of interrogation was Moeller,[3] who constantly tried to browbeat me. I remember an occasion (which must have been around 1 May, because Sonderegger and Moeller were checking about the May Day celebrations), when Moeller said, 'Whatever happens, you're going to hang; it's merely a question of whether you'll be hanged following a verdict or following an order from the Führer to liquidate you.' When he saw I kept calm he added, 'And don't forget your wife is in our hands as well, and she will die too.' I answered, 'Just because she happens to be my wife it does not follow she knows anything about politics. I can't understand you. We're supposed to be in a Supreme German Court; I only hope that there may be some vestige of justice left. If so, you cannot murder my wife.' Moeller then shrieked back, 'Why should we care? This is what we are here for—' and he made a gesture of decapitation. Then he added, 'Your secretary's in our hands, too; she will be liquidated.' I replied, 'Is this the idealism of the National Socialist Party? How can a secretary who simply takes down what's dictated to her be made responsible? I'm responsible for whatever she had taken down, not she.'

One day Roeder screamed at me, 'We have other methods to force a confession. I shall ask the Führer personally to give me permission to use them.' Whenever they threatened to put me into a Gestapo prison, I kept on emphasizing that I was still an officer. There was no doubt, though, that both Noack and Sonderegger [his interrogators] were disgusted with all this screaming and shouting, and sometimes took me into another room merely to avoid Roeder bursting in upon us. It is significant too that on more than one occasion Roeder had either interrogated me himself or had me interrogated for a whole day without a break for food, and once, when I was really famished, Sonderegger shared his sandwiches with me while Roeder was out of the room.

While I was in prison, Roeder gave instructions for me to be treated like those already under a death sentence. Following these instructions I was deprived of sleep by someone every half-hour switching on the lights and almost blinding me; then switching them off again. I complained about this repeatedly and was promised by Sonderegger and others that this treatment should be stopped. After some while my complaints seemed to have effect. I was not disturbed any more.[4]

Frau Maria Müller: On the day of my husband's arrest I too was arrested at my flat in Munich by Gestapo Chief Bauer, two other Gestapo officials and an Army officer. They made a thorough search of my flat. I was taken to a prison in Munich and kept there three or four days; then I was taken to Berlin by two Gestapo officials. There we were received by Sonderegger, and taken to the police prison in Charlottenburg. I was kept in solitary confinement and for the first few days treated very badly indeed. I was not allowed to join the other prisoners in exercise, and during all that time I only had three short walks. I was not allowed to read or write and all my property, such as sewing materials and so forth, was taken away from me. I was not allowed even to sit down or look out of the cell window.

This lasted about three weeks, and then I was interrogated for the first time. The interrogating officer was Noack, but after a little while Roeder burst into the room and shouted, 'Frau Müller, will you please note you are accused of being accessory to high treason.' It was evident he was trying to frighten me, particularly since I had already had three weeks solitary confinement. Whenever he saw me, Roeder behaved in a harsh, undignified and inhumane manner.

I was asked about my husband's activities in Munich as well as in Rome, and I told them that on principle my husband never discussed official business with me and there was virtually nothing I could tell them. As to

201

various people whose names were mentioned, all I could say was that I had met them socially in my flat or when abroad. I was asked about Fraulein Haaser, and what she might know about my husband's activities, and I simply said that being my huband's secretary and officially permitted to work on Abwehr business she had been sworn to secrecy in any case. During one of my interrogations, I told Roeder that it was senseless treating me as badly as I was being treated, since they could only use me as a witness and even as a witness there was little I could tell them. Roeder immediately flared up and said it would be better for him to forget that word senseless. I should not be so impertinent. I had no right to criticize him anyway.'[5]

What the investigators were trying to discover primarily was the place where the documents concerning Müller's discussions at the Vatican were concealed. Schmidhuber had referred to them. The need for the destruction of these and all other dangerous papers became the main concern of the conspirators whether they were inside or outside prison. Meanwhile, Roeder put every pressure on his prisoners to extract the information he most needed. After the war, Otto John made the following statement about Roeder's interrogations:

Roeder in his investigations used methods which we at the time used to call Gestapo methods. I knew that not only from what Frau Dohnanyi and Frau Müller told me after their release, but also from what my friend Captain Gehre, and Dohnanyi himself told me. . . . He put them under great mental pressure by threatening to persecute their wives if they did not make statements. I also remember the notes smuggled out of prison by Dohnanyi stating that Roeder would stop at nothing to get his way. . . . Dohnanyi lived under the constant threat that Roeder would hand him over to the Gestapo. I remember this very clearly because that would have led to Dohnanyi being tortured. None of us was under any illusion that subject to such appalling duress he

202

might well be forced to make statements which could jeopardize the entire conspiracy against Hitler.

Among those suffering anxiety that Dohnanyi might be handed over to the Gestapo were not only his wife but also General Oster, Dr. Goerdeler and other members of the conspiracy. I recall this all so well because I could never get out of my mind what Dohnanyi had once told me shortly before his arrest when we were with our friends: 'Not one of us really knows how long he can resist torture once they start doing their worst.' No wonder therefore that all Dohnanyi's friends did whatever they could to get him out of Roeder's clutches. What Roeder did constituted not only martyrdom for his victims but for their friends too.[6]

The conspirators had many useful supporters. Among those were Dr. Karl Sack, head of the military Judiciary, and the Colonel Otto Maas, commandant of the prison in which Dohnanyi, Bonhoeffer and Müller were held. "Maas had been recommended to us by Dr. Sack," declared Christine von Dohnanyi, "and he proved to be resolutely reliable." He was able to pass messages to her from her husband:

The first message Maas passed on to me from my husband was that so far as the files were concerned everything was under control. I should get in touch immediately with Oster and tell him the documents must be destroyed at once because the Gestapo were undoubtedly looking for them. . . . Oster sent my husband the message that he need not worry. He, Oster, had control of everything. Schrader had been informed, and the matter was completely in order. I should add that we had previously discussed the possibility, in case of emergency, of Schrader taking the documents to Lüneburg Heath.[7]

Frau von Dohnanyi did not have direct contact with Oster, she reached him through Clemens von Delbrück, Klaus Bonhoeffer's father-in-law and a member of the Abwehr.

203

As soon as the immediate shock of the arrests was over, Canaris decided he must act not only to protect his most intimate colleagues, now either under arrest or, like Oster, suspended from duty and under the gravest suspicion, but himself as well. He warned his officers not to be seen around with Oster while he was suspended. Canaris was determined at all costs to keep the investigations as far as ever possible out of the hands of the Gestapo. He used his influence with Himmler as well as with Keitel to achieve this, and Himmler, in particular, appeared to agree with him. He declared that he did not want to be responsible for the investigations. Canaris apparently tried to influence Keitel against Roeder in order to secure Dohnanyi's release, but in this he failed. However, during July Roeder received orders by telephone, followed by written instructions, that the investigations were to continue without any implication that the case involved treason. It was for this reason that in August 1943 the indictments of Oster, Dohnanyi and Schmidhuber remained comparatively mild—they were accused of inefficiency in the manner in which they gave political clearances, of undertaking unauthorized journeys abroad, and, in Schmidhuber's case, of being involved in currency offenses.

Oster, though still not actually arrested, had been in no position since April to undertake further action for the conspiracy, at least as far as the Abwehr was concerned. All he could do now was help in planning the details for the *coup d'état,* the initiative for which had passed out of his hands into those of General Olbricht of the Reserve Army. It was, quite naturally, dangerous even to be seen with him or to visit him in his house. In December, Keitel put his foot down about Oster's infringement of the orders he had been given:

I have been informed that you still maintain or seek to attain more or less official contacts with individual officers as well as with Division Brandenburg. I herewith expressly forbid you to have any official or private contact with *Amt Ausland Abwehr* and its members, and I order you to avoid making any attempt at such approaches, either consciously or unconsciously. The Chief of the *Amt Ausland Abwehr* has been informed of this, and has instructed the members of his staff accordingly.[8]

Oster was formally transferred from the active list to the reserve.

It had been through Oster that Hassell had learned in November about the terms of the indictment. To his relief, they seemed relatively trivial. "Nothing political has thus far been revealed," wrote Hassell, "despite the zealous efforts of the fiendish prosecutor." Oster's indictment, in fact, amounted to little more than criticism of the over-liberal manner in which he had granted exemptions from active service. Count Rüdiger von der Goltz, Dohnanyi's defense counsel, began to feel optimistic about his client's eventual release. Even Roeder himself had seen the inquiry during its earliest stages as largely turning on currency offenses, and not involving anything as serious as high treason. Nor did he for some while have any suspicion of Canaris, whom he visited in his house shortly after the arrests. He took tea with the admiral, taking his fellow investigator, Dr Noack, with him. Canaris was, said Roeder, "amiable and co-operative;" they were both convinced of his sincerity in desiring the cases to be properly investigated. Schmidhuber's allegations against Canaris, and everyone else in the Abwehr with whom he had had contact, appeared to Roeder at this earlier stage as "absurd." Only later, at the time of Italy's defection during the summer, did he begin to suspect Canaris's duplicity and have grave doubts that the admiral was covering up many irregularities and possibly even furthering schemes against the régime.[9]

The question of Dohnanyi's defense raised certain problems. As fast as counsels for the defense were chosen, Roeder, it would appear, made difficulties of such a kind that they were each in turn forced to withdraw. Dohnanyi's second defense counsel, Rüdiger Count von der Goltz, made a statement concerning the withdrawal of the first counsel, Dr Dix:

I undertook the defense of Dohnanyi in July or August 1943, when Dr. Dix had been compelled by Roeder to withdraw from the case. Dix had explained to me how Roeder constantly intrigued against hm and finally managed to persuade the authorities that Dix was not the right kind of counsel. To be on the safe side, before I undertook the case I inquired in writing whether the fact that Frau von Dohnanyi was my cousin would exclude me for the defense, and was informed that this was not so. The fact that Roeder wanted to get rid of him was the only reason why Dix did not continue Dohnanyi's defense; he wanted to avoid any danger of prejudicing his client's case. The Bonhoeffer family, and of course Frau von Dohnanyi, as well as her parents, brothers and sisters, thought that Roeder would not want me either, because Dohnanyi's brother-in-law, Dietrich Bonhoeffer, had actually asked for me as defense counsel.[10]

Count von der Goltz also described the cruel pressure brought to bear on Dohnanyi by Roeder:

Dohnanyi told me himself about Roeder, that he had caused Frau von Dohnanyi's arrest merely to be in the position to exercise pressure on her husband. 'So long as you refuse to tell us what you know, we cannot release your wife,' was what Roeder said repeatedly during the first stage of the interrogation. Dohnanyi also complained that Roeder would not let him keep the paper on which he had made memoranda and notes, and that he deliberately tried to confuse him by the manner of his questioning.

A third defence lawyer finally took over in the autumn. This was Dr. Paul Schulze zur Wiesche, another friend of the Bonhoeffer family and of Dr. Sack, who warned him about Roeder:

I knew that the examining judge in the Dohnanyi trial would be Dr. Roeder, who had been described to me as a friend of Himmler and as his man in the Reich Military Judiciary. His ambition was to reveal the alleged high treason of Dohnanyi and other collaborators of Admiral Canaris. My friend Dr. Sack told me repeatedly that Roeder was a man much to be feared precisely because he was a sort of liaison man for Himmler.

Throughout the investigations, the prisoners (apart from Schmidhuber, who tried to save himself by incriminating the others) adopted delaying tactics by wasting as much time as possible on side issues and harmless details designed to frustrate any line of investigation which might incriminate themselves and their friends. Roeder himself admitted that it was only later on that he developed suspicions that Dohnanyi was involved in a *Kassiber*, that is, smuggling letters and memoranda out of prison. His wife was permitted to visit him, but as Roeder's suspicions grew he became less and less generous in giving his permission for them to see each other. He regarded Dohnanyi as abusing the privilege granted him to write letters (limited to two a week) by trying to send out five or six a week of great length and written in a hand which it was difficult for the prison-censors to read. Moeller, the assistant interrogator, also grumbled about the way in which Dohnanyi created confusion through his denials and contradictions.

The Resistance at Bay

The spirits of the other conspirators had stood at their lowest ebb during the months following the arrests. They had expected an immediate purge to follow—"a purge like that of 30 June," as Hassell put it, thinking back some ten years to the "night of the long knives."[11] "It is to be feared that the whole project will break down," he wrote. He knew about the unfortunate incident of the compromising paper Oster had tried to conceal, and he felt his own freedom was threatened. He had been told by an associate of

207

Beck that he was "on the list of the most dangerous people," and hence in serious jeopardy. The notes in his diary, though still important for the light they throw on the atmosphere of the period, become now more intermittent. In May, a few weeks after the arrests, he writes:

> The united front of clear-sighted men is crumbling; it is partly their own fault. The whole Canaris outfit has shown weakness and in general has not quite lived up to expectations. If the 'good' people are not as wise as serpents and guileless as doves nothing will be accomplished. This is all the worse because things are storming ahead so rapidly that some 'action' becomes ever more imperative. On the one hand the political situation would not be entirely hopeless for us if the system were completely overthrown; on the other hand defeat from without and catastrophe from within draw nearer and nearer.[12]

Beck, who had had an operation for cancer of the stomach in March, was recuperating only very slowly; according to Hassell he had been watched even in the hospital, and Oster had sent him a warning about this. When his friend Ferdinand Sauerbruch, the celebrated professor of surgery who had operated upon him, had taken him to his country house to convalesce, he had been questioned about it by the police.[13]

As if Beck's illness were not enough, Olbricht told Stauffenberg and Schlabrendorff, who was on a visit to Berlin at this time, that Canaris had passed on to him an ominous remark made by Himmler. Himmler had told Canaris he was well aware that a group of influential officers was planning a *coup d'état*. Himmler added he would never, of course, let them reach the point of active revolt, but he had bided his time to find out who was behind the conspiracy. Now, he said, he had been informed; the men were Beck and Goerdeler. The conspirators were shaken by this news. They felt Himmler would reach out and take them all at any moment, and this deeply disturbed them.

Nevertheless, they knew they must continue their work and hope that they would somehow be spared.

Goeredler, in a letter written to Olbricht on 17 May, poured out his heart about the catastrophic defeats Germany had suffered, and with the kind of boldness which made so many suspicious of him even offered to confront Hitler in person:

> If there is no other way I am ready to do all I can to get an interview with Hitler. I would say to him what has to be said, that his withdrawal is asked as a vital necessity for the nation. It is not to be supposed that, if such an interview were obtained, it would of necessity be a total failure. Surprises there certainly could be, but the risk should be taken.

Later the same month Goerdeler visited Sweden and used the opportunity to send a further memorandum to Churchill through his friends the Wallenbergs.[14] He explained the intention of the future form of government which would replace that of Hitler, and at the same time urged that the bombing of the German cities should be eased since, if the means of communication were utterly destroyed, it would be more difficult to achieve a successful *coup d'état*. Once back in Germany Goerdeler toured the bombed cities and was appalled by what he found. He expressed his anguish in a long tirade addressed to Kluge on 25 July, the day Mussolini fell from power. After describing in detail the imminent collapse of Germany and its economy, he issued another astonishing challenge to the field-marshal:

> I am at your service, no matter what the risk, for any such action which simply calls things by their proper name and deals with the criminals. For this purpose I could become an officer again if only I knew that this would ensure organized quick action. I can tell you today, that I can win over to you, Field-Marshal, and to any other general resolved to take the necessary action, the overwhelming majority of the German working class, the German civil service and the German business world.

209

I can also, if you so desire, make Herr Goebbels or Herr Himmler your ally; for even these two men have long realized that with Hitler they are doomed. Therefore, all that is really required is decision, bold thinking, and right action. What is most dangerous and in the end unbearable is to shut one's ears day after day to the voice of conscience. In this I am sure that you, my dear Field-Marshal, will agree with me. . . . I only ask one more answer from you, and I know what it means if you do not give me this answer. One thing I ask you; not to refuse to answer because you are afraid. I have learned to be silent and I shall not forget the lesson. I know what I owe to the men whom I trust. Unless at least three or four men in Germany have more confidence in one another, then we can go out of business.[15]

Kluge did not venture to reply. He merely sent a message that he was no longer "interested."

Early in June Hassell met Klaus Bonhoeffer and the trade union leader Wilhelm Leuschner and gathered that Canaris was doing his best to clear Dohnanyi during the endless investigations which continued to result from the case. Hassell got some inkling of what was happening from another friend in the Abwehr, Baron Ludwig von Guttenberg, editor of *Die Wiessen Blätter,* who had himself been "grilled" during the interrogations.

Canaris, meanwhile, had been increasingly concerned about the position in Italy. As soon as he had learned about Hitler's plans for Italy (including his initial idea of capturing the King and the Pope, and both rescuing and reinstating Mussolini), he decided he must pass on certain warnings to the Italians. Taking Lahousen and Freytag-Loringhoven with him, he went to Venice in August 1943. They stayed at the hotel Canaris most favoured, the Danieli, facing the Canale di San Marco. Then, over breakfast, they talked with General Cesare Amé, Roatta's successor as chief of Italian Military Intelligence. Amé was a man Canaris both liked and trusted, and later that day, in the afternoon, the two senior officers crossed the water to the Lido, and talked together alone. They

discussed the situation in Italy very frankly. Canaris told
Amé what he knew of Hitler's intentions. Amé responded
by telling Canaris that there were signs Badoglio would
capitulate. Back in company on the mainland, Amé covered himself by declaring as loudly as possible that Italy
and Germany would remain allies until victory. Badoglio
capitulated the following month.

During the summer, Dohnanyi's anxiety about the destruction of the papers concealed at Zossen was revived.
According to Christine von Dohnanyi:

About August or September my husband asked me again
what had happened. I immediately asked Delbrück to
find out from Oster. So far as I can remember, Oster
was away from Berlin at this time, and so Perels [Dr.
Friedrich Justus Perels, a senior legal official and one of
the most useful and loyal friends of the Dohnanyis and
the Bonhoeffers] undertook to ask Beck with the help
of Dr. Sack. Beck said that the documents must not be
destroyed in any circumstances because they were of
historical importance. I believe Beck was either ill at
the time or convalescing, and my husband said that he
probably did not realize the danger. Anyway, what he
told me in effect was, to hell with history; tell them our
heads will roll. So I asked Perels to see Dr. Sack again
and insist on the destruction of the papers. Perels then
told me: 'Beck wants your husband to know that the
papers must not be destroyed, particularly those referring to the negotiations of 1939-40. It will be vitally
important for us later to be able to prove to the world
that we did not merely start acting when everything was
lost, but in those early days when the world still believed in our military victories. . . .'

I passed all this on to my husband during one of the
official visits I was allowed about September or October.
My husband said, 'This has been Beck's argument all
the time, and of course it is important. Well, let him
do what he thinks right, but for goodness' sake ask him
to take care nothing happens. We owe that to those on
the other side too.' (He meant our friends in the Vatican

211

and in England). I gave this message quite literally to Perels.

All through the winter of 1943, when my husband was ill in the hospital, this matter was constantly brought up with Perels, Delbrück [Dr. Justus Delbrück, lawyer son of the historian and Klaus Bonhoeffer's brother-in-law] and so far as I can remember, Otto John too. My husband was constantly worrying that someone might be careless, and on one occasion he told Delbrück, 'Almost every piece of paper in those files many involve a death sentence. For God's sake be careful whenever the stuff is transported.'[16]

Another immediate cause for fear was the arrest during September of the lawyer, Carl Langbehn, the friend of Popitz. Langbehn had been acting in Switzerland with Himmler's knowledge, making very veiled inquiries concerning terms for peace. By a grave mischance a message from an Allied source implicating Langbehn as an agent of Himmler sent to investigate the possibilities for a negotiated peace was intercepted by German monitors and decoded. Langbehn was arrested, and so another member of Hassell's circle of conspirators became the subject of intensive investigations. Popitz remained free for a while, and made resolute attempts to find out what was happening to Langbehn.

After his arrest, Bonhoeffer had been confined in the military section of the Tegel prison, where he was to remain for eighteen months. At the time of his arrest he was only thirty-six years old. Though he sought no favors which his fellow prisoners could not enjoy, it was known in the prison that he was the nephew of General Paul von Hase, the City Commandant of Berlin, his mother's brother. After some days of complete deprivation (crusts of bread were thrown on the floor of his solitary cell and the blankets given him were too filthy for use), conditions were considerably relaxed, and his family was permitted to bring him books, newspapers, food and clean linen. He turned his cell into a center for meditation and writing, and what he could not convey in normal letters intended for the

212

censor's eye, he managed to express in code or in letters smuggled out. Whatever he wrote revealed the greatness of his spirit and his capacity to face his condition calmly, without despair, even with a certain gentle humor. The gracious way in which he treated all men, prisoners and warders alike, won him eventually the friendship of almost everyone. On 15 May he wrote to his parents:

> People outside naturally find it difficult to imagine what prison life must be like. In itself, that is, each single moment, life here is not very different from anywhere else, so far. I spend my time reading, meditating, writing, pacing up and down my cell—without rubbing myself sore on the wall like a polar bear! The important thing is to make the best use of one's possessions and capabilities—there are still plenty left—and to accept the limits of the situation, by which I mean not giving way to feelings of resentment and discontent.[17]

By the autumn the energies of the active conspirators revived. They had experienced during the summer what could well have proved a major disaster and had been forced, in consequence, to exercise more than usual caution. One day, Major-General Helmuth Stieff's small supply of British-made bombs, which he kept under a wooden tower at Hitler's headquarters at Rastenburg, had ignited themselves and blown up. The reason for this is not known. The conspirators were fortunate that the officer appointed to investigate the explosion was Colonel Werner Schrader who, as a member of the conspiracy himself, used his skill to deflect interest from the incident and finally let the investigation peter out. But the explosion, as well as exciting unwanted attention, had deprived the conspirators of their supply of silent British bombs. Stieff managed to replace his stock with German explosives, but these were known to be unsatisfactory because their burning fuses gave off a hissing sound. Eventually, late in 1943 or early in 1944, a replacement stock of British bombs was sent to Stieff by Freytag-Loringhoven, who had supplied the original

213

bombs. These were the explosives carried by Stauffenberg on 20 July 1944.

Coup d'État *Plans Revived: the Suicide Missions*

According to Goerdeler, this, the most celebrated and by far the most spectacular of the various attempts on Hitler's life, had its origin in a long discussion he had with Beck, Kluge and Olbricht in the latter's house in September 1943. Kluge's vacillating interest in the conspiracy had revived; knowing that retrenchment and ultimate defeat were now inevitable on the Russian front, and an Allied invasion equally inevitable in the south and west at some stage in the future. Kluge wanted now to discover how far his friends in the resistance could hold out hopes of a tolerable peace for Germany if negotiations were to take place after a *coup d'état*—headed, of course, by Beck and Goerdeler. Goerdeler could only assure him that his own pre-war relations with the British led him to expect good of them, but he had to admit that all his attempts to get a reply from London to messages sent through intermediaries in Sweden had led to nothing. Goerdeler added that he was still out of sympathy with assassination—in his view, the generals must wrest the command of the Army out of Hitler's grasp and put the man on trial. Kluge and Beck disagreed. Hitler, they affirmed, must be killed. Goerdeler was forced to give way; as he put it, since it was the generals who had "allowed things to come to this pass, they themselves must find the right way to save Germany." All was agreed. The pattern seemed set. Kluge would be the commander on the Eastern Front; Falkenhausen and Stuelpnagel on the Western Front. But within a month of this meeing Kluge was badly injured in a car crash, and he did not return to his command for several months.

It was at this stage, in October 1943, that Count Stauffenberg, having recovered sufficiently from the wounds he had sustained in Africa, obtained a staff appointment in the Reserve Army.[18] He joined Tresckow in Berlin, and in effect took over from him the secret preparations for the

214

coup d'état, known as Valkyrie, on which Tresckow had been working during the summer. Very soon afterwards, Tresckow was put on active service; he was not to return to the staff of Central Group on the Eastern Front until 1944. Stauffenberg, in association with Beck and Olbricht, and helped by his aide Major Ulrich von Oertzen, prepared such details as he could for the military aspect of the *coup d'état* while Dr. Sack planned the legal action to be taken against the Nazi leaders. Goerdeler and Beck turned their attention to the final stages of forming the group who would take collective responsibility for all the main aspects of government.

Schlabrendorff, who could move relatively freely between the Eastern Front, Hitler's headquarters in East Prussia and Berlin, was kept fully informed of the plan which was developing under Stauffenberg's guidance. During the summer of 1943 he went twice to Rastenburg to study Hitler's movements when he was established in the Wolf's Lair. He also helped check on those who were prepared to undertake the assassination. Certain officers of undoubted courage nevertheless refused to place the bomb, some on the grounds of their Christian conscience. But several others were prepared to make the attempt; the gay and ironically humorous Stieff was among those prepared to place the explosive, and so were his aides, a Major Kuhn and Lieutenant Albrecht von Hagen. Tresckow was another volunteer, and tried his best to get himself transferred to Rastenburg, but failed. A plan for a "collective" assassination to be undertaken on the Eastern Front also failed; Schlabrendorff offered to join in this with a number of his fellow officers, all of whom were to fire their pistols at Hitler simultaneously. But nothing would induce the Führer to pay a return visit to the Front.

The attempt to influence the generals became the final phase of Goerdeler's work in the bare ten months of liberty he had left, though there were growing differences between him and Stauffenberg, his junior by twenty years. It seems evident that Stauffenberg was impatient at the lack of response from London and Washington and, though himself an aristocrat, thought, like Moltke, that it would

215

be both more realistic and more democratic to approach Moscow. Some peace-feelers had, indeed, been put out from Russia itself, through an agent called Klauss, who met a member of Ribbentrop's staff, Peter Kleist, in Stockholm in December 1942 and again in June and September 1943. In January 1943, Adam Trott zu Solz, known to be "Western-minded," went to Switzerland to contact Roosevelt's representative, Allen Dulles, and complain about the indifference with which all attempts to contact the Western Allies had been met. In August 1943, however, Churchill and Roosevelt met Stalin in Quebec and, as a result of their secret discussions, the fate of Germany was decided in a form which would have horrified every member of the conspiracy; whatever his point of view. Stalin sat there, upright and monolithic, an enigmatic smile on his face. Germany was to be dismembered after victory and divided into zones of occupation in which both East and West would share.

The terms of the negotiations between the Western powers and Russia, were, of course, only to be manifest in Germany after the war. Meanwhile, Trott made a second attempt to shock the Western Allies into some kind of collaboration, however remote, by visiting Dulles again in April 1944. Like the socialist leaders, Leber and Leuschner, Trott was no friend of Communism, but they all realized that some sort of revolutionary, anti-Fascist stand might in the terrible circumstances which faced them be more easily achieved with the East than with the West. Stauffenberg, it would seem, was more nearly in agreement with them than he was with Beck or Goerdeler. It was also, in part at least, a matter of the difference between generations. Nevertheless, Trott continued to try to make contact with Britain through Sweden, but he returned from a visit there in the autumn of 1943 discouraged. His British contacts had proved suspicious of a *coup d'état* that would in their opinion only lead to another form of German militarism. The matter was discussed with Hassell, who made a diplomatic point of trying to bridge the different interests and generations within the resistance. "In this game (being on good terms with both sides) I prefer the

Western orientation," wrote Hassell in August 1943. "but if need be I would also consider an agreement with Russia." The former German ambassador in Moscow, Count Friedrich von der Schulenberg, told Hassell and Goerdeler that he was willing to be smuggled through the Russian lines in order to talk to Stalin about a negotiated peace with a new régime in Germany.

Other attempts by individuals on Hitler's life continued to be planned. The best known, perhaps, of this period is that of November 1943, the suicide attempt for which Baron Axel von dem Bussche volunteered. He undertook to "model" a new kind of army greatcoat which Hitler wanted to see; the pockets were of a size suitable for concealing a bomb. Bussche was prepared to leap on the Führer and kill him while at the same time sacrificing his own life. But the attempt could never be made; on each occasion the greatcoat was to be shown the display was cancelled, and eventually the prototypes of the coats were themselves destroyed in an Allied air-raid. Bussche returned to active service, where he was severely wounded in the leg. Another volunteer was sought before the coats were destroyed. Ewald von Kleist requested permission from his father to undertake the suicide mission, but his plans came to nothing. He was only twenty when he offered his life.[19]

The Tightening Net: Canaris Dismissed

Meanwhile, confined in his prison cell, Dohnanyi suffered a severe deterioration in his health. He had never been a strong man, and the arteries in his legs had become inflamed. Roeder, the previous June, had successfully resisted the efforts of Dohnanyi's family to obtain permission for Professor Ferdinand Sauerbruch to examine him. Later in the year, on the night of 23 November, Dohnanyi's cell was struck during an air-raid and, although he was not in fact injured, the incident enabled Sack to take matters out of Roeder's hands and order the removal of the prisoner to the Charité hospital where Dohnanyi could remain under

Sauerbruch's care. It was claimed that Dohnanyi was suffering from facial paralysis and embolism of the brain. Though Roeder began to bring pressure to bear to have Dohnanyi returned to prison, Sauerbruch refused to let his patient go. Dohnanyi, with Sauerbruch's connivance, managed to receive not only his wife and children, but also many friends of the resistance who came to the Charité under cover of darkness. The visitors included his brother-in-law, Klaus Bonhoeffer, and Otto John.

Through the efforts of Sauerbruch, Dohnanyi was kept in hospital, safe from interrogation, until the following January. Roeder continued to make every possible effort to retrieve his prisoner, on one occasion even sending an ambulance without warning to fetch him away. Finally, Roeder appealed to Keitel himself, demanding that an eminent military doctor in his confidence, Generalarzt Tönjes, should make an independent examination of Dohnanyi.[20] After the examination had been made, Roeder, choosing a time when Sauerbruch was out of Berlin, arrived at the sanatorium with a high-ranking Army doctor and took Dohnanyi to the military hospital at Buch, close to Berlin. From here, on 10 February, Tönjes reported to Kaltenbrunner of the S.S. that Dohnanyi was once more "fit for interrogation." Roeder by now had taken up his appointment as Luftwaffe judge in the East.[21]

Early in the New Year, certain events had taken place outside Germany which were to prove of the utmost seriousness to the Abwehr and to Canaris personally.[22] Canaris's chief Intelligence officer at Ankara was Leverkuehn, who told Colvin that he believed Canaris had posted him to Turkey in 1942 because he knew he would be a suitable man through whom to attempt to establish relations with the Americans should peace-feelers become necessary. Leverkuehn had lived for a considerable period in the United States before the war.

For his assistants in Turkey Leverkuehn had Erich Vermehren and his wife, the former Countess Elizabeth Plettenberg. Vermehren was an intelligent but sceptical and very determined man who was regarded as showing a negative attitude to the Nazi régime; his wife, too, had the kind

218

of quick intelligence which the Gestapo did not favor outside the S.S.

Having got themselves outside Germany, the Vermehrens defected to the British during February 1944 after they had been ordered to return to Germany following the arrest in January of Moltke.[23] Their disappearance became a matter of concern and public scandal in Germany. It was widely believed they had taken the Abwehr code book with them, though when questioned by Colvin about this after the war they denied it. Their defection had serious consequences for Canaris.

Canaris's relations with Hitler were in any case growing strained. By now Hitler would only tolerate being told what he wanted to know, and not what he ought to know. He had ordered Canaris to prepare a report on the Russian front; the admiral compiled one which reflected his pessimism about the war. Hitler listened to Canaris with growing anger until he could no longer contain himself. He moved suddenly towards the admiral, overturning a table as he did so. Then he caught hold of him by the lapel of his uniform and demanded to know if Canaris was trying to tell him he was going to lose the war. Canaris, keeping as calm as he could, replied that he had said nothing about losing the war; he was only describing the situation on the Russian front as the reports he had received revealed it to be. Hitler then abused him about the defection of the Vermehrens.

The formal dissolution of the Abwehr followed soon after. Himmler, encouraged by Kaltenbrunner and Schellenberg, persuaded Hitler to sign a decree on 18 February which unified the whole Intelligence organization and placed it under Himmler's control:

I order the establishment of a unified German secret Intelligence service.
I appoint the Reichsführer S.S. to command the secret service. He will agree with the Chief of the High Command on what conditions the Military Intelligence service is to be incorporated in the secret service.[24]

Canaris was dismissed from his post. But he was neither arrested nor accused of disloyalty. Rather he was "removed" for incompetence, for allowing so many defective agents to be recruited for intelligence work, and for failing to provide the Führer with the kind of intelligence reports he wanted to receive. Canaris was in fact given extended leave of absence and for a while restricted to living in a castle in Franconia. Kaltenbrunner took over the Abwehr with alarming haste in order to forestall the removal of any incriminating or otherwise useful papers. The headquarters of the Abwehr had in any case already been moved to Zossen after the buildings on the Tirpitz Ufer had been bombed the previous April, and Canaris himself was ordered to vacate the little cottage in the military sector of the High Command where he had felt himself to be safe. He had been offered the use of a cottage by Halder when his office had been moved to Zossen. A few months later, in June 1944, Canaris was given a special position in order to cover his enforced retirement; he became Chief of the Economics Warfare Office, living alone in constant fear of arrest in his villa at Schlachtensee, and spending what time he could in the garden. He was also improving his knowledge of Russian. His family was in Bavaria, away from the air-raids. Schlabrendorff records how great was the loss of Canaris to the conspirators. "To make things worse, Admiral Canaris was forced to retire in April 1944. This was especially unfortunate because Canaris had access to much information which was valuable to us. Not least, was what he knew about the tapping of telephone lines by the Gestapo."[25]

Meanwhile, the position of Dohnanyi was less punitive than it might have been. He was confined for the first six months of 1944 in the Buch military hospital and, in spite of the report that he was fit for interrogation, he was left unmolested. Roeder had gone, and his successor, Kutzner, proved a less virulent examiner, succumbing, like Sack himself, to the policy of quiet procrastination. Christine von Dohnanyi was allowed to visit her husband, and his defence counsel also had free and official access to him.[26] But Dohnanyi's health was badly impaired. In June he had

220

a severe attack of scarlet fever, and then developed symptoms of diphtheria. He became infectious and almost paralyzed, and he was transferred to an isolation hospital in Potsdam. As the period for the hoped-for *putsch* against Hitler drew near, Sack managed to prevail on Kutzner to apply to Keitel to postpone Dohnanyi's case until "after the victory," meanwhile "interning" him in a nursing-home. This was the position on 20 July, when the blow fell not on Hitler but on those conspiring against him.

The Resistance Realigned: Stauffenberg and the 1944 Bomb Plot

The position during the spring of 1944 was one of political rather than conspiratorial action. The shift of the center of gravity away from Canaris and Oster in the direction of Stauffenberg and Olbricht was a shift towards interests which were more liberal and less right-wing. Now that Stauffenberg was in Berlin he was able more readily to assess the leadership of the conspiracy in which he had become a central figure. He shared the universal respect for Beck, but realized that he was a sick man who could be regarded only as a figurehead, not as an active leader. He found Goerdeler opinionated and at times intolerable, and he distrusted the kind of government Goerdeler wanted to establish, though he knew that he would somehow have to work in association with him; Hassell was rather more acceptable but less influential and far more cautious. So Stauffenberg looked increasingly towards the socialist leaders for support. He met Julius Leber and felt that he had discovered in him the kind of dynamic democrat whom he desired to see become a political leader in the new Germany. He pressed for the inclusion of Leber and the other outstanding socialist, Wilhelm Leuschner, in the government of the future.

The need to rid Germany of Hitler before the Western Allies landed in the north and created an impossible position for the German armies who were already falling back in the East seemed to Stauffenberg imperative. The last phases of the conspiracy which led up to Stauffenberg's personal attempt on Hitler's life on 20 July now began to take shape. Meanwhile, in order to add a popular "star" to the roster of conspirators, Rommel (back from Africa and, after a brief period of service in Northern Italy, one of the senior commanders on the Western Front) was being approached to lend his name to the *coup d'état.* Care was taken not to reveal that Hitler was to be assassinated. Rommel's attitude remained as strictly correct as possible as far as Hitler was concerned. What he wanted to see was peace restored before Germany and the German Army were dismembered by the combined attack of the Russian, American and British forces. The most he would countenance was Hitler's possible detention and trial. He was in favor of continuing the fighting in the East after an armistice had been concluded in the West. In this sense, but in this sense only, he appeared to give his special, limited approval of the idea of a *coup d'état* and the removal of Hitler from command over the German armies.

The conspirators wanted their attempt to take place before the inevitable landings on the western mainland of Europe. This seemed to them essential, especially for political reasons. As winter gave way to spring and their time ran out every possible means of accomplishing Hitler's death was examined. They seized on an offer made by Colonel von Breitenbuch to accompany Field-Marshal Busch, Kluge's successor on the Eastern Front, on a staff conference with Hitler, and then attempt to shoot him with a concealed weapon. Breitenbuch reached Berchtesgaden and stood in the same room as Hitler but this is as far as he was able to go with the plan. A protective screen of tall watchful S.S. men confronted him and made it impossible for him to take aim at Hitler.

The military plot to assassinate Hitler which came to a head on 20 July 1944 failed in the end partly through lack of firm leadership and partly through several, cumulative strokes of ill luck. In any case, far too much was left to chance in planning the take-over of Berlin, since it was assumed that various units in the Reserve Army based in and around the capital would act in proper co-ordination once they were summoned, without warning, to assist in surrounding the administrative centers—either as part of an apparent "exercise" or as a genuine protective action following some threat to national security.

The man originally intended to place the bomb was General Stieff, but in the course of his duties there seemed little or no opportunity for him to get close enough to the Führer. It was Stauffenberg's promotion in June to Chief of Staff to General Fromm, Commander-in-Chief of the Reserve Army, which gave him the necessary access to Hitler, while at the same time his disablement rendered him immune from the attentions of the S.S. whose task it was to guard the person of the Führer. What danger could there be from a man whose right hand was gone and whose left hand had only three fingers?

Stauffenberg stood face to face with Hitler for the first time on 7 June; he looked him straight in the eye and experienced no sense of fear.[27] But the Allied landings had already taken place the day before, 6 June; the dramatic despatch of Hitler on the very eve of the invasion had proved impossible because of his inaccessibility. In spite of this grave misfortune in timing, the plot was still very much alive. Tresckow, isolated on the Russian front and chafing with frustration, had sent an urgent, secret message:

The assassination must be attempted at any cost. Even should that fail, the attempt to seize power in the capital must be undertaken. We must prove to the world and to future generations that the men of the German resistance movement dared to take the decisive step and to hazard their lives upon it. Compared with this, nothing else matters.

With July came the arrest of the Socialist leader Julius Leber, and the air was charged with renewed anxiety. Matters were undoubtedly coming to a head. The conspirators did not know that they were within an ace of having their leaders arrested during the early days of July, but Himmler decided once more to procrastinate. Stauffenberg had volunteered to make the attempt at the first possible opportunity. As they waited day by day for him to be summoned, Kluge was suddenly moved to the Western front from the East in the place of Rundstedt. He refused all Tresckow's requests to accompany him. The conspirators depended on Tresckow to maintain moral pressure on Kluge and keep him within the borders of the conspiracy. Now they were to be separated.

On 3 July, Stauffenberg went to Hitler's headquarters at Berchtesgaden and there met Stieff, who was still in possession of a British bomb with a silent fuse. It was of a shape and weight suitable for hiding in a briefcase. Stauffenberg took possession of it. On 11 July Stauffenberg was ordered once again to Berchtesgaden to make a report for Hitler. It was agreed that this should be the date for an attempt, but it was abandoned because neither Himmler nor Göring was present. The conspirators believed it was essential that as many members as possible of the Nazi hierarchy should be eliminated at the same moment as Hitler. On 14 July the Führer suddenly moved his headquarters back to Rastenburg in East Prussia; the following day, Stauffenberg again prepared himself to make an attempt, but this, too, had to be abandoned. On 17 July, combined Allied offensives were expected on both the Eastern and Western fronts; on this same day Rommel, on the prestige-value of whose support the conspirators were depending, received a triple fracture of the skull from machine-gun fire from a low-flying aircraft. The following day, 18 July, Goerdeler was forced to go into hiding since rumors were circulating that he was about to be arrested. Time seemed almost to have run out when Stauffenberg received further orders to report to Hitler at Rastenburg on 20 July. With the bomb in his briefcase, he flew north soon after dawn, accompanied by his aide, Werner von Haeften, who carried a spare bomb for use in emergency. The prayers of the men in Berlin went with them.

The plan seemed clear. Stauffenberg would attend the conference in Hitler's underground bunker, place the briefcase near the Führer with the time-bomb active, and then leave as best he could on the excuse that he must telephone Berlin. Once the bomb had exploded, Stauffenberg would use the moments of confusion to bluff his way out of the compound to where Haeften was waiting with the staff car, argue his way through the two remaining checkpoints, regain the airport, fly to Berlin with Haeften and join the leaders of the *coup d'état* at about five o'clock. Only one vital factor at Rastenburg lay outside his hands —sending a signal to Berlin that all was accomplished and that the Valkyrie operation to take control of central Berlin was to be put in motion. This was done by another member of the conspiracy—General Erich Fellgiebel, head of Rastenburg's communications system. Once he had passed the signal, Fellgiebel was to close down the entire communication system, sealing off Rastenburg from the world outside.

From the outset, nothing went as planned. When Stauffenberg arrived, he was informed by Keitel that, since Mussolini was to visit Rastenburg that afternoon, the conference had been put forward by half an hour to 12.30 hours. Also, owing to structural alterations taking place in the bunker where the conferences were usually held, they were to assemble in the map-room of a wooden hutment in the central compound, and keep their reports as brief as possible. The session would be short. We can only guess now what passed through Stauffenberg's mind when he learned of these altered arrangements, but we can be certain the change of hour would have disturbed him far less than the obvious reduction in the effectiveness of the explosion inside the flimsy structure of a wooden building compared with the dire results certain within the solid walls of an underground room lined with concrete.

No one frisked Stauffenberg or asked to look inside his bulging briefcase. The bomb, the size and shape of a large square bottle of Cointreau, was wrapped in a shirt and buried among a sheaf of files. Who would suspect Stauffenberg, the briefcase hugged to his chest by his mutilated arm, of being the carrier of a bomb? How could a man with three fingers use any weapon, let alone a time-bomb? But Stauffenberg was a man of rare determination. The three fingers which had during arduous weeks of convalescence

225

learned how to knot a tie were more than capable of burrowing in the briefcase and breaking with metal tweezers the glass phial which released the acid to eat through the wire which, once it was severed, set off the firing pin of the bomb. A thin wire lasting a bare ten minutes had been inserted in the time-fuse.

As the clock neared 12.30 hours Stauffenberg, lingering in Keitel's administrative office without his cap and belt, irritated the Chief-of-Staff by pretending he was not quite ready to move over to the conference when the time came to go. Retiring for a minute, he set the acid working. Now the bomb was active with a margin of ten minutes. Stauffenberg strode across the compound in the wake of Keitel and the rest. With two minutes of his time exhausted, he entered Hitler's presence. The conference had already begun.

Stauffenberg's single eye took in the situation. The space inside the wooden room was almost filled by a huge table designed to hold the extensive maps used to record the campaigns on the various Fronts. The three large windows were thrown wide open because the day was hot and humid. Once again, the effects of blast would be seriously reduced. Hitler was leaning almost vertically across the table, studying the map of the Eastern Front while and officer reported. He took no notice of the late-comer, who moved right up beside him, set his heavy briefcase down on the floor and lodged it on the nearside of the massive plinth which supported the long table. Then, with a murmur to a fellow-officer about a telephone call from Berlin, Stauffenberg slipped from the presence of the Führer and left the gathering to their fate.

With hurried steps Stauffenberg left the building, strode back across the compound, passed the guard of the inner perimeter without difficulty, and went over to the place where Haeften was waiting in the staff car with the engine now running. As Stauffenberg reached the car there was a deafening explosion. Instinctively he glanced at his watch —the time was 12.42 hours. He was to remember this automatic act of checking and report it to his colleagues in Berlin. He leaped into the car, his mission at last ac-

226

complished. Hitler would obviously never have survived such a fearful conflagration. With two further checkpoints ahead, there was no time to be lost. The staff car passed through the first checkpoint with ease, but at the second Stauffenberg was forced to telephone the duty officer and insist on his instant permission to leave, which somehow, in the confusion of the moment, he managed to obtain. The car sped to the airport, and Stauffenberg and Haeften were airborne at 13.15 hours.

Had he been able to wait a bare five minutes, the history of this day, and perhaps of the whole war, might have been fundamentally changed. Four men were to die from the explosion, and several to be seriously injured, but none of them was Hitler. One of the dead men, a junior officer, a few moments before the explosion, had knocked his foot against the heavy briefcase and moved it over to a more convenient place on the far side of the plinth, on the side away from Hitler. This had saved the Führer from the full impact of the blast; he had staggered from the area of the wrecked building with his trousers ripped to ribbons. But he had sustained only minor injuries and a certain degree of shock, mainly because he had, at the moment of explosion, been literally lying across the table to study the situation in Kurland, which lay at the extreme north-east corner of the map. Divine Providence, his special trusted protector, had once more intervened to save him, since his body had been protected by both the plinth and the table-top. He believed at first that a lone aircraft had penetrated his defenses and bombed the headquarters, and with his instinct alert to many possible dangers, he ordered the S.S. to close down all outside communications until the incident had been fully investigated. So Fellgiebel, with only a minute on his side and uncertain what to do, found his means of signalling Berlin blocked for a period now unspecified.

It was just as if Hitler's guardian angel had contrived to cheat the conspirators in their hour of success. Hitler more or less said as much later in the afternoon when he showed the wreckage of the room to Mussolini and claimed that Providence had saved him once again. Waiting in an agony of suspense, no one at the War Office in Berlin dared to put Valkyrie into action until communications had been restored with Rastenburg and Hitler's death confirmed. Meanwhile, those conspirators still free to move had gathered, one by one, in Olbricht's office, wondering what to do for the best; the others—Goerdeler in hiding, Canaris lying low, Oster forbidden even to approach the precincts of the War Office, Tresckow isolated on the Eastern Front—could only await a signal that the time to come into the open had arrived. The hours ticked by. Obviously something drastic had happened in Rastenburg; but what? Finally, after a brief, garbled message had come through which in effect confirmed nothing, Olbricht, as Stauffenberg's close associate and the principal administrator of the *coup,* launched Valkyrie on his own initiative shortly after four o'clock in the afternoon. He issued it in the name of General Fromm, his commanding officer, who sat in his office on the second floor with no knowledge whatsoever of what was going forward.

It was in their conduct of this phase of the action that the conspirators revealed themselves at their weakest. The convergence of various units of the home-based Reserve Army from the outskirts of Berlin was believed to be a formality which would operate efficiently in the sudden emergency following the news of Hitler's death. The theory was that the units would surround the administrative centre of Berlin and act on the conspirators' orders as the newly-established military authority. What had not been foreseen was the desultory response of the Regular Army to the Valkyrie orders when no real emergency had been fully and authoritatively established. When eventually at about five o'clock Stauffenberg arrived convinced that Hitler must be dead, the flagging spirits of the conspirators were for a while revived. But no active steps had been initiated to take control of either the Propaganda Ministry or the central broadcasting system. Only the internal communications network for the Army carried the news that Hitler had been removed, and this at so late a time that little more than two hours afterwards, at 18.45 hours, Goebbels's

228

official announcement that Hitler was alive and well was broadcast to the nation.

Counter-action by the Nazis followed its own effective line. With Rastenburg sealed off, Hitler summoned Himmler, who was based only twenty miles away, to investigate the incident. The S.S. soon discovered that no aircraft had penetrated Rastenburg, but they assumed at first that a single killer, identified as Stauffenberg, had used a concealed bomb to make the attempt on Hitler's life. There was no suspicion during the early stages of the investigation that the attempt was part of an organized *coup d'état*, and when Olbricht demanded Fromm's support for the insurrection at about 4.30 in the afternoon, Fromm as the commanding general found no difficulty in making contact with Keitel at Rastenburg. He was told the Führer was alive. Only the arrival of Stauffenberg prevented Olbricht's immediate suspension. Stauffenberg, announcing that he himself was responsible for Hitler's certain death, placed Fromm under arrest, and also arrested the Gestapo agents who arrived later to take him into custody. Among the many people he telephoned in the late afternoon with the news of Hitler's death was Canaris. The Admiral, well aware his telephone was tapped, exclaimed at once, "Dead. For God's sake who did it? The Russians?" The Admiral was right. His words were automatically recorded, and appeared later in the interrogation files.

Goebbels, the only senior Minister in Berlin, soon turned the tables on the conspirators, who had failed to arrest him and seize his administration and broadcasting facilities. Seeing units of the Reserve Army in the streets below, Goebbels asserted his authority with a young officer, Major Otto Ernst Remer, a Nazi loyalist, who was in the streets on duty, but disturbed by the recent events. Goebbels immediately reached for the telephone and put Remer into direct contact with Hitler himself in Rastenburg. Remer was staggered to hear the inimitable voice, and elated to be made a colonel on the spot in return for his active loyalty. By six o'clock it was clear that the conspirators were losing what indifferent military support they had managed to bring in. Valkyrie had never functioned as it should have in

229

the streets. The units, given no firm direction, were seen returning to their bases in the suburbs not long after the first broadcast announcing the failure of the attempt.

The conspirators at the War Office—Beck, Stauffenberg, Olbricht, Hoepner and many others, both Army and civilian—could not sustain the *coup* so long as there was any doubt that Hitler had been killed. Only in France (and to some extent in Vienna) was some action taken which could have been effective had Berlin won the day. Here the planning lay with Stuelpnagel, and the senior S.S. and Gestapo officers were actually rounded up and placed under arrest by the Army during the later evening. But Kluge, most cautious of the senior commanders who knew an attempt was in the air, refused his old friend Beck any definite support. While Beck was pleading with him on the telephone, the text of Goebbels's broadcast was placed in Kluge's hand. "The bloody thing's misfired," cried Kluge, and at once held back from any kind of association with any kind of plot. There followed an almost silent meal by candlelight at which Stuelpnagel admitted to his supreme commander what he had ordered to be done. Kluge was appalled. He demanded the prisoners should be freed at once, and left Stuelpnagel with the task of explaining the hideous mistake. Stuelpnagel, his hours numbered, did as he was told.

In Berlin it was only a matter of time before retribution took its toll. Fromm, released by loyalists in the War Office, placed Beck and his associates under close arrest. To clear himself of the least suspicion of complicity in the plot, Fromm held a summary court-martial towards midnight. Beck he permitted to try suicide, but the old man's nervous state was such he was unable to succeed. After a second attempt at shooting had failed, a sergeant was ordered to dispatch him. Stauffenberg, Olbricht and Haeften were shot in the courtyard down below before the S.S. had time to intervene and round up the remaining suspects for imprisonment and prolonged interrogation.

No sooner had the S.S. and the Gestapo grasped the fact that Stauffenberg was not an individual assassin but an agent of the conspiracy which they had for so long known to be at some stage of preparation, the great wave of arrests began. The remaining men of the former Abwehr organization who were under any kind of suspicion were not spared. Oster was arrested on 21 July; Canaris was taken prisoner by Schellenberg, his friend, two days later. With a complete disregard for his state of health, Dohnanyi was removed to Sachsenhausen concentration camp. Among those involved in the conspiracy who chose suicide were Tresckow, who walked into the no-man's-land of the Russian front on 21 July, and Kluge, who died by his own hand in August. Stuelpnagel attempted suicide, but failed; he was arrested and, though in no physical condition to do so, stood his trial with the rest of those whose names were directly linked with the conspiracy. On 28 July Hassell was arrested in his office in Berlin. On 12 August Goerdeler, on the run from his pursuers, was finally betrayed by a woman who recognized him, and was taken into custody. Gisevius was more fortunate; he disappeared into hiding and, after spending the greater part of six months in Germany, fled across the border into Switzerland in January 1945. Most fortunate of all was Otto John, though his brother, Hans, was to be arrested and executed. John used his position with Lufthansa to board a plane for Madrid on 24 July, and he left Germany without the slightest difficulty.

Many of those arrested faced Freisler's persecution in the People's Court during the August trials and died the same month—among them Stuelpnagel, Stieff, Helldorf, Witzleben, Trott zu Solz and Peter Yorck. Hassell was also involved in this particular series of trials which extended into September. He was hanged on 8 September, a fortnight before the incriminating documents about which Dohnanyi had been so deeply concerned were discovered in the basement at Zossen.

II

After 20 July

The Resistance Archives: Gestapo Finds and Losses

Dohnanyi's secret papers were discovered on 22 September at the Army headquarters at Zossen. According to Bartz, all the safes at Zossen had been rifled during the preceding weeks for incriminating evidence. Only one safe remained unopened—a safe the key of which was unaccountably missing. The makers, at Dortmund, were ordered to send a locksmith to open it. In the presence of Sonderegger, the main lock was laboriously filed away and the contents of the safe revealed. The files neatly stacked inside contained records of the Vatican negotiations and other attempts to reach the Allied governments, as well as many papers prepared for use at the time of the *coup d'état,* including the names of those who might form the new government.[1]

Sonderegger was staggered by what he had found. Even a cursory glance through the files was sufficient to reveal the paramount importance of these papers. Without further delay, he took possession of the files and, driving back to Berlin, placed them in the hands of Walther Huppenkothen,[2] the notorious Gestapo Commissioner who was now in charge of the investigations. Huppenkothen made a detailed examination of the files and compiled a report of some 160 pages of typescript on the *Zossen Aktenfund.*[3] This he sent to Hitler, together with photostat copies of many of the principal documents.

The papers at Zossen formed only a part of the accumulation of documents the conspirators had assembled to use as evidence against the Nazi régime when the trials of the guilty men would, as they hoped, take place. One important collection, contained in a number of cases, included

Canaris's celebrated diary in typescript and was hidden on a farm in Gross Denkte near Brunswick. This farm belonged to Franz Bracke, brother-in-law of Colonel Werner Schrader, the member of the conspiracy who had covered for Stieff at the time of the spontaneous explosion of the hidden bombs at Rastenburg.[4]

Colonel Schrader became one of the principal custodians of the conspirators' documents. His son, Dr. Wolf Schrader, recalls how, as a soldier aged twenty, he was summoned by his father to their apartment in Berlin to help him, as Dr. Schrader has put it, "go through all of Canaris's diaries, cutting out passages which might have proved dangerous if discovered by the Gestapo. These passages were then put into large yellow envelopes and sealed." He does not know what happened in the end to these envelopes, but after her husband's suicide Frau Schrader burned the entire contents of the cases concealed at Gross Denkte. According to her son:

My mother took this decision in order to protect Canaris, Oster, Strünck, Gehre and others who were at that time still alive, some of them being under arrest. While she hurriedly burned the papers, she tried to memorize sections of them. After the war, seeing Schlabrendorff as well as Frau Canaris and Frau Oster, my mother justified what she had done. Since my uncle's farm was twice visited by the Gestapo, the possibility was that they would have found the cases. Moreover, my father had left no instructions as to what to do with the documents in the event of his death. . . . It was well known that my father was anti-Nazi; ever since 1933 we had had our fill of the Gestapo. It was due only to Oster and Canaris that my father was saved from certain death in a concentration camp.

Among the files burned there were parts of Canaris's diary as well as documentation of Nazi crimes. My father had explained to my mother that after a successful *putsch* these files would be helpful in telling the German people the truth about the National Socialists. Probably the files contained the famous 'Oster collection' for which my father provided many items. After Oster's suspension, my father managed to get some of these documents out of Oster's office. I suspect the Fritsch files (still undiscovered) were also included. My mother also remembers a great many films and photographs of mass-shootings, executions and the torture of Jews in the East.[5]

Dr Wolf Schrader has written for us the following comment on Canaris's diaries as he remembers them, and what he learned of Canaris, whom he already knew well, during the two days he spent with his father "purging" the diaries:

We were quite unprepared for the sudden task of looking through all these volumes (I don't remember quite how many, six or eight) within two days. Our attention was focused on critical remarks about the régime, as well as names of friends; these were the sections to be 'purged'. From time to time, while working against time, we would read out passages of particular interest to each other. Time was very short. So I cannot recall many points of detail. But I did gain a fairly clear impression of the diaries as a whole, and I have retained this fairly exactly to this day. . . . My view of Canaris differs considerably from much I have read. It differs with regard to the character and motives of the man rather than historical fact.

Take, for instance, the very substantial reports on and comments about his dogs, thoughts occupying a great deal of space throughout the volumes of the diary. His love of dogs appears again and again in a manner which seems almost whimsical and precious. Frequently he makes the point that he prefers dogs to human beings— but all this would, I think, interest a psychologist rather than an historian. . . . One always saw more of Canaris himself than the people he happened to be dealing with. He was not the kind of politically-minded man who would put down details concerning important people in order to get a general picture of their minds and motives.

234

One might almost claim that what really mattered to him was to be entertained.

Frequently the entries would start: '21h. 18; Anhalt Station; sleeper to so-and-so'. What followed might as well have been copied from the railway timetable. He arrives, encounters such-and-such a situation, comes to some quick decision about what to do or not to do, and he departs quickly, taking with him a favourable or a displeased impression. There is hardly ever any self-criticism. He seems always to be right. When meeting prominent people, he describes whether or not they were good listeners, whether or not they showed some charm of manner. He liked intelligent, worldy-wise, much-travelled people; he disliked Nazis. But he never attempts to analyze his reasons. He never put down in the diary any point he was trying to clarify in his own mind, or anything which might contradict some previous observation. He was always well-informed, and he could see through everyone he met. After that, they ceased to interest him. Oddly enough, considering his naval career, there was hardly a word about the sea or naval matters, let alone any love for the sea.

I think that all his activities in the resistance were foisted on him by Oster. As for the Nazis, Canaris considered them to be thugs and crooks, but he had no objection to observing them. It was like getting absorbed in some well-written crime story. Canaris had a strongly developed sense of adventure, including the adventure of evil itself. Oster would say that in the German government and in German history such things were not to be tolerated. Canaris would find this quite irrefutable. So, he became active in the resistance, even though it must have irked him as it would anyone who is not by nature cut out for conspiracy or direct political action.[6]

Dr Schrader concludes that he came to realize through reading the diaries how deeply and directly Canaris involved himself in the conspiracy. He writes:

It was not merely that Canaris covered Oster and gave

235

him all facilities for action, but there was a definite, genuine agreement on the need for this activity against evil. The only difference was Canaris did not expect to end on the gallows, whereas Oster never had any illusions about it at all.

Dr Schrader has also revealed something of the plans for escape which had been prepared for certain members of the resistance, but which were never realized:

I know that foreign currency and other facilities were fully prepared for their escape. Some years ago the Princess Calma von Coburg, who was at the time married to a test pilot, reported that my father had made definite arrangements with her husband for Canaris's and Oster's escape abroad whenever it might be necessary. The pilot's name was Schnirring, and it happened that he crashed his aircraft shortly before 20 July. After the July plot, the princess was interrogated sadistically by the Gestapo.

In all probability I too was intended to be involved in one of the escape routes. On 20 July I happened to be posted to an Abwehr unit in Yugoslavia. A few days previously the paymaster had told me that the supreme Abwehr Command had sent him an astonishingly large sum in dollars, together with six bars of gold. He had no idea at all what he was supposed to do with all this. At exactly the same time I was assigned new quarters in the vicinity of the paymaster. This is all I can say; indeed, all I know. I can only guess that my father had certain plans which he never put into effect or had the opportunity to reveal to me.

When Fretag-Loringhoven shot himself, my father, very distressed and excited, exclaimed to his secretary: 'Surely he didn't have to do that!' Here again escape routes had been prepared. Here's the enigma; why did the two supreme chiefs of the Abwehr let themselves be arrested, or, in my father's case, commit suicide? After all, they still had their foreign contacts and their facilities, financial and otherwise. Right up to his end, my father could command aircraft, U-boats and un-limited supplies of foreign currency. But nothing happened. Still, I dare say one can gather from Canaris's diary that they felt they could not, or would not cope any longer after the failure of the July plot. They were worn out and had given up all hope.[7]

Canaris in Prison: Arrests, Interrogations, Torture

Schellenberg has left an almost sentimental account of Canaris's arrest,[8] which he was ordered to carry out by Kaltenbrunner himself:

I went to Canaris's house in Berlin-Schlachtensee and he himself opened the door. . . . Canaris was very calm. His first words to me were, 'Somehow I felt it would be you. Please tell me first of all, have they found anything in writing from that fool Colonel Hansen?' (This officer had been involved in the affair of 20 July.). Truthfully I answered, 'Yes; a notebook in which there was among other things a list of those who were to be killed. But there was nothing about you or participation on your part.' 'Those dolts on the General Staff cannot live without their scribblings,' Canaris replied.

I explained the situation to him and told him what my assignment was. 'It's too bad,'' he said, 'that we have to say goodbye in this way. But'—and here he made an effort to throw off his apprehension—'we'll get over this. You must promise me faithfully that within the next three days you will get me an opportunity to talk to Himmler personally. All the others—Kaltenbrunner and Müller [of the Gestapo]—are nothing but filthy butchers, out for my blood.'

I promised to do as he asked and then said in a completely official voice, 'If the Herr Admiral wishes to make other arrangements, then I beg him to consider me at his disposal. I shall wait in this room for an hour, and during that time you may do what you wish. My report will say that you went to your bedroom in order to change.'

He understood at once what I meant. 'No, dear Schellenberg,' he said, 'flight is out of the question for me. And I won't kill myself either. I am sure of my case, and I have faith in the promise you have given me.'

We discussed quietly whether it would be wise for him to put on his uniform, what things he should take with him, and other details. Then he went upstairs. He returned after about half an hour, having washed, changed, and packed a handbag. Again and again he shook his head saying, 'Those devils—they had to draw you into this thing too! But be on your guard—I've known for a long time that they are after you too. When I talk to Himmler I'll tell him about your case as well.' He embraced me with tears in his eyes, and said, 'Well, then, let us go.'

We drove in my open car. After we left the city, the road led through the lovely countryside of Mecklenburg. The sky was slowly darkening. Our conversation grew increasingly monosyllabic, for each of us was pursuing his own thoughts. Canaris assured me several times that he knew very well I had no share in bringing about his dismissal. He hoped that fate would be kinder to me, and that I would not one day be hunted down as he had been. . . .

It was about eleven o'clock when I said goodbye to him. He accompanied me to the anteroom, and we stood there talking for another five minutes. Once more he reminded me of my promise to arrange an interview with Himmler. . . . The next day I had a long telephone conversation with Himmler. . . . He assured me that he would have an interview with Canaris, for there is no other explanation of the fact that Canaris was not sentenced to death until the very last days before the collapse of the Third Reich. . . . Himmler was still powerful enough to protect Canaris from the death sentence.

Why should Himmler have wished to protect Canaris?

238

According to Schellenberg, who has every reason, writing after the war, to represent himself as astute and on the side of the angels, he, Schellenberg, had realized Canaris's guilt long before Roeder. Canaris was also guilty, according to Schellenberg, of gross inefficiency in the field of Military Intelligence, and was suspected, at least by Schellenberg, of playing a double game. Meanwhile he claims that Himmler was himself playing a double game with Canaris.

> Himmler had decided to employ a sort of snowball tactic against him. He never spontaneously expressed his opinion on Canaris to Hitler, but always waited until the problem of Canaris was raised by Hitler himself. Meanwhile, he saw to it that other leaders, both political and of the Wehrmacht, who were for one reason or another opposed to the Admiral, continually kept the subject of Canaris in the limelight. Himmler regularly furnished this anti-Canaris clique with new material against him, and so added continually to the stiffening opposition.

Yet Himmler would never take direct action against Canaris himself:

> Again and again I raised these matters because of their importance to Germany's war effort, but Himmler obviously did not wish to be burdened with the responsibility. Like Heydrich, he seemed to have some inhibitions with regard to the Admiral. I am certain that at some time or other Canaris must have got to know something incriminating against Himmler, for otherwise there is no possible explanation of Himmler's reaction to the material I placed before him.

However, we have it on the authority of Roeder himself, that most ruthless of investigators, with his special interest in the Abwehr, that he had no real suspicion whatsoever of Canaris's guilt until after the attempt in July and the discovery of the documents at Zossen. According to both Schellenberg and Bartz, Colonel Georg Hansen (who,

239

although remaining in touch with the conspirators, had been put in charge of the shadow Abwehr which had survived Canaris's downfall) was responsible after his arrest for giving the information which involved Canaris in the network of the plot. Bartz claims that Hansen, who was absent from Berlin on 20 July because his wife was having a child, wrote voluntarily a 'confession' offering evidence in which Canaris was involved.

The prisons in Berlin were overflowing as the hundreds of men and women implicated in one way or another with the conspiracy were brought in for interrogation. The principal prisoners were confined at Gestapo headquarters in the Prinz Albrechtstrasse; others were sent under Gestapo control to the Lehrterstrasse prison. A section of the Police Training School at Fuerstenberg, near Berlin, was converted into another prison, and it was here that Canaris was for a while confined. Oster was examined initially by Huppenkothen, as were Canaris and Dohnanyi; Huppenkothen claimed after the war that he obtained a form of confession from Oster:

> After I had confronted Oster with the confession of Count Marogna-Redwitz he was quiet for some fifteen minutes. Then he asked for a cigarette and said, 'Well, it's no good denying things any longer. I will tell you the truth.' And then he made a partial confession. Oster admitted that he knew about certain things from General Olbricht, and that both Canaris and his assistant Dr. Dohnanyi were well informed. He had no secrets from Dohnanyi.[9]

According to Huppenkothen, this partial confession was obtained during August.

Those already in custody—but not before 20 July in the hands of the Gestapo—Dohnanyi, Josef Müller, Dietrich Bonhoeffer, and Moltke, were now removed from their places of confinement by the Gestapo. Müller was taken to Gestapo headquarters in the Prinz Albrechtstrasse. Dohnanyi had been taken by Sonderegger from the Army prison hospital at Potsdam on 22 August and put in the

240

hospital ward of Sachsenhausen concentration camp, where his health immediately began to deteriorate. It was now that he began to add to the effects of genuine illness various forms of simulation to assist his policy of procrastination. The prisoners were acutely aware of how badly the war was going for Germany. Their problem, as they saw it, was to prolong the interrogations so that the endless checking and counter-checking their statements involved would serve to keep them alive until an Allied victory would deliver them from their tormentors.

Pastor Bethge, himself to be arrested during September, writes of Dohnanyi's condition after his removal to Sachsenhausen:

From this day Dohnanyi used illness as the only weapon left to him. With a concentration which seemed almost superhuman he studied and practiced the symptoms so as to prolong his illness and make use of it every time it proved necessary. He hoped in this way to avoid the betrayal of his friends until the general breakdown of the Reich. And he almost succeeded.[10]

At 7.30 in the morning of the day after the attempt on Hitler, 21 July, Sonderegger was on the telephone to both Professor Bonhoeffer and to Dohnanyi's wife, Christine, to probe into the relationship between Oster and Dohnanyi. Christine von Dohnanyi said she knew nothing at all about Oster. Professor Bonhoeffer, however, as Dohnanyi's father-in-law, was allowed to visit him before his removal to Sachsenhausen, and wrote about him to Bethge on 30 July:

I saw Hans last week. He is in a deplorable condition, his diphtheria making him practically immobile. The paralysis in his face and gums is slightly better, but unchecked in his arms and legs. There is some hope, but it is a great anxiety for him and Christel. Dietrich is all right as far as his health is concerned. We hope to see him one of these days.[11]

241

As soon as he had received Huppenkothen's resumé of the documents from Zossen, Hitler issued a directive that the whole matter of the conspiracy was to remain a State secret and was never to be brought before the People's Court. The examination of the conspirators was henceforth to be conducted in private. This meant that from the conspirators' point of view further prolongation of the interrogations became even more possible. Canaris, Oster, Dohnanyi, Bonhoeffer, Müller, Goerdeler and Schlabrendorff (who had been arrested on the Eastern Front on 17 August and brought the following day to the cells of the Prinz Albrechtstrasse) were all treated as prime witnesses whose potential value as informants meant that they must be kept alive to testify. Among those taken into custody following the discoveries at Zossen was General Thomas, whose arrest took place on 11 October. He was taken to the Prinz Albrechtstrasse and placed in a cell with Schacht, who, arrested on 23 July, had also been brought to the Prinz Albrechtstrasse from Ravensbrück concentration camp, his first place of confinement, late in August.

At Sachsenhausen, Dohnanyi was fortunate to be in the care of a medical orderly called Max Geissler. When he had arrived at night on a stretcher in the charge of a group of S.S. men, a Norwegian prisoner-doctor was detailed to look after him. The orders were that he was to be treated as a prisoner confined under a strict security control, and that Geissler was forbidden to converse with him. Geissler, however, took no notice of these orders, and not only talked to Dohnanyi but did all he could to relieve his sufferings.

Dohnanyi was subjected once more to severe interrogations in spite of his condition. According to Geissler:

The first Gestapo interrogation on the day after his admission to the camp lasted more than eight hours. It took place in the office of the security service in R 1, although all other interrogations took place in the sick room. The Gestapo always took security measures so that I could not overhear anything, as I could in many other cases. But of course the abuse by the Gestapo

242

could be heard through the thin walls. These uneducated boors tore into him unspeakably, in their frustrated rage. It can be said without any doubt that Dohnanyi proved both the better and the stronger party in this unequal contest.[12]

Dohnanyi was still concerned about the files hidden at Zossen—at this stage, of course, still unknown to the Gestapo. Christine von Dohnanyi said later:

After the July plot, the Gestapo had forbidden me to visit my husband in the Potsdam hospital, but he informed me through his reliable nurse that I should take care of his books—books being our camouflage word for the Zossen files. . . . Early in November, I had a letter from my husband from the concentration camp. In this, in disguised phrasing, he informed me that 'some weaklings must have betrayed everything. Now all that matters is to gain time.'[13]

According to Huppenkothen, Dohnanyi's principal interrogator, "it was very difficult to get anything out of him, particularly during the initial period. It was different, of course, after the discovery of the Zossen files. He just could not help confessing then, because after all much of it was in his own handwriting."[14] In a further letter smuggled out to his wife, Dohnanyi described his feelings when he was confronted with certain of the papers from Zossen: "I do not know who the traitor is, and after all it does not really matter any longer. They have got us in the hollow of their hands." Later he was able to tell her what had happened, and she recalled what he had said:

On 5 October 1944 Huppenkothen had come to see him in Sachsenhausen concentration camp and showed him photostats of the report by Dr. Müller from the Vatican and also photostats of a draft for General Beck of an appeal to the German people. Well, he threw all these documents on my husband's bed, shouting: 'That's what we've been looking for for two years.' My husband told

243

me that he kept quite calm and replied: 'Have you indeed. Where on earth did you get that from?' Huppenkothen told him they had found the papers at Zossen. When my husband refused to believe this—and indeed from all the assurances he had received from his associates he had no reason to believe it—Huppenkothen (or perhaps Sonderegger) named the officer alleged to have betrayed the whereabouts of the papers. Huppenkothen then told my husband that there was no value in denying anything, and my husband indeed took his point. From then on they kept him under pressure for a long while to force him to name the people connected with the plot of 1939-40. They promised him proper hospital treatment and contact with the family. They told him that everything was known anyway, and he would not be incriminating anyone if he talked.[15]

Huppenkothen was the initial interrogator, he was later succeeded by Stavitsky, a huge man with an artificial leg who had a reputation for maltreating his prisoners, and finally by the regular interrogator, Sonderegger. According to Dr. Tietze, a local physician in whose care Dohnanyi was placed early in 1945, he never gave away anything of importance to the Gestapo:

He was an uncannily shrewd and clever man when it came to interrogation. As soon as things got what we called 'too hot' he simply pretended to lose consciousness and fall asleep, and in other ways use his physical condition to sabotage further interrogation. I learned of this from various sources, and certainly from what he told me himself he never made a genuine confession.[16]

As the range and depth of the conspiracy was gradually uncovered, the investigations themselves went further underground at Gestapo headquarters. It was certainly not in the best interests of the régime to make public the extent of the network of opposition which had grown up in every section of German society, or to execute men from whom it was always hoped to obtain further details in evidence.

Though the trials had been suspended, the interrogations by Himmler's team of investigators, Huppenkothen, Sonderegger, and their assistants, Stavitsky, Panzinger and Lange, continued.

In September, after the discoveries at Zossen, a plan to liberate Bonhoeffer came near to being put in action. The plan turned on the assistance of one of Bonhoeffer's warders, a working man from north Berlin called Knobloch, who was serving in the prison as an N.C.O. He said that he was prepared to accompany Bonhoeffer through the gates of the Tegel prison, where he was still confined, and then, like certain other members of the resistance (among them Jacob Kaiser and Ludwig von Hammerstein) go into hiding with him. Suitable working-man's clothes were obtained for Knobloch to smuggle into prison, and on 24 September Bonhoeffer's sister Ursula, together with her husband Rüdiger Schleicher and her daughter Renate (Pastor Bethge's wife), met Knobloch and gave him a parcel containing the clothing and also money and food coupons.

The date of the escape was fixed for early October, but it was never effected. When Dietrich Bonhoeffer's brother Klaus returned from his office on 30 September, he saw a Gestapo car drawn up outside his suburban house. He did not go in; he went straight to Ursula Schleicher's house. Here he found that his aunt, the widow of General von Hase (who had been among those executed the previous month) had also come to take refuge after being released that same day from prison. When Knobloch arrived to discuss obtaining false passports from the Swedes for himself and Dietrich, it was decided that before anything further was done, Dietrich should be told that his brother was in imminent danger of arrest.

The family did not know what to do for the best. Klaus's wife and children were away in Schleswig-Holstein. Klaus himself, distracted, faced the alternatives of attempted flight, arrest, or even suicide. He was still uncertain what he should do when, the following day, the Gestapo arrived and took him away as, eighteen months previously, they had come to take Dietrich into captivity from the same

245

house. Knobloch returned the next day. He had come to say that Dietrich had decided to abandon his attempt to escape because he did not want to add to his brother's difficulties. Two days later, Rüdiger Schleicher was arrested in his office at the Ministry.

On 8 October Dietrich was removed from the Tegel prison to the Gestapo cellars at Prinz Albrechtstrasse where his friend Josef Müller had also been moved a few days previously, on 27 September. The prisoners at Gestapo headquarters were shackled at night, ostensibly to prevent them committing suicide. Schlabrendorff has described in detail how he was tortured in order to force him to abandon his persistent denial he had any knowledge of other people involved in the plot. He reports that Carl Langbehn, a fellow prisoner, was among those similarly treated. The tortures only stopped when he made a carefully calculated minor admission concerning Tresckow which could harm nobody—this was, that Tresckow had wanted Hitler to surrender his position to one of the field-marshals. The Gestapo investigators, says Schlabrendorff, suddenly appeared satisfied, and the interrogations were stopped for a while. Later, however, he was taken to Sachsenhausen concentration camp and forced to view Tresckow's remains; the coffin had been exhumed, and the Gestapo had hoped through this macabre display to force a real confession from Schlabrendorff. He said nothing, and Tresckow's body was cremated before his eyes.

Other prisoners whom Schlabrendorff recognized at the Prinz Albrechtstrasse—they included Canaris, Oster, Hassell (soon to die), Bonhoeffer, Müller and Goerdeler—were not at this stage subject to torture. They were all guarded by special Gestapo men who for the most part wore civilian clothes and, in some cases, assumed a friendly manner towards the prisoners in order to create an atmosphere of confidence out of which they might manage to extract a few scraps of interesting information. Schlabrendorff adds that a few of the guards were genuinely sympathetic and tried to make life for the prisoners more bearable.

The prisoners did what they could to help each other. In

246

spite of the intense cold from which he always suffered, Canaris loaned Schlabrendorff his precious overcoat when he was taken from his cell to see the body of Tresckow. It is typical of Canaris's assiduous collecting of information in the prison that in the overcoat pocket Schlabrendorff found a note warning him that his case was shortly to be heard.

Canaris was kept in solitary confinement, and in chains. His cell door was left permanently open, and the light burned continually, day and night. He was given only one third of the normal prison rations, and as the winter set in his starved body suffered cruelly from the cold. The cells were frequently unheated. Occasionally he was humiliated by being forced to do menial jobs, such as scrubbing the prison floor. Josef Müller remembers one of the jailers mocking him, calling him "little sailor" and adding, "I guess you never thought you'd have to scrub floors one day." No one outside the prison was told anything about Canaris, or even where he was; the only information about the prisoners was contained in messages smuggled out of the prison itself. Abshagen records how a friend of Canaris, whom he does not name, managed to get to see Huppenkothen on the grounds that Canaris's housekeeper was in financial difficulties and need the Admiral's signature on some checks. It was Huppenkothen's secretary who took the check book and came back with the necessary signatures. So now it was known definitely that Canaris was in Prinz Albrechtstrasse.

Although the rigid prison discipline forbade the prisoners to speak, they were at least neighbours and could see each other during exercise, washing and other activities which took them from their cells. Among these were the frequent journeys to the air-raid shelter. On all these occasions the prisoners did what they could to speak and pass messages to each other.

Schacht has given some idea how his interrogations were conducted by Stavitsky in a room on the third floor at Prinz Albrechtstrasse. Schacht claims he replied in the following manner to the questions he was asked:

247

STAVITSKY: You attended meetings of a committee at which the political situation was regularly discussed?

SCHACHT: Which committee do you mean?

STAVITSKY: The chairman of the committe was Reusch; those present were Voegler, Bücher, Wentzel, and others.

SCHACHT: I can't help laughing if you really think that this committee discussed politics. It was a gathering of about twelve persons, half of them industrialists, the other half farmers, who met at regular intervals to talk over the problems connected with the industrialization of agriculture.

STAVITSKY: That is not correct. Herr Goerdeler has told us that this committee also discussed politics.

SCHACHT: I presume that if you have arrested me because I was a member of this committee you have taken all the others into custody as well. When you come to question these gentlemen you will find that my statements are correct. If by chance someone let drop a political word or so it will have been during a personal conversation, but not as a matter of committee business.

STAVITSKY: On 13 July you had a discussion with Gisevius in Berlin.

SCHACHT: That is quite untrue.

STAVITSKY: We have proof that you did.

SCHACHT: This cannot be correct. Please let me see the proof.

STAVITSKY: We will not let you see it. But we know that at that date you saw and spoke with Gisevius.

SCHACHT: I don't know how you came by your inforation, but if Gisevius was in Berlin at that time you must surely have arrested him meanwhile. Kindly allow me to meet him face to face.

STAVITSKY: You also discussed a plan to escape with Goerdeler.

SCHACHT: I would urge you to let me confront Herr Goerdeler and you shall learn what it was we discussed.[17]

Schacht has also described in some detail the limited

way in which the prisoners were able to communicate with each other:

In the Prinz Albrechtstrasse, the only time we left our cells was when we dressed in the morning. Two men at a time were taken to the wash-house, while in a recess two more went under the cold shower. In spite of the icy water we never missed it, for it was our only chance of exchanging a few whispered words. The lavatory, with its row of four or five seats, offered far less opportunity as there were no doors, and a warder patrolled up and down the whole time.

The only other occasion on which we left our cells was when we were questioned, and when there was an air-raid warning and we made for the shelter. When that happened we stood close together in a narrow passage, drawn up in two rows along both walls, and were absolutely forbidden to whisper or speak to one another. Sometimes we might pass a fellow-prisoner on the way to the toilet or to a hearing; otherwise these gatherings in the shelter were our only opportunities for catching sight of the other inmates of the prison. . . .

In the shelter, the officials on guard over the two rows of us kept a strict look-out to prevent any talking, and it was not easy to glean anything from the blank expressions of one's fellows, since each endeavored to present a stony mask. Most of them displayed only an iron determination to hold their own in the mental and psychological conflict with the Gestapo.

Of all the faces I saw there none impressed me so painfully as those of Canaris and Goerdeler. The last, and comparatively recent, time I had seen Goerdeler he was still at liberty, alert and full of confidence; now he was in a state of complete collapse. His face expressed his whole inner disillusion and despair. Canaris was at bottom a great patriot; his face, too, revealed how the man's divided outlook, brought about by necessity, had convulsed his whole inner nature and shattered his balance.[18]

249

On 6 December, the day Schacht's wife was permitted to visit him for the first time since his arrest in July, he was taken back to Ravensbrück concentration camp.

In Freisler's Court

Schlabrendorff was not brought before Freisler's secret court until 21 December. Even then his case, most fortunately for him, was postponed until February. Nevertheless, he had been able to watch Freisler in action, shouting his accusations at the prisoners he was, at least technically, supposed to examine impartially. Schlabrendorff wrote:

> Roland Freisler, the president, deliberately avoided all judicial objectivity by describing as high treason the smallest offenses against National Socialism. In most cases the sentence was death, usually by hanging. Freisler did not hesitate to make long-drawn-out, cheap propaganda harangues, delivering them in a voice which would easily have carried through several large courtrooms. He had acquired these tactics by studying the performance of Andrei Vishinsky during the Soviet purge trials of the 1930s. Freisler had been a prisoner of war in Russia during the first world war and an ardent Bolshevik before later becoming an ardent Nazi; he had great admiration for the terror methods of the Soviets.[19]

Another description of Freisler was left by Father Alfred Delp, the Catholic priest who belonged to Moltke's circle:

> Freisler is clever, nervous, vain and arrogant. He is performing all the time, in such a way that the player opposite him is forced into a position of inferiority. . . . All the questions were neatly prepared, and woe betide you if the answers you gave were not what Freisler expected.[20]

Moltke, a formidable debater whose trial did not take

250

place until 10 January 1945, seemed to take an almost masochistic pleasure in withstanding Freisler's onslaughts. In a letter to his wife[21] after the hearing at which he was condemned to death, Moltke described Freisler as 'talented, with some genius in him, and withal unintelligent, all three in the highest degree.' He described the climax of his trial as "a sort of dialogue between Freisler and me—a dialogue of the spirit, since I did not get the chance to say much—in the course of which we got to know each other through and through. Freisler was the only one of the whole gang who thoroughly understood me, and the only one of them who realized why he must do away with me." The other defendants of the moment, including Father Delp and Eugen Gerstenmaier, were for a while forgotten as these two, like devil and archangel, became locked in isolated argument. But Moltke could only postpone the moment when he was to receive the inevitable death sentence. He died by hanging on 23 January, 'steadfast and calm'.

Freisler himself had only a few days left to live. On 3 February, Schlabrendorff's case was due to be heard. After pronouncing sentence on Ewald von Kleist, whose hearing preceded Schlabrendorff's Freisler picked up the file papers which contained such evidence as the Gestapo had managed to compile against Schlabrendorff. As he did so, the air-raid sirens began to wail. The bombing which followed was one of the heaviest daylight raids by American aircraft Berlin experienced. The court had to be adjourned and the court-room evacuated. Schlabrendorff, manacled, was hurried down with the rest into the cellars. Freisler, the file under his arm, was in the cellar when the building received a direct hit. A beam fell and fractured Freisler's skull.

By an extraordinary chance, on the same day, Rolf Schleicher, a physician, who had come to Berlin from Stuttgart in order to help his brother Rüdiger's family, was travelling by underground to the Prinz Albrechtstrasse, where he hoped to be allowed to leave a parcel for Dietrich Bonhoeffer, his brother-in-law. The Gestapo headquarters and the court-room building were close together. By the

251

time Schleicher arrived, the raid was so intense the police forbade anyone to leave the shelter of the underground station. However, a message came that a doctor was urgently needed to attend "a very prominent casualty," and Schleicher volunteered at once to help. He was hurried to the ruins of the People's Court, where he found that it was Freisler whom he had been called to attend. He arrived in time only to confirm the death of the man who the day before had ordered the execution of his brother and brother-in-law.[22] He refused to sign a death certificate, and immediately went to see Otto Georg Thierack, the Minister of Justice, whom he knew, obtaining from him a promise that Freisler's verdicts would be re-examined, and the executions delayed.

Freisler, then, was dead, and in the event the file containing the evidence against Schlabrendorff was destroyed. When his case was finally reheard on 16 March and he pleaded, with great emotion, that any admission he had made had been obtained under torture, he managed to win an acquittal from the new examiner, Dr. Krohne. This was not, however, to lead to his release.

The raid which on 3 February had destroyed the courthouse also destroyed the Gestapo headquarters in the Prinz Albrechtstrasse, except for the prison cells below ground. Many of the prisoners had to be removed, and only a hard core of men already condemned to death, or considered as good as condemned, were kept in the cells without light, heat or water. A skeleton guard watched over them. Schacht has described the conditions after the raid:

The cellar . . . looked bleak and hopeless in the extreme. Those parts of the building above ground had nearly collapsed under the bombing. Light and water no longer functioned. We undressed by the flickering light of a candle-end, in spite of which each of us was once again confined in a separate cell. For nature's needs, a pit had been dug in the yard with a bar nailed across it. It was here, sitting next to him on the bar, that I had my last talk with Dietrich Bonhoeffer. Our glance fell on

252

the barred window of a cellar, behind which a woman wrung her hands in despair and implored us, by signs, to help her.[23]

Tactics of Goerdeler and Canaris

Among those still confined in the Prinz Albrechtstrasse was Dohnanyi, who, a few days before the raid had been brought in from Sachsenhausen on a stretcher. His legs were paralyzed, and says Schlabrendorff, he "suffered unspeakably." His only comfort in these fearful conditions of imprisonment was that he was close now to his brother-in-law Dietrich, and to his friends.

Dietrich Bonhoeffer's presence in the dungeons of the Gestapo had given inspiration if not hope to everyone. As we shall see, he was to remain there only until 7 February, when he, together with nearly all the remaining prisoners, was to be sent to continue his imprisonment in a concentration camp. Schlabrendorff, who had been in the prison since 18 August, had first noticed that Bonhoeffer was among his fellow-prisoners when he had seen him one night during October in the air-raid shelter in the prison yard. For the moment, Schlabrendorff was shocked at the sight of his friend, for any sign of recognition from Bonhoeffer would have been fatal to him. Bonhoeffer, alert and serene, made no sign that he knew Schlabrendorff, whose cell proved to be only a few doors from his own. The following day they exchanged a few surreptitious words in the washroom. Bonhoeffer whispered that he would reveal nothing to the Gestapo. A few days later Bonhoeffer was removed to cell 24, next door to Schlabrendorff. From now on they met regularly, using the noise of running water in the showers to drown their conversation. They whispered to each other when they were lined up at the cell-doors, and took advantage of the disturbance caused by the recurrent air-raids. Schlabrendorff learned that Bonhoeffer had been threatened with torture, but that the Gestapo had so far failed to realize the importance of his activities and even the significance of his meeting with

253

Bell. Bonhoeffer remained completely self-possessed and cheerful, never appearing to lose hope, and his nature was so radiant that the guards themselves succumbed to his influence. He continued to be less harshly treated than most of the prisoners, and was not usually manacled at night. He and Schlabrendorff always shared whatever presents reached them from their families; Bonhoeffer normally received a parcel of clean underwear, cigars, apples and bread each Wednesday.

Goerdeler's response to his imprisonment was no less remarkable in its own distinctive way. He had been condemned to death by Freisler at the same time as Hassell and Leuschner on 8 September. While the other two had been hanged the same month, Goerdeler was set up with writing materials in the condemned cell and encouraged to continue with the composition of his interminable memoranda for the enlightenment of the S.S.

According to his friend and biographer Gerhard Ritter, who shared his imprisonment, Goerdeler was determined to give his captors the impression that he was the most co-operative prisoner they had in their control, and then to confound them with his garrulity. He certainly inspired a favorable reaction in Kaltenbrunner, who noted "Goerdeler's extremely comprehensive statements," but unfortunately he was misrepresented by the Gestapo to the other prisoners as an ideal witness from whose information they had everything to fear. Goerdeler's reputation was already dubious; he was known to be indiscreet. The other prisoners therefore feared that he would eventually give everything away, and turn State's evidence. In spite of his "co-operation," he was ill-treated like the rest, as Ritter himself observed. The food he was given was both bad and insufficient, his manacles were so tight they caused the utmost discomfort at night, and his cell light was kept burning and added to the difficulty of sleep. Schlabrendorff managed to speak to Goerdeler from time to time, and they agreed not to reveal that they knew each other.

It would seem that Goerdeler's "confessions," whether true, part-true or wholly invented, primarily involved people whom he knew to be already dead. Goerdeler's delaying tactics involved the fabrication of a network of evidence of a kind which it might take months to investigate. Ritter, too, was confronted with Goerdeler and says that he was "astonished at the fullness of his statements," which none the less were so colored as to tell in Ritter's favor. It was evident that the Gestapo interrogator had succumbed to Goerdeler's technique and accepted every word he chose to utter. It was thought by some, however, that Goerdeler's statements led to further arrests.

The greater part of Goerdeler's oral evidence was completed during the weeks between his arrest in August and trial in September. But he was regarded by them as far too valuable an informant to be put to death. During the period of respite which followed, his cell door was left open in case he should be tempted to commit suicide. Suicide, however, was far from his mind. Once more, the prisoner became the master of his jailer. Goerdeler dedicated the whole of his time to writing, part of which was "official," part unofficial. His warder, S.S. man Wilhelm Brandenburg, became his confederate and confidant; Goerdeler wrote of his "noble humanity and Christian charity" when in November, Brandenburg became the executor of Goerdeler's political testament, and smuggled the unofficial section of his manuscripts and letters out of prison. Goerdeler's ambitions knew no bounds, and he had visions of his essays on economics and social policy becoming worldrenowned. He became obsessed, and his appearance disturbed Ritter:

It was a man grown old who stood before me, shackled hand and foot, in the same light summer clothes as he had had on when he was captured, shabby and collarless, face thin and drawn, strangely different. But it was his eyes that shocked me most. They were once bright grey eyes and had flashed beneath the heavy eyebrows; that had always been the most impressive thing about him. Now there was no light in them; they were the eyes of a blind man, yet like nothing I had ever seen before.[24]

255

Goerdeler, in fact, felt that his God had failed him; his family was being persecuted on his account, his brother condemned as his accomplice.

Yet the Nazis, responsive to his reputation, seemed anxious to keep him alive and productive. The official part of his writings, which he undertook in order to keep himself alive, was work set him by the "intellectuals" of the S.S. on the future administration of the State under Nazism. Other "expert" prisoners, notably Schulenberg and Popitz, were also employed in the same way, and their ideas actually became the subject of a conference of S.D. officials at Wannsee towards the end of 1944. There is evidence, too, that Dohnanyi's views were sought, probably at a later stage than this. The execution of men as able, willing and productive as Goerdeler and Popitz before they had been milked of their ideas seemed wasteful, and Kaltenbrunner, who was scarcely an intellectual, was somehow persuaded to keep them alive. However, the time had come for them to die. Müller remembers the morning of 2 February when the executioners arrived to hurry Goerdeler away; he heard the voice of the executioner shouting. "Come on, come on, come on." Goerdeler was hanged at Plötzensee on 2 February, the same day as Popitz. Goerdeler's brother Fritz was executed a month later.

According to Colvin, Canaris became the main source of outside information for the prisoners, and adopted his own technique to obtain the latest news from the jailers. He would ask his guards the most seemingly stupid questions in order to trick them into talking, extracting from them whenever possible the latest communique from the Wehrmacht, "I suppose by now we're pushing the Russians back over the Vistula?" Schlabrendorff heard him ask one day, and he also heard the reply, "Rubbish! The Russians are approaching the Oder." It would appear that after these discoveries at Zossen, Canaris, like Goerdeler, blinded his captors with an excess of conflicting evidence. Colvin quotes Schlabrendorff as saying that "for months Canaris baffled them with one ruse after another." His skill in acting a part, his cunning, his imagination, the ease with which he affected naïve stupidity and then emerged into the most subtle reasoning disarmed the security agents who interrogated him. "It was not so much lying," Lahousen commented to Colvin, "more an artistic distortion of the truth."[25]

Meanwhile Oster's interrogation had been taken over by Huppenkothen, although, according to Sonderegger, his previous interrogator, he had asked for the investigation to be conducted by someone else. There was no doubt at all in the mind of the Gestapo officials that Oster was fully implicated in the conspiracy; there was ample evidence revealed in the files at Zossen. Oster's son, Major Achim Oster, managed to reach Sonderegger and request that, if his father were condemned, the fact would not be published. Sonderegger believed that Oster's case was hopeless; in any event it was out of his hands. He knew that Oster's wife and daughter, Barbara, who was a nurse, were continually pressing for permission to see Oster. They were unsuccessful. "The women were severely but decently dealt with," was Sonderegger's comment.

The maltreatment of the prisoners under interrogation continued. Christine von Dohnanyi testified:

My brother Klaus Bonhoeffer and also my brother-in-law Rüdiger Schleicher have been maltreated, too, but not by Sonderegger, I think. I know this from my brother Klaus because he informed me by a letter smuggled out of prison and he also sent laundry which was covered in blood. But as I said both my brother and brother-in-law were maltreated not by Sonderegger, but by the officials Baumert and Gunther. My other brother, Pastor Dietrich Bonhoeffer, during the entire period of his arrest, from 5 April 1943 until his assassination in Flossenbürg in April 1945 was constantly under the supervision of Sonderegger. Ever since the day in February 1945 when my brother Dietrich was taken away I never heard a word from him or about him, though I repeatedly asked Sonderegger to give me his address. I did not even know where he was. I could not say either whether Sonderegger maltreated him. I doubt it,

257

because I had the impression that unlike so many of the others Sonderegger was not completely devoid of human emotions and a touch of decency.[26]

Later when she had, as we shall see, a brief moment with her husband, in Dr. Tietze's hospital, Dohnanyi told her about his experiences in prison:

He told me Sonderegger had not tortured or maltreated him, but through letters which my husband smuggled out of prison to me I had learned at the time he was left without any medical care in spite of being practically paralyzed from diphtheria. But I cannot say whether Sonderegger should be made responsible for this. For a period, Sonderegger was represented by the notorious Stavitsky, who was known for his cruelty. But while Sonderegger did not physically hurt my husband, he did not do much to help him either.

Dr. Tietze, the doctor who had been called in at the time Dohnanyi was for a while transferred from the Prinz Albrechtstrasse to a police hospital in Berlin, has described the condition in which he found him:

There is no doubt that Dohnanyi was for a considerable period completely neglected, and since he was unable to look after himself he soon declined into a horrible state of physical decay. His nails were long and dirty, his hair untidy and uncut. When we had the opportunity to take charge of him, we first of all washed him and saw he had decent food. I had the chance to talk to him for some hours each day. I had him taken down from his cell to the medical wards so that we could talk undisturbed. He had special guards, but some of these were decent enough men who during the medical examinations left the room without any trouble, although they had been ordered not to do so. On such occasions when we were alone Dohnanyi told me about his sufferings.[27]

258

Dohnanyi's Letter to his Wife

A letter written by Dohnanyi to his wife on 8 March and smuggled out of prison has survived. The letters he sent to Christine were all written in his tidy, minute handwriting and, like the letters his wife wrote to him, were carried in a Thermos flask and other containers put in the parcels or suitcases which the prisoners were allowed to receive and send back out of prison. The letter of 8 March is one of the most moving statements to come from those still left alive in the Gestapo's hands:

My dear, you can hardly imagine how my heart beat when I opened the case and saw that jar with its little red cap, then the book, and then again the Thermos flask, which I opened with unseemly haste. At long last a few lines from you after more than six months, a gift for which I thanked dear God in my evening prayers. Thank you, my dear.

By the way, before I forget, in your letters don't even mention Sonderegger's name, because the letters might well come to the knowledge of his superiors. I don't want him to be suspected of being insufficiently tough, let alone granting me privileges. After all, I did mention him repeatedly in letters which were sent directly through him, and I dare say he feels flattered about it.

The interrogations go on and on, and I have no illusions about what I am facing unless some miracle happens. The misery all round us is so oppressive that I would gladly throw away the fragment of life left to me if it were not for you. But the very thought of you, of your great love, my dear, and my love for you gives me the will to live so strongly that sometimes I think it must win out. . . .

I am not afraid of any infectious disease. I know that I would lie down feeling that this may be a means of saving life not only for me but for many others whose cause is linked to mine. Certainly for Dietrich.

259

Of course, I put the diphtheria thing into my mouth immediately and chewed it, but it was not possible before seven-thirty in the evening since Ense had been sitting at my bed all the time, and I fear that the cotton-wool was dried out by then. Now I will eat the sweets infected with the diphtheria bacteria as quickly as possible.

For all I know, I may well be by now immune against diphtheria, but there can be no harm in trying once again, so do send me more. And if you can get something else different by all means send that too, but for goodness sake take care of *yourself,* because I am in constant fear that you might catch something. Be particularly careful with the colored handkerchiefs. I may well be infected even though I don't get ill myself.

I *must* get out of here and into a proper hospital. But in conditions where they cannot interrogate me any longer. I am trying to impress them with fainting-fits, bogus heart attacks and so forth. But the trouble is they are not impressed, and should I be taken to a hospital *without* some genuine new illness this might even be dangerous because they would make me fit again pretty quickly.

Sonderegger said today: 'It's in your best interest to have the interrogations concluded as quickly as possible. The Reichsführer [Himmler] is not interested in keeping you here. He wants you well again quickly.' Do you want me to translate this into plain language? 'Himmler wants the interrogations finished as soon as possible. Then while the indictment is being concocted they would like to put me in hospital, possibly in central Germany or Bavaria, and make me fit again very quickly. They know, of course, that in my present condition they cannot very well put me up for public trial, but in three or four weeks they would manage it.' That is what they want, and this is what I want to frustrate for these people. Believe me, dear, there is no proper solution except a genuine new illness. Don't fear for me; I'll get over it. But even if I don't, much would be achieved for the others and really nothing lost for me, for I have

260

nothing more to lose; *but I must try to preserve myself and live, if this be possible, for you.* That's why I prefer this uncertain form of life to certain death.

Forgive me, my sweetheart, for writing such ugly things to you. But I believe they don't frighten you. You know how things are, you probably know better than I do, and probably better than you would admit to me, because you are so very kind, my dear. But you don't have to be; I have come to terms with everything. I have seen and experienced so much here that there is really only one thing that would completely finish me, and that would be if, God forbid, anything happened to you, my dear. That must not happen; I pray God for this every day and every night, and that's why, apart from asking help for myself, I always think of you, your liberty, and your health. Never forget this, I beg you. Don't think that, because I am beyond ordinary help, I have become indifferent. Quite the contrary; I want to defend myself, I do indeed, but there is just nothing left now but a new illness, and there is little enough time left. For the trouble is, they've got everything, really everything, in their hands; there is no use denying this. Who the traitor is I still do not know; and in the last resort I don't really care.

I heard from Sonderegger today that Eberhard [Bethge] has been arrested too. He was arrested in our house in September, and I really cannot understand this at all. Luckily they don't connect him with me in any way. Sonderegger merely asked why he was staying with us. Apparently Sonderegger is unaware of the fact that he is Schleicher's son-in-law, and his acquaintance with Perels at least by reputation. Incidentally, it seems that Perels has made rather indiscreet statements about Dietrich. Well, by now they have so many statements to juggle with that things are getting more and more difficult, particularly since they are pretty thorough about it. I don't think that I can help very much more.

As for our code, let's stick to this: red indicates infected nourishment, such as a blot of red ink on the cup, for instance. I always have a good look at the Thermos flask as well as the cup, and I suppose you are doing the same. If 'regards from' appear on a wrapper even without particular emphasis, it means that it contains some news. If you indicate the items otherwise, for instance coffee, tea, or whatever it may be, just do it for me to see who is at home, and I lay particular stress on seeing your own handwriting—my dear, I long to send you a proper love letter, and all the time I have to mention these horrible things—but then we have to work on this together, and I do think sometimes we succeed. I think there must be very few men who are as happy as I am. The many many terrible things that have happened which I have been aware of during the past month have given me a deeper awareness. The one comfort which makes up the wealth of my life is you, you, you. You know, my dear, for a while I wondered if I shouldn't simply pretend to be quite cheerful, rather than let you share in the ugly thoughts so often uppermost in my mind, but I believe this would not be right. You have a strong heart, my darling, and I know you would rather live *with* me than *beside* me—or am I being selfish? For my part, I am wonderfully strengthened by the feeling that you know all about me. Above all, my dear, so long as we can act, we must act; the war situation or the S.S. can ruin us at any time, but what I am more afraid of than anything else is to be removed from Berlin. I want, in all circumstances, to stay here, as near to you as possible. For this makes me feel I am not quite helplessly in the hands of those swine. So it all comes back to the one and only remedy, a new illness. What I am also very much worried about is what might happen to the parents. I wish I could help, but can I? My angel, my dear, that you love me is really my greatest happiness, I should like to kneel before you and thank you. I pray that God will fulfil this wish. Kisses. H.

And now, my darling, I must send you a love letter after all. Why on earth not! I destroyed your letter immediately—but not really immediately, only after I could recite it almost by heart. My sweet angel, if I think of all the others, I keep on realizing that no one is as well off as I, no one has a wife like I have, and if sometimes I was being unfair or in a hurry, or had 'no time' to show you how fond I was of you, you've surely known it all the time, haven't you, my dear?

What you have been and are to me and to the children could have made me one of the happiest men under God's sun. Still, I believe we were right to worry about the fate of others, which is what makes one become political. Oh, how I would like to talk to you, really talk with you! One other thing, I have come to realize that your suggestions codifying the inscriptions is much better than mine. So let's stick to this. Flour, coffee means news, but 'regards from' is quite unnecessary. Otherwise, let's stick to what we have already agreed. But do please be careful. I just heard that Brigitte has been arrested, because they think she knows where Gisevius is. I take it that the children are absolutely sure that they have to keep silent! Renate too! My darling heart, love me as I love you. Somehow, I feel everything will turn out all right. Kisses, kisses, kisses, my dear. Hans.[28]

During one of the heaviest of the air-raids, Dietrich Bonhoeffer had managed to slip unobserved from the line of prisoners standing ready to be led to the air-raid shelter. He reached Dohnanyi's cell, and stayed with him for the duration of the raid undiscovered by the guards. But by the time Dohnanyi had managed to smuggle his long letter of 8 March to his wife out of prison, Dietrich had left the Prinz Albrechtstrasse. After the greater part of the prison had been destroyed the previous month, Himmler had ordered the removal of most of the prisoners remaining in this virtually unusable building. The war situation was in any case very grave; by mid-January the Russian armies had broken through to the Oder, and the evacuation of prisoners from the camps and other places of detention to centers in the south and west was taking place.

The Final Weeks: Dohnanyi's Indictment and Execution

Among the first to leave the Prinz Albrechtstrasse were

the former members of the Abwehr staff. On 7 February several of the prisoners were loaded into a motorcoach and taken under the supervision of Sonderegger to the concentration camp at Flossenbürg; among them were Canaris, Oster, Schacht, Thomas, Halder, Sack and Strünck; Schacht had been taken back to Berlin from Ravensbrück on 3 February, the day of the heavy raid on Berlin. The journey now to Flossenbürg, in south-west Germany, lasted fifteen hours, and the condition of the camp when the prisoners finally arrived seemed ominous. Schacht whispered to Thomas: "Not one of us will get out of here alive."

Stavitsky, the Gestapo interrogator, had recently been appointed commandant of the camp. Every morning at about six o'clock the condemned prisoners, both men and women, were stripped naked before being marched to their place of execution. After they had been shot in the back of the head or hanged on a gallows set up in a shed at the end of the courtyard, their bodies were carried in the sight of everyone to a pyre where they were burned. The prisoners who stayed alive were often ill-treated; Thomas on several occasions saw Canaris endure having his face slapped by the guards.

According to evidence collected by Abshagen from one of Canaris's fellow-prisoners at Flossenbürg, Colonel Lunding, former director of Danish Military Intelligence, the Admiral remained always neatly dressed in spite of what he had had to endure at the Prinz Albrechtstrasse. He was for some reason allowed to keep his civilian suit, while the other prisoners were clothed as convicts. Canaris wore a grey suit and a grey, tweed overcoat, which he always put on when he left his cell, and except on the day of his death, he always wore a tie.

At Flossenbürg the prisoners were better able to make contact with each other through tapping on the walls of their cells. They did not use the morse code, but adopted the simpler prison system of dividing the alphabet into five groups of five letters each, omitting the letter "j"; they tapped the group number first, then the number of the letter in the group. Men with any connections with military Intelligence were housed in a separate block, and Lunding

264

found himself imprisoned in the cell next to Canaris. They introduced themselves at night by the tapping code. The interrogations continued in the supreme effort to trap Canaris completely in the act of conspiracy. At Flossenbürg, Lunding noticed, he was still not treated as utterly condemned, and during the latter part of March Kaltenbrunner himself came to question him. Lunding saw them walking up and down in the prison courtyard—Kaltenbrunner, large and uncouth, talking in loud, angry tones, and Canaris, slender and elegant, arguing with emphatic gestures.

On 7 February Bonhoeffer and Müller were taken from their cells at the Prinz Albrechtstrasse and driven to Buchenwald. Bonhoeffer still hoped that he might be acquitted, since the evidence against him remained very slight. Notable prisoners of many nationalities had been brought to Buchenwald and, with the end of the war in sight, their treatment became much more lenient.[29] The prisoners could move about and talk freely. Among them was the Englishman, Captain Payne Best, who has written a full account of his imprisonment; he was deeply impressed by Bonhoeffer, who seemed to him possessed by "humility and sweetness;" in a letter written to Leibholtz in 1951 he wrote of Bonhoeffer:

... without exception the finest and most lovable man I ever met . . . . quite calm and normal, seemingly at perfect ease . . . . his soul really shone in the dark desperation of our prison . . . . we were in complete agreement that our warders and guards needed pity far more than we and that it was absurd to blame them for their actions.[30]

Schlabrendorff was among the prisoners who remained in the Prinz Albrechtstrasse. His case was due for secret hearing on 16 March when, as we have seen, he defended himself successfully and was acquitted. But he was sent back to the Gestapo prison and told later by Habecker, a Gestapo officer, that the outcome of the trial was an "error" and that he must, in consequence, continue in captivity. A few days later he was taken, with several additional prisoners, to join the others in Flossenbürg. Here he was manacled and kept in solitary confinement.

Dohnanyi remained at the Prinz Albrechtstrasse until 19 March, when he came under the care of Dr. Tietze and was removed to hospital and kept there under guard. His health improved under medical care, and he was able to see his wife once more as well as unburden himself to his doctor. Dr. Tietze has testified:

> He asked me to do everything I could to enable him to see his wife. This was of course outside my official powers and rather difficult. But we managed to do it by putting him in a bathtub and then hiding his wife in a cupboard. That way they could have a brief glimpse of each other.[31]

Both Christine von Dohnanyi and Dr. Tietze have revealed that there was an abortive plan to rescue Dohnanyi from confinement when, early in April, Tietze was warned that Dohnanyi was to be taken away. According to Christine von Dohnanyi:

> On the night from 4 to 5 April there was a plan to liberate my husband. . . . . Evidently Sonderegger had learned of it, and during the late evening of 4 April he arranged a very much stronger guard. Considering the chaotic conditions in Berlin at this time, such measures were really no longer necessary; Sonderegger need not have feared being made responsible, or being punished by his superiors. At least this is my opinion. Instead when Sonderegger came to fetch my husband from the police hospital on 5 April and was asked by Tietze what was going to happen now to Dohnanyi, he simply said: 'Dohnanyi has only himself to blame'. And when Tietze asked him point blank, 'Does this mean that Dohnanyi is to be killed?', Sonderegger merely shrugged his shoulders. He knew quite well that my husband was to be murdered.[32]

According to the evidence of Dr. Tietze, Dohnanyi was removed early on the morning of 6 April, not the day before. He had had the chance to see his wife for the last time on 4 April. When he left the hospital on a stretcher, he was barely conscious. Dr. Tietze has described his condition:

> I remember distinctly that on 5 April Dohnanyi had received a dose of morphia from me; also he was under the influence of a very strong dose of luminal, and he had half a gram of morphia in his hand. It is inconceivable, according to my medical judgment, that he was fit for trial on either 5 or 6 April.[33]

Sonderegger had received Gestapo orders to transfer Dohnanyi to Sachsenhausen concentration camp for trial on 6 April by a "special order of the Führer." Tietze had given Dohnanyi the drugs as a final attempt to delay the trial; as he put it: "This as a matter of fact was one of our regular tactics to delay action being taken against people in great danger." He gave him both luminal and morphia in the middle of the night, a few hours before Sonderegger came to remove him.

Huppenkothen went to Sachsenhausen the same morning to present the indictment at Dohnanyi's "court martial," as the hearing was termed. Dohnanyi was carried in on a stretcher; Huppenkothen averred later that he was fully conscious of the proceedings, although Dr. Tietze remained certain that he could not possibly have been in a fit state to plead. The court martial lasted until eight o'clock that night, and Dohnanyi was faced with many incriminating documents written in his own hand. It would appear that he did what he could to defend himself and postpone receiving a death sentence, but the evidence against him was in any case conclusive. He was condemned to death. Prior to his trial, he had tried to win time by offering to meet Himmler and discuss the situation with him and the need to institute peace negotiations.[34] It was of no use. He was hanged on 9 April at Sachsenhausen. When Christine von Dohnanyi went to see Sonderegger to ask about him, he merely handed her her husband's clothes. She knew then that he was dead.

It was Hitler himself who ordered the destruction of the men who had conspired to remove him. During the endless shuffling of prisoners of distinction from camp to camp which characterized the last, uncertain days of the war, Bonhoeffer was finally reunited with his friends at the extermination camp of Flossenbürg on Sunday 8 April. He had been moved from Buchenwald five days before, crowded into a prison van powered by a wood-burning engine, and taken to Flossenbürg, only to be sent on again to some undefined destination since the camp was too crowded to receive more prisoners. The following day, Sunday 8 April, Bonhoeffer is described by Payne Best as holding "a little service" and speaking "in a manner which reached the hearts of us all." As the service finished, officers of the Gestapo arrived to take the pastor on the journey back to Flossenbürg. "This is the end," said Bonhoeffer, as he took his leave of his fellow-prisoners, "but for me it is the beginning of life!"

There had already been a panic search for Bonhoeffer at Flossenbürg during the night of 7 April. The Gestapo's records were in chaos. Schlabrendorff was wakened by a guard who insisted that he was Bonhoeffer. Müller, in fact, had been detached from the group of prisoners in the prison-van before it had left the area of Flossenbürg a few days before. Evidently Bonhoeffer should have been detained as well, or Müller had been kept back in error for him. They had for a while been handcuffed together.

"Court Martial" at Flossenbürg: Canaris, Oster and Bonhoeffer Executed

Kaltenbrunner, on direct orders from Hitler, had demanded that a summary court-martial be held at Flossenbürg and the senior members of the former Abwehr condemned and executed. Huppenkothen was once more to act as prosecutor, and Otto Thorbeck, the S.S. judge, was to preside. On 7 April Huppenkothen hurried to the camp and the court was set up. The first hearing took place during the afternoon of Sunday 8 April. Huppenkothen presented the case first of all against Oster, who was forced to admit his complicity in the conspiracy, though he denied that he had ever plotted to assassinate Hitler. He asked to be sent to the front to fight as an ordinary soldier.

The trial of Canaris started at eight o'clock in the evening, and he denied all personal complicity in the conspiracy, although he admitted knowledge of it. At one stage he was confronted with Oster, whose own admissions were said to have implicated him.[35] In any case, Canaris had to be condemned; these were the orders from the Head of State. Canaris also asked to be sent to the front. The others whose cases were heard, all without the help of any defense counsel, included Sack, Gehre and Bonhoeffer. All alike were condemned.

Canaris, Oster and Bonhoeffer were tried and condemned to death a few days before the American armies arrived to liberate Flossenbürg camp. They were executed in the courtyard on Monday 9 April. Like the rest of those sentenced, they walked naked to their deaths.[36]

The evidence of how they died had to be pieced together later from fragmentary records which survived the war. At the time Schlabrendorff questioned the guards at Flossenbürg after the executions and discovered the identity of those who had died, Bonhoeffer's Bible and his volume of Goethe were left lying in the guard-room.

Josef Müller has given us the story of his experiences on the morning of the execution:

Just before six o'clock there was a great noise; I heard the numbers of cells being shouted out. I listened for my own because one of the warders had told me the night before, 'They've forgotten you this time'. Then I heard Canaris's voice, but I couldn't understand what he was saying. Later Peter Churchill and two other British prisoners told me that my friends were dead. 'Their bodies are being burned behind the cells,' he said. I could see the smoke through the little cell window. It was nauseating to see fragments of unburned skin in

269

the air, a last physical contact, as it were, with my friends Canaris and Oster.

After the trial, Lunding remembered that Canaris had said: "This is the end. Badly mishandled. My nose broken. I have done nothing against Germany. If you survive, please tell my wife." Lunding watched the naked figure of Canaris being led to execution.[37]

The doctor on duty at Flossenbürg was to describe later the manner in which Bonhoeffer met his death:

Between five and six o'clock in the morning the prisoners, including Admiral Canaris, General Oster, Dr. Sack and Pastor Bonhoeffer, were taken from their cells, and the verdict was read to them. Through the half-open door of his cell, I had seen the pastor kneeling in prayer. I have never before been so moved as I was then. His devotion was absolute; he appeared almost cheerful. Later, in front of the gallows, he repeated a short prayer, and then climbed up to the rope with complete composure. He was dead in a few seconds. During my fifty years' experience in medicine, I have never seen anyone die so calmly and so trustingly.[68]

Notes

Principal Sources. Of the many books on the German resistance movement to Hitler and the leading personalities involved, we have drawn particularly on: *The Nemesis of Power* (1953) by J. Wheeler-Bennett; *The Secret War Against Hitler* (1966) by Fabian von Schlabrendorff (a revision of his earlier book, *Revolt against Hitler,* 1948); *Chief of Intelligence* (1951) by Ian Colvin; *The von Hassell Diaries* (1947); *Canaris* (1949) by Karl Heinz Abshagen; *Goerdeler und die Deutsche Widerstandsbewegung* (1954; revised 1963, and translated as *The German Resistance,* 1958) by Gerhard Ritter; *To the Bitter End* (1948) by Hans Bernd Gisevius (revised 1960); *Dietrich Bonhoeffer* (1967) by Eberhard Bethge; *German Military Intelligence* (1954) by Paul Leverkuehn; *Germans against Hitler* (1964) by Terence Prittie, and *Hitler* (revised edition 1964) by Alan Bullock, and our *The July Plot* (1964). In addition, we have drawn, with the reservations pointed out elsewhere, on *The Downfall of the German Secret Service* (1956) by Karl Bartz. The text recorded verbatim at the Nuremberg Trial of 1945-6 was published in Britain by H.M. Stationary Office in 23 volumes with the title: *Trial of the German War Criminals: Proceedings of the International Military Tribunal*; reference to this below is abbreviated as *I.M.T.*

Other books referred to or quoted from are mentioned individually in the Notes below, together with the sources of the various unpublished documents on which we have drawn. Statements made to us by individual witnesses are credited in the appropriate Notes; the authors are referred to by their initials, R.M. and H.F.

INTRODUCTION

WAS IT RESISTANCE?

This chapter, which portrays the principal men involved in the German resistance movement and outlines the special problems which faced them, owes its general line of argument to all the sources quoted above, and especially to prolonged discussion by H.F. with survivors from the movement.

In addition to the books already listed, we have drawn for the three chapters of Part One on Margret Boveri's, *Treason in the Twentieth Century*; Gert Buchheit's, *Ludwig Beck*; Gerald Reitlinger's, *The S.S.*; Hjalmar Schacht's, *My First Seventy-Six Years*. We are also particularly grateful to Otto John, Dr. Werner Best, Admiral Patzig and General Achim Oster for the help they have given us on points of detail connected with the chapters in this Part.

1. Various accounts are given of how Canaris reached Europe. According to Abshagen, he fled from Chile, using a Chilean passport, on a Dutch ship bound for Plymouth. Here he is said to have satisfied the British authorities, left for Holland to reach Germany by the spring of 1916. Bartz says that he fled to the Argentine from Chile and then, using a Chilean passport, sailed to neutral Holland, from where he made his way to Germany. Colvin claims that he fled direct from Chile with a Chilean passport, but sailed by a British ship to Europe.

2. Documentation of Colonel Heinz preserved in the Munich *Institut für Zeitgeschichte*.

3. For the background to the Freikorps movement, see Wheeler-Bennett, *The Nemesis of Power*, pp. 33-44. The Reichswehr was the surviving German Army; the Freikorps were, in effect, members of a volunteer army formed in individual units from disbanded servicemen with strong nationalist sympathies and for a while tolerated by the Allies as a further protection against Communism. For the Kapp *putsch* see also Wheeler-Bennett, *op. cit.*, pp. 75 *et seq.* This *putsch* was an abortive right-wing movement which made an attempt to take over the government after the war; Canaris, among other fellow-officers, was one of those who openly opted for the rebel "government" of Kapp and Lüttwitz. Thanks to a general strike, it lasted only a few days. Canaris later justified himself by claiming that he *would* have been loyal to the movement if Noske, the Minister of Defense, had stayed in Berlin and made an appeal to the Army, rather than take flight with the rest. When the *putsch* failed, Canaris was among those arrested; he was however released after a few days. The rightful government (at that time Social Democrat) realized that it needed the support of these officers under arrest, such as Canaris, and let them go. Gessler, a Democrat, succeeded Noske as Minister of Defense, and established good relations with Canaris, so that he was not among the 170 officers, including twelve generals, who were dismissed or reprimanded after the *putsch*. In the Navy only four officers were retired.

4. It must be made clear from the outset that Canaris was never suspected of being directly involved in the murder; he was not in Berlin when it happened. He denied helping the murderers to escape. When he had to face the parliamentary com-

mission of inquiry early in 1926, he came under heavy attack from the Left. It is ironic that one of the principal men involved in this attack was Dr. Julius Leber, who was later to be so prominent a member of the resistance.

5. The official reports on Canaris before he took over the Abwehr still survive. Admiral Bastian, reporting on him in 1934, said that he had "special talents and inclination" for diplomatic rather than purely service interests. In 1931 he had been praised as stern but warmhearted, though this report adds that his standards are, perhaps, too high, "because he is liable to demand too much of himself as well as those under his command." Copies of these reports are held by the Military Archive in Freiburg.

6. Quoted by Boveri, *Treason in the Twentieth Century*, p. 254.

7. Notes on Canaris written or completed by Best in Copenhagen in 1949 and given by Dr. Best to the authors.

8. See the authors' book, *Himmler* p. 62. Frau Heydrich claimed in conversation with H.F. that her husband had, she was certain, no Jewish blood. However, the threat of investigation was always a sword of Damocles, and probably, in so far as he knew about the threat, it determined him to harden still further his attitude to the Jews, which was exactly what Hitler and Himmler wanted.

9. In *Germany's Underground*, Allen Dulles describes (pp. 31-2) how Goerdeler visited both Britain and the United States during 1937, "to find out whether there would be any support abroad for anti-Hitler activity within Germany." He adds that during his stay in the States Goerdeler wrote a political testament to be published in the even of his death (or, with his approval, before that) which was an "indictment of Nazi acts, policies and intentions."

10. Field-Marshal Milch told H.F. that on the day of Blomberg's wedding there was a ceremonial luncheon for the Luftwaffe at which Göring was presiding. Göring asked Milch to take over from him at around 2.30 hours because he had to attend the wedding. Milch is convinced Göring knew all about the "past" of the woman Blomberg was marrying. This is supported by Gisevius in his book, *Wo Ist Nebe?*, p. 178 *et seq.* As for Frau von Blomberg's behavior when Oster was waiting with her while Blomberg read the papers announcing his dismissal, this was described to H.F. by Oster's son, General Achim Oster.

11. For fuller accounts of these cases see the authors' biographies, *Göring* pp. 152-5 and *Himmler* pp. 63-7. A transcript of the Fritsch case, not before published, appears as an Appendix in Schlabrendorff's book *The Secret War against Hitler*.

12. At one stage, apparently, Beck considered resigning at the same time as Schacht, to make the effect more pronounced. See Gisevius's evidence at Nuremberg, *I.M.T.*, XII, p. 236.

13. For this and the quotation which follows. See Schacht, *My First Seventy-Six Years*, pp. 388-9.
14. Arthur Nebe has found his principal protagonist in his friend Gisevius. But it must be remembered that Nebe led one of Himmler's notorious Action Groups which massacred Jews and Communists in the East. According to Gisevius, Nebe did everything he could to stem the slaughter, but none of the Action Groups could escape taking part. See the authors' book, *The Incomparable Crime*, pp. 107-29.
15. See *I.M.T.*, XII, p. 210
16. See *I.M.T.*, I, pp. 272-3 for this and the following quotations.

PART ONE   II FIASCO IN 1938

1. See *I.M.T.*, XII, p. 235.
2. See Boveri, *Treason in the 20th Century*, p. 243.
3. See *I.M.T.*, XII, p. 237.
4. We are most grateful to Otto John for giving us this account of the meeting with Professor Bonhoeffer, at which he was present.
5. Dohnanyi also met his future wife, Christine Bonhoeffer, at this school. We are grateful to members of the Dohnanyi family for certain details which appear in this chapter.
6. For this and subsequent quotations from official memoranda, etc., and also for the text of Winston Churchill's letter, see Woodward and Butler, *Documents on British Foreign Policy*, Series III, Vol. II, pp. 683-9.
7. For a somewhat differing account of the passage of the Churchill letter from Britain to Berlin, see Schlabrendorff, *op. cit.*, p. 95, and Wheeler-Bennett, *The Nemesis of Power*, p. 413, note.
8. F. W. Heinz's *Stosstrupp* consisted of some thirty completely reliable young officers, students and working men. The unit was to enter the Chancellery, arrest Hitler and take him to some secure spot while units of the 23rd Division occupied key centres in Berlin. This was to be done at the moment Hitler gave the order to attack Czechoslovakia. Heinz was anxious to involve Leuschner, the labor leader, in the plot. See also Schlabrendorff's detailed account of the plan, *The Secret War against Hitler*, pp. 100-101, and Gisevius's evidence in *I.M.T.*, XII, pp. 238-9.
9. Halder testified after the war that:

> Even among Hitler's opponents in the senior-officer corps his success made an enormous impression. I do not know if a non-military man can understand what it means to have the Czechoslovak army eliminated by a stroke of the pen. ... I want to emphasize once more the extreme importance which must be attributed to this Munich agreement. . . .

274

From this time on you could always hear the saying: 'Well, the Führer will do it somehow, he did it at Munich.'

Goerdeler wrote to a friend in the United States: "The development of the past weeks can only be called very dangerous. . . . Hitler and Göring have bluffed the entire world. But the world had been warned and informed in time. . . . By shying from a small risk Mr Chamberlain has made war inevitable." (See Allen Dulles, *Germany's Underground*, pp. pp. 47-8.) When Halder was interrogated by American Army officers after the war, he explained that although at this time he wanted Hitler to be removed, he was not satisfied with the vague political program under discussion by the conspirators. He felt that it was the duty of the politicians to get rid of Hitler, not the generals,' since it was the politicians who had put him in power. See Dulles, *op. cit.*, pp. 43-4.

10. *I.M.T.*, XII, p. 242.

PART ONE   III ANTI-WAR EFFORT

1. *Von Hassell Diaries*, pp. 14-5. The quotations following are pp. 32 and 43.
2. Schlabrendorff, *The Secret War against Hitler*, p. 72.
3. Schacht in *My First Seventy-Six Years* claims at this particular time he was on his way to India.
4. Schlabrendorff, *op. cit.*, pp. 97-8. On p. 98 Schlabrendorff writes:

   Details of that conversation of 1939 vividly came back to me when, exactly ten years later, in 1949, I once again met with and talked with Churchill at his country estate. He showed me the entry of my name in the guest book of ten years before, and I was amazed at his keen memory. Later, while reviewing the years that lay between our two meetings, he told me that he afterwards realized that during the war he had been misled by his assistants about the considerable strength and size of the German anti-Hitler resistance.

5. *Von Hassell Diaries*, pp. 58-60.
6. For 'Operation Himmler', also known as Operation Gleiwitz, see below, page 64.
7. Quoted by Colvin in *Chief of Intelligence*, pp. 81-2.
8. There was, of course, a strong working-class element in the German underground, but it was only at a later stage that it had close connections with the right-wing upper-class element. A very critical assessment of resistance on the right is contained in a recent book, *Der Deutsche Widerstand gegen Hitler*. (see Selected Book-List under Schmitthenner.)
9. As an instance of the blind eye which the generals turned to the imminence of war, Colonel Bernd von Brauchitsch early in 1939 asked his father whether or not he should get married

in view of the possibility of war. Brauchitsch told him not to postpone his wedding. War was unlikely, he said, before 1941 or 1942. (Bernd von Brauchitsch in conversation with H.F.)

10. *I.M.T.*, XII, p. 246.

11. Gisevius, *To the Bitter End*, p. 358.

In addition to the books already listed, we have drawn on J. Lonsdale Bryans' *Blind Victory*, Gert Buchheit's *Ludwig Beck*, Allen Dulles's *Germany's Underground*, and Hjalmar Schacht's *My First Seventy-Six Years*. More especially we have drawn on Sas' unpublished report on his dealings with Oster and on the recollections of Otto John, Dr. Werner Best, Dr. Josef Müller, the Dohnanyi family, Friedrich Wilhelm Heinz and Alexander von Pfuhlstein.

1. *I.M.T.*, I, pp. 276-7. See also *I.M.T.*, III, pp. 191-2 for the full story.

2. According to Leverkuehn (*German Military Intelligence*, p. 46) the birth of what were to be the Brandenburg commando units, and later the Brandenburg Division, followed the Polish campaign. The first units of volunteers for special duties were raised in Brandenburg in October 1939; the corps developed into a battalion by 1940, and a division in December 1942. Men of German racial stock from the Sudetenland, Poland, Czechoslovakia, and so forth, who were fluent linguists and fitted to penetrate as agents into territory where special operations had to be carried out (often by men in mufti posing as local people) were the kind the Brandenburg units needed. Initially, these men were regarded as "confidential agents in uniform," and came under the control of Abwehr II. As their strength increased they came directly under Canaris's control, even though they were nominally under the command of the Army Group in whose area they might be operating. The Brandenburgers in the end spent a great deal of the war period in Yugoslavia. Both Colonel Heinz and Major-General Pfuhlstein were commanding officers of the Brandenburgers, Pfuhlstein established the full division in January 1943, and was its commanding officer.

3. *I.M.T.*, I, pp. 274-5.

4. See Leverkuehn, p. 29, for a diagram illustrating the structure of the Abwehr.

5. Grosscurth's importance is not restricted to his prominent rôle in the resistance. He was a prodigious diarist and note-taker, and a substantial selection of his documentation is to be published during 1969. After his dismissal from O.K.H. on 1 February 1940, he passed his papers to his wife before leaving for the front.

6. Bamler is one of the few survivors of the Abwehr still on active service. He is a general in the East German Army.

7. In addition to the various departments in the central Abwehr office, there were a number of regional centers. According to

Colvin, the Abwehr office in Königsberg directed their attention to Russia, that in Munich kept watch on the Balkans and Mediterranean, that in Cologne looked after France, and that in Hamburg, Britain, Scandinavia and the American continent. Canaris also kept his agents in foreign capitals and other cities where Germany had diplomatic representation, and some cities where she did not.

8. There was some suggestion that Dohnanyi was not a pure "Aryan" in Himmler's sense of the term; be that as it may, there was a special *'Führerbefehl'* that any blemish of this kind in Dohnanyi's case was to be overlooked. One of Dohnanyi's children was to become the distinguished conductor Christoph von Dohnanyi.

9. The Oster Study is referred to in some detail in the Huppenkothen files as *Ausarbeitung* (an elaborate paper) with the Nazi leaders indicated as: HI, RIBB, HEY, etc. The Oster study was discovered among the papers at Zossen. See below, Part III, Chapter II.

10. *I.M.T.,* XII, p. 249. For the reference to the Vatican discussions see ensuing pages.

11. It should be pointed out that it was common for businessmen and others to "acquire" a consulship of this kind for purposes of prestige. The title did not necessarily mean they carried out normal consular duties.

12. This memorandum, preserved at Freiburg, fills 21 pages of typescript and forms a part of the voluminous Grosscurth papers.

13. The authors received a letter from Sir Francis D'Arcy Osborne (later Duke of Leeds) shortly before his death in which he stressed that he never met Müller personally and, though aware of this approaches being made, he realized that the British government remained quite unaffected. See the authors' book, *The July Plot,* p. 225. When told of this letter, Professor Deutsch wrote to the authors:

> I agree, of course, that there were no real 'negotiations' and specifically emphasize this in my book. Yet the British government in the end did make a very real and rather formal commitment—little hope as it may have had by January that it would lead to anything. That his reports must have been full of references to the exchanges is indicated by their skeleton character after the reports that carried them had been sifted out at the request of the Vatican. Father Leiber said that 'about seven' from the British government were passed on to Müller by him and that about twice the Pope showed him communications in Osborne's hand. From these he then made his own notes for Müller. When interviewed by my friend Father Robert A. Graham, Osborne recalled that he had passed on a Vatican request to the

277

British government to destroy in its archives all vestiges of the exchanges, though he did not know much of this had been done. That was at the time of Dunkirk.

14. Memories differ as to the exact nature of the terms set down in the X Report, which appears to have been in the end a combination of what the notes from Rome held to be the British view and the kind of terms Beck, in particular, considered to be just. Memories of the survivors who saw the original document are carefully analyzed by Professor Deutsch in Chapter VII of his book *The Conspiracy against Hitler during the Twilight War.* Colonel Werner Schrader, in whose charge the key copy of the X Report was placed, according to evidence given us by his son, Dr. W. W. Schrader, had been a Stahlhelm leader in Brunswick at the time Hitler came to power, and had been held responsible for dissensions and bloodshed in that area owing to differences between the Party and the local Stahlhelm movement, which was strongly nationalist. Schrader had openly criticized the excesses of the storm-troopers in Hitler's presence at the Harzburg Congress of nationalists held in October 1931. He was arrested in 1933, but escaped the following year. When his re-arrest seemed imminent in 1936, Canaris stepped in and "rescued" him by making him a captain in the Munich Abwehr, from which he was later posted to Vienna. At the beginning of the war he was sent to O.K.H. at Zossen. Schrader had for long been responsible for collecting together the kind of evidence against the régime which Beck and Dohnanyi favored. The material had been stored originally in big metal containers and concealed in his mother's house. The files were eventually absorbed during the later 1930s into Oster's and Dohnanyi's main collection.

15. Hassell, *Diaries,* pp. 117-8.
16. Hassell, *op. cit.,* pp. 125-6. The quotation which follows will be found on p. 130.
17. For the meeting between Beck and Halder on 16 January, see Schlabrendorff, *The Secret War against Hitler,* p. 107.
18. The record of this conversation is preserved in the Freiburg archives, among the Grosscurth papers. Helldorf, a former officer in the Hussars and a post-war member of the nationalist Freikorps movement, had also been a Brownshirt leader in Berlin during the early Nazi campaigns. He became Police President in Berlin in 1935, but his 'turn round', as it was called, began in 1937. He was fully involved in the Army conspiracy of 1938.
19. Count von der Goltz told H.F.
20. The authors possess a copy of the German version of the Sas statement, originally recorded after the war in Dutch. The German version is preserved in the archive at Freiburg.

21. Sas is, of course, wrong in naming General Student in this connection. The Luftwaffe officer who made a forced landing in Belgium was Major Helmut Reinberger. The documents he was carrying gave the complete plan of attack in the West. Reinberger attempted to destroy the documents, which he was carrying to a staff conference, but he was only partly successful. For the repercussions in Germany, see the authors' *Göring*, p. 220.

22. A close personal friend of Oster was Franz Liedig, a naval captain who died in 1967. In conversation with H.F. shortly before his death, he said how much he hated to talk of those sad days. He told Professor Deutsch that he had accompanied Oster on one of his visits to Sas's residence and waited for him outside. When Oster returned after a very brief absence he was at first too moved to speak. Then he begged Liedig to keep his regard for him whatever might happen. It would be easier, he said, to kill a man for a cause than do what he had done. How many people, he wondered, would even begin to understand his motives.

PART TWO   II THE ABWEHR NETWORK

In addition to the books already listed, we have drawn for this chapter on the Schellenberg *Memoirs*, the Goebbels *Diaries*, and our own book *The July Plot* (*The Men Who Tried to Kill Hitler*). We are also particularly indebted to the *Institut für Zeitgeschichte* in Munich for making available extensive unpublished material relating to Canaris and the Abwehr from Colonel Friedrich Wilhelm Heinz.

1. *I.M.T.*, XII, p. 250.
2. Heinz records, Munich Institute.
3. *I.M.T.*, XII, pp. 272-5.
4. *I.M.T.*, I, pp. 277-8.
5. The ex-Kaiser was offered refuge in Britain on the fall of Holland, but he refused. He kept himself as aloof as possible from any potential involvement in German or any other political activity.
6. Baldur von Schirach after his release from Spandau confirmed this in conversation with H.F.
7. Several young officers associated with Tresckow were dedicated anti-Nazis. Among them were Graf Heinrich von Lehndorff, Graf Hans von Hardenberg, Colonel Freiherr von Gersdorff, Colonel Schultze-Brettger, Colonel Alexander von Voss (son-in-law of the resistance leader in France, von Stuelpnagel), Major Ulrich von Oertzen, Captain Eggert and Lieutenant Hans Albrecht von Boddien. See Wheeler-Bennett, *The Nemesis of Power*, pp. 514-5.
8. Hassell, *Diaries*, pp. 219-20.
9. According to Abshagen in *Canaris*, p. 273 *et seq.*, after a

foolish attempt to land ten "saboteurs" in the U.S.A. who had been immediately captured, Hitler blamed Canaris. When Canaris countered that they had, after all, been Party volunteers, Hitler replied: "You should have used criminals or Jews!" Canaris immediately seized on this, made it a *Führerbefehl* (a special Hitler order), and started at once to use Jews on alleged work for the Azwehr.

10. *I.M.T.*, XII, p. 246. The quotation immediately following is on p. 288.
11. Schellenberg, *Memoirs*, pp. 399-400.
12. *Schellenberg, op. cit.*, pp. 403-4.
13. For a full account of Schellenberg's career in the S.D. and his relations with Himmler, see the authors' book *Heinrich Himmler*.
14. Schellenberg, *op. cit.*, p. 160. The quotations which follow are on pp. 405-6.
15. *I.M.T.*, I, pp. 284-6.
16. See above, Chapter I, note 8.
17. For a full account of the meeting between Bonhoeffer and Bell, and of the parallel visit to Sweden of Dr. Hans Schönfeld, research director of the World Council of Churches in Geneva, see the authors' book *The July Plot*, pp. 29-37. Also Bethge, *Dietrich Bonhoeffer*, pp. 850 *et seq.*
18. Hassell, *op. cit.*, p. 236. The quotation following is from p. 237.
19. Schlabrendorff, *The Secret War against Hitler*, p. 146.
20. *I.M.T.*, XXI, pp. 60-1. Halder also explained the dilemma he was in, and the effect of the oath of personal loyalty to Hitler on the will of the Army officers who might otherwise have more readily defected, when he was interrogated after the war. He said:

> I am the last masculine member of a family who for 300 years were soldiers. . . . In the dictionary of a German soldier the terms 'treason' and 'plot against the State' do not exist. I was in the awful dilemma of one who had the duty of a soldier and also a duty which I considered higher. Innumerable of my old comrades were in the same dilemma. I chose the duties I esteem higher. The majority of my comrades esteemed the duty to the flag higher. You may be assured that this is the worst dilemma that a soldier may be faced with.

See Dulles, *Germany's Underground*, p. 38. The oath to Hitler was mostly used as an alibi for inactivity.
21. *I.M.T.*, XII, pp. 256-7.
22. Hassell, *op. cit.*, p. 214.
23. Hassell, *op. cit.*, p. 232.
24. Hassell, *op. cit.*, p. 245.

25. Hassell, *op. cit.*, pp. 256-7. Late in April 1942, Weizsäcker finally broke his friendly contact with Hassell on the grounds that neither the former ambassador nor his wife were any longer safe to know. Hitler regarded them, he said, as "peculiarly impossible people." When at the end of the following year, 1943, Weizsäcker became Hitler's representative at the Vatican, he resumed his exhortations to the conspirators to take action against the Führer, whom he continued nevertheless dutifully to serve from the relative security of his place beside the Pope.
26. Schlabrendorff, *op. cit.*, pp. 196-7.
27. This statement by Greta Kuckhoff is preserved in the Munich archive.

In this chapter we are particularly indebted to the *Institut für Zeitgeschichte* in Munich for the unpublished affidavits made by Josef Müller and many others during the successive cases heard post-war concerning Sonderegger, Roeder and Huppenkothen, and more especially in this chapter in relation to Schmidhuber. We are particularly grateful to Pastor Bethge and to the Dohnanyi family for records of statements made by Frau Christine von Dohnanyi.

1. This man was called David; he was arrested carrying dollars and jewellery intended for an emigré Czech Jewess who had gone to Switzerland.
2. According to a statement made by Frau von Dohnanyi after the war, Schmidhuber was

> finally arrested by a man called Captain Brede who had participated in his currency deals to a considerable extent by appropriating substantial sums of foreign currency made available by Schmidhuber. He had recently quite definitely come over to the side of the prosecutors, presumably in order to make up for his alleged anti-Nazi past, and was consequently tougher than ever. It was he who was sent to Italy and who brought Schmidhuber back in handcuffs.

3. Affidavit made by Christine von Dohnanyi. A V-man was a confidence man, "V" standing for *vertrauen* (trusted).
4. Müller explained his position carefully to H.F. After the war, having survived after being for so long on the point of death, he wanted to forget the worst aspects of the past. He therefore did not attempt to answer Bartz's book point for point where he knew it was inaccurate. Some further background to the Schmidhuber affair is given in an affidavit made by Nicholas Ficht who, from May 1942, was in charge of the Abwehr in Munich. Müller, he claims, received his orders direct from Berlin; Schmidhuber up to 1941 held the rank of captain in the Abwehr; then for a period he was released in

281

order to carry on with his normal work, returning to service with the Abwehr "late in 1941 or early in 1942" with the rank of major. Ficht says that when looking into Schmidhuber's case after his escape to Italy, he proposed that Schmidhuber be charged with desertion because he could find no record that he had ever been officially released from active service. It was with Ficht's knowledge that Schmidhuber went to Czechoslovakia with an assistant called Ickrath, a captain, in order to organize the transference of the Czech Jewess's money to Switzerland. While they were still in Prague, Ficht received a warning from the customs officials that Schmidhuber and Ickrath were involved in currency offenses. It was Ficht who sent Müller to Italy to persuade Schmidhuber to return after his refusal to obey the initial orders he had received to do so. When Ficht was later interrogated by Roeder and Noack he gained the impression that they were trying to saddle Müller, then himself under arrest, with the offenses of which Schmidhuber and Ickrath were guilty.

5. Statement made by Roeder on 2 October 1950 during the investigations into his own and Sonderegger's conduct during the war. For Ickrath, see previous note.
6. Statement made by Dr Müller on 22 September 1950.
7. Affidavit made by Karl Süss, 19 December 1946.
8. The White Rose movement became a national one among intellectuals opposed to Hitler.
9. Hassell, *op. cit.*, pp. 295-6. The quotations which follow are from pp. 281-6. For Eugen Gerstenmaier's notable participation in the resistance movement see *The July Plot*. Dr. Gerstenmaier is the equivalent in the Bundeshaus of the British Speaker to the House of Commons.
10. See Schlabrendorff, *op. ct.*, pp. 223-34 on the moral issue of breaking one's oath of allegiance to a head of State.
11. Gisevius says of Olbricht:

> In the spring of 1942, Oster had won over General Olbricht, the man who from now on directed the technical headquarters of our conspiracy. In the O.K.W., Olbricht held the office of chief of the *Allgemeine Heeresamt* (the general army office.) As such—and this was of prime importance— he was the permanent deputy of the commander-in-chief of the home army [i.e. the Reserve army]. He held a real key position, one that was even more important than Oster's, for he not only saw and heard a great deal, but also had the power of command over active troops.

> (*To the Bitter End,* p. 464.)

12. Schlabrendorff, *The Secret War against Hitler*, p. 226.
13. Brandt was unlucky in his association with the anti-Hitler bombs. Though he escaped on this occasion, he was to be among those killed on 20 July 1944.

282

14. Statement made by Frau von Dohnanyi after the war.
14. For Arthur Nebe, see above page 24, and Chapter 1, note 14.
16. Statement made by Frau von Dohnanyi after the war. Captain Ludwig Gehre was on active service with the Abwehr, a member of the resistance and a friend of Otto John. Baron Carl Ludwig von Guttenberg and Justus Delbrück were close associates of Oster in the Abwehr office. The removal of the key documents to Zossen took place towards the end of 1942. Oster and Heinz sifted the filed material and extracted the most incriminating material. With the help of Schrader, the dangerous documents were taken and at first deposited in an underground strongroom in the Prussian State Bank; this was done with the help of a bank director who was a brother of Heinz. The files were later removed by Heinz and Schrader and taken to Zossen, where a Colonel Radke placed them in an underground safe belonging to Army Reserve headquarters. A driver called Kerstenhan had undertaken the work of chauffeur on these various journeys. A short while after, Heinz passed on an order to Schrader to destroy the files, since danger of discovery seemed to be imminent. Schrader reported that he had done so, and Heinz passed this information on to Oster. But in fact Schrader left the files intact not, it would seem, through any disloyalty to the opposition, but because Beck wanted them preserved for research purposes of his own. This for what it is worth, is the account given by Bartz.
17. Statement made by Frau von Dohnanyi after the war.
18. There are many variant versions of the manner in which this search and arrest was carried out. See the various books already cited—by Colvin, p. 188, Schlabrendorff, p. 242, Hassell, p. 300, and Reitlinger's, *S.S.* p. 292. In our version we have checked what happened with statements made by Sonderegger after the war, and by Roeder to H.F. We are satisfied that the version now given is the correct one. The documents discovered in Dohnanyi's possession were relatively incriminating— sufficiently so to warrant the arrest which followed. Roeder says that the paper Oster tried to spirit away contained "ideas and suggestions for the shape of a post-Hitler Reich." Most of the papers found in the safe dealt with similar matters, and evidence that Bonhoeffer had visited Sweden and Müller the Vatican. Other papers dealt with exemptions from military service which went beyond Oster's reasonable powers. According to Bartz, other papers were concerned with the extradition of Jews. Several papers, including that spirited away by Oster, bore his initial "O" inscribed with the same kind of pencil as those Roeder took from Oster's desk.
19. Statement made by Christine von Dohnanyi after the war.

PART THREE   I THE DESPERATE YEARS

In addition to the books already cited, for this chapter use has also been made of Dietrich Bonhoeffer's *Letters and Papers from Prison* and Eberhard Bethge's *Dietrich Bonhoeffer*. We are particularly indebted to Major-General Alexander von Pfuhlstein, to Barbara and Klaus von Dohnanyi and to Dr. Eberhard Bethge for their personal assistance, and we have drawn on the Dohnanyi *Kassibers* as well as the post-war statements preserved in the Munich archive described in the head-note to the previous chapter.

1. Statement made by Christine von Dohnanyi after the war.
2. Reproduced by courtesy of Dr. Bethge and the Dohnanyi family.
3. Walther Moeller was one of the assistant interrogators.
4. From an affidavit made on 21 October 1948 by Josef Müller.
5. From an affidavit made on 12 November 1948 by Frau Maria Müller. Anny Haaser, Dr. Müller's secretary (who was later to become Frau Achim Oster), also made an affidavit on 22 October 1948. In this she stated that she followed Müller and his wife to Berlin, where they were imprisoned, in order to bring them food and linen. She demanded to see Dr. Roeder, who refused to let her visit the prisoners, but agreed to see that they received the things she had brought. On 29 April she was herself arrested, taken back to Berlin and imprisoned in the Charlottenburg Kantstrasse, sharing a cell with Hannelore Thiele of the *Rote Kapelle*. She was interrogated by Sonderegger and Noack. She was released after her third interrogation. Dr. Noack was a colleague of Roeder and a member of the Judiciary staff.
6. Statement made by Otto John after the war, when resident in London. Captain Ludwig Gehre of the Abwehr was a close friend.
7. Statement made by Christine von Dohnanyi after the war.
8. Military Archives, Freiburg.
9. Roeder in conversation with H.F.
10. Statements made in connexion with the Roeder hearings, 1948-9. Dr Rudolf Dix, who is now dead, was counsel for the defense of Schacht at the International Military Tribunal in Nuremberg, 1945-6.
11. The story of the Roehm purge in the summer of 1934, with its vengeful massacre known as "the night of the long knives," is told by the authors in their book *Göring*, p. 113 *et seq.*
12. Hassell, *Diaries,* pp. 301-2.
13. Professor Sauerbruch was also a good friend of Dohnanyi, as well as his medical adviser. He was later to show great courage when he insisted upon proper medical care for him during the period of his imprisonment.
14. The Wallenbergs, Jacob and Marcus, were wealthy Swedish bankers who frequently served as liaison with the Allies.
15. The whole letter is quoted in Wheeler-Bennett, *The Nemesis of Power,* pp. 573-4.
16. Statement made by Christine von Dohnanyi after the war. Dr

Friedrich Justus Perels was a senior legal official, and legal adviser to the Confessional Church. He was a trusted member of the resistance.

17. Bonhoeffer, *Letters and Papers from Prison*, Fontana Books edition, pp. 16-7.

18. For the background to Colonel Claus Schenk Count Stauffenberg, see the authors' book, *The July Plot*. The plans for the *coup d'état* on which Stauffenberg worked are discussed in some detail by Schlabrendorff in *The Secret War against Hitler*, pp. 248-57.

19. Of the men who are known to have been prepared to make the attempt to take Hitler's life during the period of the war four survive: Schlabrendorff, Gersdorff, Bussche and Kleist. Günther Gereke, now resident in East Germany, also planned an attempt on Hitler's life. This was to have been achieved by shooting at him with a telescopic rifle from the window of a bedroom in the Kaiserhof hotel, which was some 200 yards from the balcony of the Chancellery on which Hitler was due to appear. The Führer did not oblige.

20. Not Professor de Crinis, as usually stated. The title *Generalarzt* is a medical rank, the equivalent of a general on the staff.

21. Roeder retained his position as examining magistrate until 25 August 1943, by which time his investigations were complete and his indictment against the prisoners filed. Roeder was subsequently promoted to the position of judge with the Luftwaffe. He did not leave Berlin nor completely sever his connexion with the case until the New Year. It has been represented that Pfuhlstein's visit to Poland where he slapped Roeder's face because of an alleged insult to the courage of the Brandenburg division he had just taken over, followed a hint from Sack to Canaris that something should be done to degrade Roeder. Whether this was so or not, Roeder lost little from the sharp gesture, whereas Pfuhlstein received a minor reprimand. Schlabrendorff has a somewhat different version of this incident, *op. cit.*, p. 242.

22. The curious and much-told story of the secret agent Cicero has little direct connection with the Abwehr or Canaris. Ankara, like Lisbon, was a center for intrigue and spying precisely because the warring nations were all represented in the embassies and legations based on the neutral capital of Turkey. The British ambassador, Sir Hughe Knatchbull-Hugessen, and the German ambassador, Franz von Papen, were both old-fashioned diplomats whose security sense scarcely matched the unethical activities of the more advanced Intelligence services. Sir Hughe's Albanian valet, Diello, made contact with a German security agent in Ankara called Moyzisch and through him from October 1943 to April 1944 supplied the German embassy with photographs of highly secret documents for

which he received vast payments largely in sterling notes counterfeited in Germany. The documents he secured included records of the Teheran discussions between Stalin, Churchill and Roosevelt (during which the period for the invasion of Europe was discussed) and meetings with President Inonü of Turkey in Cairo at which the possibility of Turkey joining the Western Allies in the war against Germany was debated. The information gained by Cicero reached Germany by Ribbentrop's Foreign Office, but was ultimately studied by Kaltenbrunner, who proved sceptical about Cicero's motives and therefore doubted the value of the information he was passing on—though his rewards, certainly, were costing Germany little but the work of her counterfeiters, most of whom were prisoners in the concentration camps. Eventually, Moyzisch's secret source of information was uncovered by his secretary, Nelly "Elizabeth" Kapp, who was a British agent. Cicero fled with his counterfeit fortune. Leverkuehn, who was Canaris's agent in Turkey, told Colvin that he believed Cicero was a Turk. He also told him that Canaris employed deaf-mute lipreaders to watch Allied diplomats talking together in restaurants. H.F., who has met the original "Cicero" and investigated the whole story, denies that this unusual spy was a Turk. He was Albanian.

23. Moltke's arrest was linked with Schellenberg's exposure of the Solf circle. Dr. Wilhelm Solf, a former German ambassador in Japan, was an opponent of Hitler. After his death his widow and daughter formed their own group, the Solf circle, which had many distinguished members, including Elizabeth von Thadden, a noted headmistress, Otto Kiep, a former consul-general in New York, and other intellectuals and diplomats. They, like Moltke, who knew them well, were arrested in January 1944.

24. Quoted by Colvin in *Chief of Intelligence*, p. 195. Huppenkothen made a note of the original wording.

25. Schlabrendorff, *op. cit.*, p. 275.

26. Barbara (Bärbel) and Klaus von Dohnanyi have explained to H.F. that this was by far the best period of Dohnanyi's imprisonment both for him and his famly. The children were able to slip in through a backyard and had many hurried glimpses of their father. Among the many things they have said about him was that he remained always an "inveterate civilian" (*passionierter Zivilisl*) in spite of his position in the Abwehr. If for any reason he had to wear a uniform, he would joke about it. It will be remembered that Canaris and Oster preferred to wear mufti.

27. The full story of the July plot is told by the authors in their book *The July Plot (The Men Who Tried to Kill Hitler)*.

The main sources for this chapter in addition to the books already mentioned are the interrogations and proceedings for the post-war investigations of Roeder and the successive trials of Huppenkothen and Sonderegger. In addition, we are once more indebted to the Dohnanyi family and to Eberhard Bethge for the *Kassiber* material which was smuggled out of prison, and is quoted in this chapter in connection with Dohnanyi's imprisonment, and to Dr. Wolf Schrader for his invaluable information. It was revealed during the Huppenkothen hearings that the S.S. had made microfilm records of those parts of the Canaris diary which emerged at Zossen. Many German archivists are convinced that the papers discovered by the S.S. at Zossen eventually passed into British hands at the end of the war. Extensive inquiries have so far failed to find any evidence to support this view.

1. During his post-war interrogations Huppenkothen gave some information about the Zossen files. Among other material discovered were two large folders about the Fritsch and Blomberg cases, and evidence that an Army *coup* was due to succeed the Court of Honor. Beck, Oster and Dohnanyi were compromised in many documents connected with the abortive peace negotiations directed to the West. Huppenkothen also claims there were papers written by Oster in pencil (the so-called 'Oster Study') containing a precise plan for an attempt on Hitler's life, and for a *coup d'état*, followed by suggestions (purely Oster's own) for the offices various men of the resistance might occupy. (Their names were indicated by initials.) [See Part II, Chapter I, p. 70.] The other documents discovered included memoranda by Beck, Goerdeler, and others examining the war situation in negative terms, and sometimes counter-signed by Dohnanyi, Oster and Canaris. Bartz, *The Downfall of the German Secret Service*, gives a categorized list of the *Zossen Aktenfund*, pp. 157 *et seq.* He includes, in addition to the above, records of the Vatican negotiations, the Bonhoeffer discussion in Sweden, Müller's "X" Report, notes on Hassell's attempted negotiations, a letter incriminating Halder (written by him to Beck) and sections of Canaris's diary (see Notes 4 and 6 below).

2. After the war, Huppenkothen was three times put on trial; in February 1951 and again in October 1952 and October 1955.

3. This document does not appear to have survived in any of the archives in Germany. Giving evidence in court during one of the hearings of his case, Huppenkothen said:

    It took about three weeks to finish the report. . . . One went to Hitler via Bormann, one went to Himmler, a third to Kaltenbrunner, anda fourth remained in my office. We had direct orders from the Führer and from Gestapo Chief Müller and Himmler to maintain the utmost secrecy and

287

never to mention the files to anyone connected with the People's Court. Hitler reserved judgment on how the matter should be dealt with.

4. We owe to Dr. Wolf Schrader, son of Colonel Werner Schrader, the opportunity to publish for the first time details of the destruction of the papers originally in Schrader's possession, which included, as we have seen, Canaris's diary in typescript. Frau von Dohnanyi stated after the war, when her husband had been warned about his secret files, Dr. Justus Perels told her that Schrader had buried them on the site of a hunting lodge on the Lüneburg Heath, between Hamburg and Hanover. See p. 163 above. (The Heath was a popular area for shooting and open-air recreation.) Dr. Schrader assures us the papers were not buried there; in any event, there was never a hunting lodge on the Heath. His father had for a while rented a shoot during the mid-1930s, though he had not returned there after 1936. In a letter to H. F. he adds:

> I can see no logical reason why my father would not have enlisted my help had he wished to bury the papers. In such an event he would certainly have called on me as well as on his loyal driver Kerstenhan. My last visit to the H.Q. was in April 1944, and I well remember how at that time, after Gehre's arrest, we discussed everything that could endanger us or our friends. As I was much concerned with the Canaris diaries I asked my father what had become of them and he told me they were at Gross Denkte. The shoot in Ösingen was never mentioned. It would be interesting to trace how the error about the hunting lodge arose. Presumably, among friends, my father had mentioned Lüneburg Heath which he knew well and where, as a young man, he discovered a lake which was not on the maps. Perhaps he simply said, 'the documents are at home', and Frau von Dohnanyi might have thought of Lüneburg Heath; or perhaps he mentioned the Heath in order to conceal the real hiding-place at Gross Denkte.

Dr Schrader in 1944 was an officer cadet aged twenty-one, serving in the section Abwehr II. He was arrested after his father's suicide. He writes:

> I repeatedly served as messenger for my father and his friends, a few times in the H.Q. of O.K.H. and once in the Wolf's Lair [Hitler's headquarters in Rastenburg]. I was usually given my instructions by Captain Gehre, and I also delivered messages in sealed envelopes—once to Oster when he was under house arrest, once to Canaris when he was sent for by Keitel in connection with the Solf affair, once to Count Marogna in Vienna (through his secretary, Frau Müller). On one occasion I had to hand a sealed envelope to a

288

field-marshal who was to meet me in the hall of a nursing-home. It was Witzleben.

Bartz has a supplementary story to tell about another copy of the Canaris diaries. He says (p. 154, *op. cit.*) that soon after 20 July 1944, the Gestapo came into possession of Canaris's diaries covering the years after 1942. Canaris, according to Bartz, believing that Schrader had destroyed all of the diary that remained, told his interrogators that Schrader had possession of the pages covering the missing years. When the Gestapo went to question Schrader, they found that he had committed suicide. However, the following year, 1945, 2,000 pages of typewritten material bound in 12 black folders came to light at Zossen, and reached Huppenkothen on 11 April 1945. (See Bartz, *op. cit.*, p. 165.) They were found to be Canaris's diaries starting 1 September 1939. The diaries were then photocopied by the police, but destroyed at the end of the war, according to Bartz, "to efface all trace of the conspiracy in history."

When interrogated about the diaries after the war, according to Huppenkothen, Gestapo Müller brought him the diaries in Wannsee after his return from Flossenbürg on 11 April. He received them in fact, "probably on April 12 or 13." He immediately connected them with the other section already discovered at Zossen. He examined the new documents, and then claims that he destroyed them in Mittersil in Austria, to which he had been sent. Müller was deeply interested in the diaries and studied them himself; he had received them from Brigadier Rattenhuber of the Security Service. He ordered Huppenkothen to preserve them as historical documents, but Kaltenbrunner countermanded this order and said that they were to be destroyed. A reel of photographic negative containing copies of the diaries was also burned by Huppenkothen in Austria. Müller was present and helped with the burning of both the documents and the microfilm.

5. Letter to H.F.
6. Memorandum written by Dr. Wolf Schrader for the authors.
7. Letter to the authors.
8. Schellenberg claims he drove Canaris to Fuerstenberg and handed him there to the police authorities. For the quotations which follow, see *Memoirs,* pp. 408-12.
9. Huppenkothen interrogation.
10. Bethge, *Dietrich Bonhoeffer,* pp. 909-10.
11. *Ibid.,* pp. 909-10.
12. See the authors' *The July Plot,* pp. 203-4.
13. Statement by Christine von Dohnanyi.
14. Examination of Huppenkothen during trial.
15. Statement by Christine von Dohnanyi.
16. Statement during trial by Dr Tietze.

17. Schacht, *My First Seventy-Six Years*, pp. 429-50.
18. Schacht, *op. cit.*, pp. 432-3.
19. Schlabrendorff, *The Secret War against Hitler*, p. 318.
20. See the authors' *The July Plot*, p. 205.
21. For a fuller consideration of this contest between Moltke and Freilser, see *The July Plot*, pp. 206-11. The full text of Moltke's letters to his wife from prison appear in Count Helmuth von Moltke's *A German of the Resistance*.
22. Klaus Bonhoeffer, Rüdiger Schleicher, Friedrich Justus Perels (who had been arrested on 5 September 1944), and Hans John (brother of Otto) were all condemned to death during Freisler's last full day in court.
23. Schacht, *op. cit.*, p. 436.
24. See *The July Plot*, p. 214.
25. Colvin, *Chief of Intelligence*, p. 205.
26. Statement made by Christine von Dohnanyi in connection with the Sonderegger case, and signed 26 August 1948. The quotation immediately following comes from the same document.
27. Statement made in court by Dr Tietze.
28. This letter comes from the Dohnanyi *Kassibers*. Ense, referred to in the letter, was a doctor, a helpful fellow-prisoner. Brigitte was one of Canaris's two daughters.
29. For the fuller story of the confinement of notable prisoners during the last phase of the war, see *The July Plot*, Schlabrendorff's *The Secret War against Hitler* and Captain S. Payne Best's *The Venlo Incident*. Captain S. Payne Best was one of the two secret agents captured by Schellenberg at Venlo.
30. Bethge, *Dietrich Bonhoeffer*, p. 1029. Leibholz was Bonhoeffer's brother-in-law.
31. Statement in court by Dr Tietze.
32. Signed statement by Christine von Dohnanyi (see Note 26 above).
33. Statement in court by Dr Tietze
34. Statement by Christine von Dohnanyi referred to in court.
35. There are a number of different versions of this confrontation of Canaris by Oster. Colvin implies (*op. cit.*, p. 212-3) that Oster, possibly drugged, hid nothing, while Canaris tried to claim he had only "pretended complicity." Bartz (in *The Downfall of the German Secret Service*, p. 195) claims that Canaris simply denied everything and that Oster in effect called him a liar. Sources are not given for this final scene. We have not traced a Gestapo record to this effect.
36. The guards told Schlabrendorff that Canaris had to be hanged twice. See Colvin, *op. cit.*, p. 211. Both Müller and Schlabrendorff escaped execution. (See also the final general note on those who escaped death, below.)
37. Bartz, *op. cit.*, p. 198.
38. Bethge, *op. cit.*, p. 1238.

Schlabrendorff, who was at Flossenbürg camp on 10 April when Bonhoeffer, Canaris and Oster were executed, was transferred two days later to Dachau camp. It was here that Josef Müller, Schacht and members of the families of Stauffenberg and Goerdeler were confined, together with many other celebrated or otherwise distinguished prisoners. Among these, for example, were Pastor Niemöller, Léon Blum, the former Prime Minister of France, and his wife, and Kurt von Schuschnigg, the former Chancellor of Austria. As the Allied armies closed in, these variously distinguished prisoners, over a hundred in number, were moved from place to place, and finally liberated by the American Army on 4 May. Accounts of these last days are given in their books by both Schlabrendorff and Payne Best. Other prominent survivors from the resistance movement who were liberated were Dr. Eugen Gerstenmaier, who had managed to win only a seven-year sentence at the same hearing at which Moltke and others were condemned to death, and Pastor Eberhard Bethge, later to become the biographer of Bonhoeffer.

We are grateful to Pastor Bethge for the following details concerning his deliverance in the last days of the war:

> My trial was fixed for 15.5.45. But on Tuesday morning April 24 the few of us left of 45 political prisoners in the Lehrterstrasse prison noticed that our S.S. guards had left us and been replaced by the original prison warders who had 'normally' been in charge. In some of the cells we discovered S.S. uniforms, evidently discarded by some of the men who were trying to avoid trouble by changing into mufti. But it took us another twenty-four hours to persuade the prison guards to let us go, our argument being that once the approaching Russians had arrived, they were likely to hurt *them* rather than *us*.
>
> So on Wednesday 25 April, in the afternoon, we persuaded them to open the prison gates to us. One could already hear the Russian guns. Some of us were still apprehensive about being made to join a *Volkssturm* company, but there was no one to conscript us. So we were able to rush home, almost delirious with joy at being free and alive, though we had to run through a hail of shot.
>
> Home for me meant the Marienburger Allee, the Schleichers' house next to the Bonhoeffers. Only one of us had nowhere to go, a Jewish-Russian doctor whom the S.S. had taken from the concentration camp at Sachsenhausen to do all the most menial chores in the Lehrterstrasse prison. I took him to my mother-in-law's house, little realizing how useful this would turn out to be a few days later, when the Russians started on their brief period of unchecked raping and plundering. It was this Russian who saved us all from any form of molestation when the 'front' engulfed the Ma-

291

rienburger Allee. Of course we had to take shelter in the
cellar like everyone else, since the bombardment was still
going on. But, thanks to our protector, the Russians treated
us with every consideration.

Among the prisoners held under death sentence at the Lehrterstrasse prison until April 1945 in addition to Eberhard Bethge, were
Rüdiger Schleicher, Hans John and Klaus Bonhoeffer. All except
Bethge were in the group of prisoners taken to the Prinz Albrechtstrasse prison during the night of 22 April 1944 and executed.

Frau Erika Canaris went to live in Spain in 1948 at the invita-
tion of General Franco and later retired to Hamburg. She had
never tried to play a part in her husband's resistance work, and
has preferred to keep silent about it. Of the leading members of
Canaris's staff who survived the war, Lahousen was discovered in a
prisoner-of-war camp and gave evidence at the International Military Tribunal at Nuremberg, Leverkuehn became defense counsel
at the trial of Marshal von Manstein and Pieckenbrock fell prisoner
to the Russians. Bentivegni shot himself after the failure of the
July plot of 1944.

Chronology of Events during Hitler's Régime

with special reference to the German resistance

1933

30 January. Hitler becomes Chancellor.

January. *Dohnanyi joins staff of Ministry of Justice and begins
compilation of evidence against the régime.*

27 February. Reichstag fire leads to direct action by Nazis against
their opponents, especially the Communists.

5 March. Last free election for Reichstag. Nazi Party gains a mere
288 seats, only 44 per cent voting in their favour.

14 March. Goebbels appointed Minister of Propaganda and Public
Enlightenment.

23 March. Enabling Law gives Hitler dictatorial power; with Communists excluded, Social Democrats become only party voting
against bill.

1 April. Persecution of Jews begins with national boycott of Jewish
professional men and Jewish-owned shops.

April. All but Nazi-controlled journals virtually abolished.

2 May. Abolition of trade unions.

10 May. The public "burning of the books" organized nationally by
Goebbels.

14 July. The Nazi Party (N.S.D.A.P.) the only legitimate political
party.

20 July. Concordat with Vatican signed.

22 September. Reich Chamber of Culture established to control all forms of art and expression.

4 October. Journalists' Law; all journalists become in effect licensed civil servants.

19 October. Germany quits League of Nations.

1934

30 June. Night of the Long Knives. Many opponents of the régime assassinated during the Roehm purge. *Oster disillusioned by this savage reprisal.*

25 July. Murder of Dollfuss during attempted Nazi *coup d'état* in Austria.

2 August. Death of Hindenburg. Hitler proclaims himself German Führer and Chancellor, and imposes a personal oath of loyalty on all officers and men in the Army. *Beck disillusioned.*

24 October. German Labour Front formed.

28 November. Winston Churchill warns British Parliament of the menace of growing German air power.

1935

5 January. *Canaris put in charge of the Abwehr.*

16 March. Universal conscription ordered. Germany repudiates disarmament clauses in Versailles Treaty.

15 September. Nuremberg Racial Laws proclaim the Jews outlaws. The swastika becomes the official German flag.

1936

7 March. Occupation of the demilitarized Rhineland in violation of Versailles Treaty. *Disillusionment of Canaris increased.*

18 July. Spanish Civil War starts with Army revolt led by Mola and Franco.

19 October. German Four-Year Plan initiated by Göring.

1 November. Rome-Berlin Axis proclaimed.

24 November. Germany and Japan sign anti-Comintern Pact.

1937

April. *Goerdeler, disillusioned with Nazism, resigns as Lord Mayor of Leipzig.*

August. *Schacht, supplanted by Göring and disillusioned with Nazism, resigns as Minister of Economics.*

13 October. Germany guarantees inviolability of Belgium.

6 November. Italy joins anti-Comintern Pact.

With Gisevius acting as intermediary between the various branches of the growing resistance, Oster, Schacht, Goerdeler and Thomas attempt during the latter part of the year to persuade Blomberg,

293

commander-in-chief of the Army, to support the arrest of Hitler.
Helldorf joins the resistance movement.

1938

January. "Exposure" and dismissal of Blomberg following his marriage to a former prostitute. Fritsch, Blomberg's successor as commander-in-chief, framed by bogus charge of homosexuality.
4 February. Hitler becomes Minister for War and commander-in-chief of the armed forces. Ribbentrop appointed Foreign Minister; Ribbentrop removes Hassell from his post as ambassador in Italy.
11-13 March. Austrian Anschluss completed; Austria incorporated into the Reich.
10 and 17 March. Military Court of Honor convened under Göring to examine charges against Fritsch brings together the future resistance leaders and organizers, Canaris, Oster and Dohnanyi. *The Abwehr, under the influence of Canaris and Oster, begins to centralize disaffection. Hassell keeps in close touch, more especially through Beck, Goerdeler and Schacht, Schlabrendorff, opponent of Hitler before the régime was established, joins the movement.*
May. Operation Green (preparations for the subjection of Czechoslovakia) secretly initiated by Hitler.
June. *Breck fails to persuade Brauchitsch, commander-in-chief of the Army, to oppose Hitler's war preparations.*
July. *Goerdeler meets Vansittart in Britain; meeting a failure.*
August. *Resignation of Beck as Chief of Army General Staff as final act of protest against Hitler's policy.* Replaced by Halder.
18 August. *Kleist sent by Beck and Canaris to London. Meets Vansittart, Churchill and Lord Lloyd.*
19 August. *Churchill writes a letter which in effect gives unofficial recognition to the German resistance movement.*
5 September. *Theodor Kordt of the German embassy in London, but prompted by Weizsäcker in Berlin, warns Lord Halifax of an October deadline for the Nazi invasion of Czechoslovakia.*
September. *An Army putsch against Hitler to be led by Beck, Halder and Witzleben collapses at the news that Chamberlain is to visit Hitler in Germany.*
29 September. The Munich agreement. Sudetenland incorporated into Germany.
9/10 November. *Kristallnacht*; national pogrom against the Jews.
6 December. Franco-German pact on inviolability of existing frontiers.

1939

15 March. Annexation by Hitler of Bohemia and Moravia, which become a German protectorate.
21 March. Annexation by Hitler of Memel.

22 May. Hitler and Mussolini sign the Pact of Steel, a ten-year political and military alliance.

Summer. *Churchill visited by Kleist, Goerdeler, and Schlabrendorff and given full information of the German anti-Nazi movement. Erich and Theo Kordt visit Vansittart. Trott and Moltke visit the Oxford historian Wheeler-Bennett. Bohm-Tettelbach sees Sir James Grigg. Moltke and Yorck found the peace-loving, anti-Nazi Kreisau Circle.*

23 August. Russo-German non-aggression pact signed.

25 August. Anglo-Polish treaty of mutual assistance signed.

August. *Dohnanyi directly recruited to serve in Abwehr.*

1 September. Hitler launches attack on Poland (campaign ends 1 October). Hitler annexes Danzig.

3 September. France and Britain declare war on Germany.

17 September. U.S.S.R. invades Poland.

30 September. Partition of Poland.

8 October. Western Poland incorporated into the Reich.

October. *Oster decides to give advance warnings of Hitler's future acts of aggression, and begins to feed information through Sas.*

October-November. *Josef Müller joins Abwehr in order to initiate peace-feelers through the Vatican.*

November. *Oster invited by Beck to "bring the 1938 plan up to date" for study by himself, Canaris and Halder.*

Müller succeeds in enlisting the sympathetic help of the Pope, who offers to act as intermediary for peace. Indirect contact with official channels in Britain encourages Müller to draw up an initial draft of the future "X Report" on viable peace terms for submission to leading generals in the High Command. Final X Report drafted by Dohnanyi and Thomas at the turn of the year.

1940

January-April. *Resistance endeavors to bring pressure to bear on Brauchitsch to depose Hitler and bring about peace. Brauchitsch refuses; Halder through divided loyalty begins to cool towards resistance.*

February. *First meeting between Hassell and the unofficial peace negotiator Bryans in Arosa.*

March. *Sumner Welles visits Germany and makes contact with Schacht. Goerdeler has contact with the King of the Belgians.*

3 April. *Oster reveals to Sas the dates of the invasion of Denmark and Norway.*

9 April. German invasion of Denmark and Norway.

Mid-April. *Second and final meeting between Hassell and Bryans.*

Early May. *Warnings of Hitler's intentions to invade West sent by Müller to Britain via the Vatican; Sas also warned again by Oster. Coded messages to Belgium intercepted by the Gestapo.*

10 May. German invasion of Holland, Belgium, France and Lux-

embourg begins. Churchill becomes Prime Minister of Britain and forms a national government.

Late May. *Heydrich orders the investigation of Dohnanyi and Müller in relation to their dealings with the Vatican.*

22 June. The Franco-German armistice.

27 June. The U.S.S.R. invades Roumania.

9 July. Romania places herself under German protection.

23 August. All-night raid on London; the "blitz" begins.

7 October. Germany seizes Romanian oil-fields.

1941

18 April. The collapse of Yugoslavia.

22 April. The British evacuate Greece.

22 June. The German invasion of Soviet Union.

3 July. Göring orders Heydrich to undertake the total removal of Jews from Germany and eventually from Europe.

12 July. Anglo-Russian agreement for mutual assistance signed.

28 July. German armies enter the Ukraine. *Tresckow begins at Army Group Center in Russia his long campaign to win Kluge's wholehearted support for an attempt to arrest Hitler.*

11 August. The Atlantic Charter signed by Churchill and Roosevelt.

25 October. Failure of the German offensive against Moscow.

18 November. The British begin their attack in the Western Desert.

7 December. Japanese bomb Pearl Harbor.

8 December. Britain and the U.S.A. declare war on Japan.

11 December. War declared between United States and Germany.

1942

2 January. Britain, the U.S.A., the U.S.S.R. and other Allies agree not to sign a separate peace with Germany.

20 January. The Wannsee Conference convened by Heydrich and Eichmann to discuss the 'final solution' for the Jews in Europe. Full-scale extermination such as that of Auschwitz receive their secret authorization.

April. *Hassell warned officially by Weizsäcker that the Gestapo is watching him.*

May. The start of the thousand-bomber raids by the R.A.F. on Germany. The death of Heydrich following a shooting incident in Prague.

Pastors Bonhoeffer and Schönfeld meet Bishop Bell in Sweden. Eden refuses to respond to specific appeals for public recognition of the resistance.

August. The *'Rote Kapelle'* communist network in Germany jointly uncovered by the Abwehr and the S.D. Roeder, the investigator attached to the Luftwaffe division of the Army Judiciary, conducts interrogations.

296

23 October. The battle of El Alamein initiates the defeat of Germany in North Africa.

2 November. The arrest of Müller's associate Schmidhuber on currency charges. The interrogation by Roeder reveals the complicity of Müller and Dohnanyi in certain areas of negotiations through the Vatican.

Winter. *Plans for the actual assassination of Hitler begin to mature. Goerdeler penetrates to Smolensk to discuss action with Kluge. Beck, Goerdeler, Olbricht and Tresckow, with Berlin as their center of discussions, accept that they must make their* coup d'état *follow on the killing of Hitler, not his arrest.*

1943

January. *A conference of resistance leaders at Yorck's house to determine shape of German constitution after the* coup d'état. *Beck operated upon for cancer. Trott meets Allen Dulles in Switzerland to urge direct contact between Allies and German resistance.*

30/31 January. The defeat of the Germany Army at Stalingrad; Paulus surrenders.

13 February. Goebbels's notorious "total war" speech in the Berlin Sportspalast.

22 February. *The trial and execution of Hans and Sophie Scholl, members of the independent "White Rose" movement against Hitler.*

28 February. Heavy R.A.F. raid on Berlin.

13 March. *Tresckow and Schlabrendorff smuggle a time-bomb on to Hitler's plane set to explode during his flight from Smolensk to Rastenburg. The bomb fails to ignite.*

March. *Baron Gersdorff offers to undertake a suicide mission to kill Hitler, which fails through force of circumstances.*

5 April. *The arrest of Dohnanyi, Müller and Bonhoeffer. Interrogation by Roeder. Oster rusticated.*

May. *Goerdeler sends a memorandum on the intentions of the post-Hitler German government to Churchill via Sweden.*

10 July. The Allied invasion of Sicily.

25/26 July. Mussolini falls from power.

August. *Roeder completes his indictment on Oster, Dohnanyi and Schmidhuber.*

Summer. *Tresckow, on sick leave in Berlin, works on Valkyrie, the cover plan to be used for the 1944 attempt on Hitler's life.*

3 September. The Allied invasion of Italy.

8 September. The Italian government surrenders to the Allies.

September. *Goerdeler, Beck, Kluge and Olbricht meet in Berlin and work on their plan for the 1944 coup d'état. Infiltration by a Gestapo agent into the Solf "tea-party" betrays the identity of several anti-Nazis. Cold-shouldered, as it seems, by the Western*

Allies, certain members of the resistance begin to favour over-
tures being made to Moscow.
13 October. Italy (Badoglio) declares war on Germany.
October. *Stauffenberg, recovered from severe war injuries, joins the*
Reserve Army staff and takes over Tresckow's work of planning
for the 1944 coup.
November. *Axel von dem Bussche's abortive suicide mission to as-*
sassinate Hitler. A similar mission by Ewald von Kleist also fails
to mature.

1944

27 January. The relief of Leningrad.
January. *The arrest of Moltke and Otto Kiep (the latter the first*
Army officer to be arrested by the Gestapo).
February. *Erich Vermehren of the Abwehr staff in Turkey defects*
to the British with his wife. The Abwehr absorbed into the S.D.
(S.S. Intelligence) under *Schellenberg. Canaris dismissed and for*
a while restricted in his movements.
April. *Second meeting between Dulles and Trott in Switzerland.*
4 June. The Fifth Army enters Rome.
6 June. D-Day. The Allied invasion of France.
13 June. The first V.1 flying-bomb dropped on London.
June. *Canaris given sinecure to cover his enforced retirement.*
4/5 July. *The arrest of Leber, and of another prominent Socialist*
member of the resistance, Adolf Reichwein.
14 July. Hitler moves his headquarters from Berchtesgaden back
to Rastenburg, East Prussia.
18 July. *Goerdeler forced to go into hiding. Pressure to undertake*
coup d'état *now at its height.*
20 July. *Stauffenberg's attempt on Hitler's life fails. The action for*
the coup d'état, *started in both Berlin and Paris, and to a minor*
extent in Vienna, collapses. Suicide of Beck; execution of Stauf-
fenberg, Olbricht and others immediately implicated after sum-
mary court-martial. The failure of the bomb-plot breaks the en-
tire resistance movement, and leads to wholesale arrests and a
long succession of trials under Freisler.
21 July. The suicide of Tresckow, Oster arrested.
23 July. The arrest of Hassell, Canaris, Schacht.
24 July. Otto John escapes to Madrid.
12 August. Goerdeler arrested.
24 August. Measures for total war and total mobilization.
25 August. De Gaulle enters Paris in the wake of the Allied armies.
30 August. The Russian armies enter Bucharest.
August to February 1945. The trial and execution of many resistance leaders and supporters, including Hassell, Witzleben, Yorck,
Stuelpnagel, Hoepner, Helldorf, Trott, Stieff, Leuschner. Kluge
commits suicide in August.

298

22 September. The discovery by the Gestapo of Dohnanyi's secret papers.

29 September. Russian armies in Yugoslavia.

11 October. Thomas arrested.

12 October. The execution of Langbehn.

14 October. Rommel forced to commit suicide for his involvement in the abortive *coup d'état*.

27 December. The Russian armies surround Budapest.

1945

17 January. The Russians take Warsaw.

23 January. The Russians reach Oder.

January. Moltke and Leber executed. Escape of Gisevius to Switzerland.

2 February. Execution of Goerdeler.

3 February. Death in an air-raid of the notorious Nazi judge Freisler.

15 February. British troops reach the Rhine.

March. British and Americans cross the Rhine.

6 April. The "court-martial" of Dohnanyi at Sachsenhausen concentration camp, followed by his execution on 9 April.

8 April. The "court-marital" of Oster, Canaris, Bonhoeffer, among others.

9 April. The execution of Canaris, Oster, and Bonhoeffer at Flossenbürg concentration camp.

22 April. Hitler retires to his bunker in Berlin.

28 April. Mussolini assassinated.

30 April. Hitler commits suicide in Berlin.

1 May. The suicide of Goebbels and his wife.

2 May. Berlin surrenders to the Russians.

7 May. Germany surrenders unconditionally. The liberation of Müller, Schlabrendorff, Bethge, Thomas, Schacht during May.

Appendix

THE ESCAPE OF CANARIS, 1916

As this book was going to press we learnt about Canaris's dramatic escape in a U-boat sent to Spain to pick him up in September 1916 (an operation which, having been betrayed to the French, very nearly failed). But for the fifty years' rule having recently been reduced to thirty, the information would have remained 'top secret' until 1969. The report to the German Admiralty made by the U-boat commander and duly confiscated by the British Admiralty in 1919, was made available about a year ago, and we are much indebted to Gabriele von Arnauld, niece of the U-boat commandant concerned, for allowing us to read the full text of her uncle's report.

The report is headed: "Orders to pick up Captain-Lieutenant Canaris near Cartagena," and it starts: "The pre-arranged rendezvous with the sailing boat carrying Canaris and his two companions was for the early hours of the morning on 30 September."

Captain von Arnauld reports how, at 2.30 a.m. his U-boat surfaced at the northern end of Salitrona Bay heading for Tinoso lighthouse. The bay was quickly filling up with brightly illuminated fishing craft, but the pre-arranged morse signal remained unanswered: Canaris had evidently been delayed. At 6.45, as dawn broke, the U-boat left the bay, passed Cape Tinoso at a distance of a little over 500 yards and went up and down the pre-arranged rendezvous line. Encountering various suspicious craft (including one unidentified vessel which he rightly assumed to be a "U-boat trap") Captain von Arnauld had to submerge frequently, leaving the rendezvous line at 11 a.m. and heading south-east. At 3 p.m., about thirteen nautical miles from Tinoso, he had to surface to recharge his batteries. "I realized," the report continues, "that I

300

might be observed and reported, but the risk had to be taken as I had to be operative on the rendezvous line from late afternoon till dusk."

At 5.30 p.m. he sighted at some distance a low vessel which suddenly disappeared, thereby confirming the suspicion that it was an enemy submarine. The report continues:

Night of 30.9 to 1.10. From 7 p.m. till dusk at 8.30 I

stood surfaced on the rendezvous line in sight of Tinoso. No fishing craft to be seen. . . . At 2.10 a.m. I sighted a small vessel with its lights dimmed which suddenly started to send morse signals seawards. I submerged into the Bay of Salitrona where I felt fairly safe as this would be the last thing the enemy would expect.

Later that day morse and signaling contact was made with what, indeed, was the sailing boat carrying Canaris, but the contact was lost. It was next morning only, soon after dawn that the sailing craft was spotted again, the proper signals leaving no doubt as to its identity. The U-boat followed and caught up with it submerged, surfacing when only fifty yards away and less than two miles from land. To take on Canaris and his two companions took less than five minutes, and the U-boat submerged again immediately.

There was no doubt in Captain von Arnauld's mind (and this was later confirmed by the French submarine commander) that the operation was observed by the enemy and that there just was not time enough for an attack to be mounted. In concluding his report von Arnauld makes practical suggestions as to how best to avoid the fearful risks he had had to take if any similar operation was to be considered in the future.

(Again thanks to Gabriele von Arnauld's courtesy), we have seen the report of Commandant Pradeau, as published in *Les Marins* (*'Souvenirs maritimes, sociaux et politique d'un ancien Officier de Marine'*). In his uncommonly chivalrous report the French officer explains that during the crucial few minutes the blinding sun was against him, thus favouring the rescue operation. Having met both Canaris and von Arnauld many years later, he expresses his delight at having been prevented from destroying so gallant an enemy.

301

Selected Book-List

ABSHAGEN, KARL HEINZ: *Canaris, Patriot und Weltbürger.* (Stuttgart: Union Verlag, 1949)

BERBEN, PAUL: *L'Attentat contre Hitler.* (Paris: Editions Robert Laffont, 1962)

BARTZ, KARL: *The Downfall of the German Secret Service.* (London: William Kimber, 1956)

BEST, S. PAYNE: *The Venlo Incident.* (London: Hutchinson, 1950)

BETHGE, EBERHARD: *Dietrich Bonhoeffer.* (Munich: Chr. Kaiser Verlag, 1967)

BLEICHER, HUGO: *Colonel Henri's Story.* (London: Kimber, 1954)

BONHOEFFER, DIETRICH: *Letters and Papers from Prison.* (German edition, *Widerstand und Ergebung*; Munich: Chr. Kaiser Verlag, 1951, edited by Eberhard Bethge. English edition: London: S.C.M. Press, 1953; Fontana, 1959)

BOVERI, MARGRET: *Treason in the Twentieth Century.* (London: Macdonald, 1961)

BUCHHEIT, GERT: *Ludwig Beck.* (Munich: List, 1964)

BUCHHEIT, GERT: *Der Deutsche Geheimdienst.* (Munich: List, 1966)

BULLOCK, ALAN: *Hitler: a Study in Tyranny.* (London: Odhams, 1952; revised 1964)

COLVIN, IAN: *Chief of Intelligence.* (London: Gollancz, 1951)

DEUTSCH, HAROLD C.: *The Conspiracy against Hitler in the Twilight War.* (London: Oxford University Press, 1968)

DULLES, ALLEN WELSH: *Germany's Underground.* (New York: Macmillan, 1947)

FITZ-GIBBON, CONSTANTINE: *The Shirt of Nessus.* (London: Cassell, 1956)

FRASCHKA, GUNTER: *20. Juli.* (Baden: 1961)

302

GISEVIUS, HANS BERND: *To the Bitter End.* (Boston: Houghton Mifflin, 1947)

GISEVIUS, HANS BERND: *Wo ist Nebe?* (Zurich: Droemersche Verlaganstalt, 1966)

GOEBBELS, JOSEPH: *The Goebbels Diaries.* (London: Hamish Hamilton, 1948)

GOERLITZ, WALTER: *The German General Staff.* (London: Hollis & Carter, 1953)

GRAML, H.: *'Der Fall Oster'.* (Munich: *Vierteljahrshefte,* 1966)

HASSELL, ULRICH VON: *The Von Hassell Diaries.* (New York: Doubleday, 1947)

HENK, EMIL: *Die Tragödie des 20. Juli.* (Heidelberg, 1946)

INTERNATIONAL MILITARY TRIBUNAL: *The Trial of the German Major War Criminals.* 22 volumes. (London: H.M. Stationery Office, 1946)

KALTENBRUNNER, ERNST: *Spiegelbild einer Verschwörung.* (Stuttgart: Seewald, 1961)

KORDT, ERICH: *Nicht aus den Akten.* (Stuttgart: Deutsche Verlagsanstalt, 1950)

KOSTHORST, ERICH: *Die Deutsche Opposition gegen Hitler zwischen Polen und Frankreichfeldzug* (Bonn: Bundeszentrale für Heimatsdienst, 1955)

KRAUSNICK, HELMUT, and others (Editors): *Vollmacht des Gewissens.* (Frankfurt: Metzner Verlag, 1960)

LEBER, ANNEDORE and FREYA COUNTESS MOLTKE: *Für und Wider.* (Berlin: Mosaik Verlag, 1961)

LEVERKUEHN, PAUL: *German Military Intelligence.* (London: Weidenfeld and Nicolson, 1954)

MANVELL, ROGER and FRAENKEL, HEINRICH: *Doctor Goebbels.* (London: Heinemann, 1960)

MANVELL, ROGER and FRAENKEL, HEINRICH: *Hermann Göring.* (London: Heinemann, 1962)

MANVELL, ROGER and FRAENKEL, HEINRICH: *The July Plot.* London: The Bodley Head, 1964)

MANVELL, ROGER and FRAENKEL, HEINRICH: *Heinrich Himmler.* (London: Heinemann, 1965)

MANVELL, ROGER and FRAENKEL, HEINRICH: *The Incomparable Crime.* (London: Heinemann, 1967)

MELNIKOW, DANIEL: *20. Juli. 1944.* (Berlin: Deutscher Verlag der Wissenschafften, 1944)

MOLTKE, COUNT HELMUTH VON: *A German of the Resistance.* (Oxford University Press, 1947)

PECHEL, RUDOLF: *Deutscher Widerstand.* (Zurich: Eugen Rentsch Verlag, 1947)

PETER, J. K.: *Der 20. Juli.* (Buenos Aires: Dürer Verlag, 1951)

POELCHAU, HARALD: *Die letzten Stunden.* (Berlin: Verlag Volk und Welt, 1949)

POELCHAU, HARALD: *Die Ordnung der Bedrängten.* (Berlin: Käte Vogt Verlag, 1963)

PRITTIE, TERENCE: *Germans against Hitler.* (London: Hutchinson, 1964)

REITLINGER, GERALD: *The S.S., Alibi of a Nation.* (London: Heinemann, 1956)

RITTER, GERHARD: *Goerdeler und die Deutsche Widerstandsbewegung.* (Deutsche Verlagsanstalt Stuttgart, 1954). Translated as *The German Resistance.* (London: 1958)

ROTHFELS, HANS: *The German Opposition to Hitler.* (London: Wolff, 1961)

ROYCE, HANS: *Germans against Hitler; July 20 1944.* (Bonn: Bundeszentrale für Heimatsdienst, 1952; revised 1960)

SCHᴧCHT, HJALMAR: *My First Seventy-Six Years.* (London: Wingate 1955)

SCHELLENBERG, WALTER: *The Schellenberg Memoirs.* (London: André Deutsch, 1956)

SCHEURIG, BODO: *Stauffenberg.* (Berlin: Colloquium Verlag, 1964)

SCHLABRENDORFF, FABIAN VON: *The Secret War against Hitler.* (London: Hodder and Stoughton, 1966)

SCHMITTHENNER and BUCHHEIM (Editors): *Der Deutsche Widerstand gegen Hitler.* (Cologne: Kiepenheuer und Witsch, 1966)

SCHRAMM, WILHELM VON: *Der 20. Juli in Paris.* (Bad. Woerishofen: Kindler Verlag, 1953)

SCHRAMM, WILHELM VON (Editor): *Beck und Goerdeler.* (Munich: Gotthold Müller, 1965)

SHIRER, W. L.: *The Rise and Fall of the Third Reich.* (London: Secker and Warburg: 1960)

THOMAS, GENERAL GEORG: *Gedanken und Ereignisse.* (Article in *Schweizer Monatshefte*, Dec. 1945)

TRENTZSCH, MAJOR DR: *Der Soldat und der 20. Juli.* (Darmstadt: Wehr und Wissen, 1956)

TREVOR-ROPER, H. R.: *The Philby Affair.* (London: Kimber, 1968)

WEIZSÄCKER, ERNST VON: *Erinnerungen.* (Munich: Paul List Verlag, 1950)

WHEELER-BENNETT, JOHN W.: *The Nemesis of Power*. (London: Macmillan, 1953)

WOODWARD and BUTLER (Editors): *Documents on British Foreign Policy, 1919-39*, Series III, Vol. II. (London: H.M. Stationery Office)

ZELLER, EBERHARD: *Geist der Freiheit*. (Munich: Hermann Rinn Verlag, 1954)

attitude to assassination of Hitler 137; excessive optimism and theorizing, according to Hassell 156, 160, 180; leading part in later coordination of German resistance 158-62, 214, 215; thought reactionary by younger wing of German resistance 161, 216; opposes destruction of documents incriminating Nazis 188, 211; operated upon for cancer of the stomach, March 1943 208; suspected by Himmler 167; suicide following failure of bomb attempt of July 1944 230

Bell, George, Bishop of Chichester 154-55

Beneš, Eduard, President of Czechoslovakia 79-82

Bentivegni, Colonel Egbert von 61, 103, 105, 165, 292

Bernstorff, Count Albrecht 124

Best, Dr Werner 46, 105

Best, Captain S. Payne 121, 265, 268

Bethge, Pastor Eberhard 140, 241, 245, 261, 291

Bloch, Colonel (Abwehr) 140

Blomberg, Field Marshal Werner von 42, 45, 54, 64, 273

Boeselager, Colonel Baron Georg von 183

Böhm-Tettelbach, Colonel Hans 77

Bonhoeffer, Christine (see Frau Christine von Dohnanyi)

Bonhoeffer, Pastor Dietrich xxi, 68, 69, 109, 133, 140, 154-55, 173, 176, 191 *et seq.*, 192, 203, 212-13, 241-42, 245-46, 251, 252-54, 257, 259, 263, 265-70

Bonhoeffer, Professor Karl 69, 241-42

Bonhoeffer, Klaus 69, 203, 210, 212, 218, 245, 257, 290, 292

Boris III, King of Bulgaria 139, 162

Bormann, Martin 87, 189

Brandenburg Division 101, 276

Brandenburg, Wilhelm 255

Brandt, Colonel Heinz, 185-86

Brauchitsch, Field Marshal Walter von 55, 65, 81, 87, 94, 107, 108, 112, 116-18, 136, 276

Brede, Captain 281

Bredow, Major-General Kurt von 44

Breitenbach, Colonel von, 222

Brockdorff, Countess Erika von 166

Bryans, J. Lonsdale 113-18

Buerkner, Rear-Admiral Leopold 103

Busch, Field-Marshal 222

Bussche, Freiherr Axel von dem 217

Cadogan, Sir Alexander 88

Calma von Coburg, Princess 236

Canaris, Frau Erika 41, 46, 292

Canaris, Admiral Wilhelm. At centre of German resistance organization xxi, xxvi; assumes deliberate ambivalence xxvi-xxviii, 64, 138-39; character 40, 48-50, 105, 139, 140-43, 149; unsuspected by Gestapo until 1944 xxvii; as patriot xxviii; and weakness of German resistance movement xxxii; career before taking charge of Abwehr 37-42; background 38; service in Naval Intelligence during first World War 38-40; escape from internment 272; Intelligence work in Spain 39, 301; commands U-boat 40; postwar paramilitary activity 41, 272; later promotion in Navy

307

41; political outlook 38, 40-41, 51, 52, 114; pride in assumed Mediterranean links 38; hatred of cold 38; marriage and domestic life 41, 46; recommended by predecessor at Abwehr, Admiral Patzig 42; relations with Hitler 43, 47; relations with Oster 45, 61, 64, 235-36; relations with Himmler and Heydrich 40, 45-49, 141-42; relations with Werner Best 46; residences in Berlin 46; relations with General Franco 49; travels in Europe 49, 77; modest office at Abwehr 50; and the Fritsch affair (1938) 53-56

Joined in opposition by Schacht 57; in Vienna after *Anschluss* 60; recruits Lahousen 60; relations with staff at Abwehr 61, 105, 140-41; association with Beck 63; association with Nazi hierarchy 64, 143-45, 149-50, 183, 239-40; briefs Kleist before latter's 1938 visit to England 70; and Czech crisis 1938 78; and Schlabrendorff 86; warns Keitel 92; despair over failure of approaches to O.K.W. to stop impending war 95; on declaration of war 1939 96; reaction to German invasion of Poland 99-102, 106

Wartime organization of Abwehr 102-04, 140-41; part in wartime plots for *coup d' état* 106-08; and Müller's peace negotiations at Vatican 108 *et seq.*, 123; and Oster's 'treason' 120; probably issues personal warning of German invasion plans 124; tours German-occupied France 128; love of cooking 128; wartime visits to Mediterranean countries 128, 134, 140; his constant travels 140; withholds Intelligence concerning potential Allied action 128; his reports withheld from Hitler by Keitel 129-30; resists pressure to assassinate Weygand 131-32; interest in restoration of German monarchy 132-33; meets Tresckow and Schlabrendorff 134; attitude to assassination of Hitler 137; probably leaks information concerning projected invasion of Britain 138; possibly keeps Spain out of war 138; possible attempt to keep Bulgaria neutral 139; in Yugoslavia 1941 139; recruits Jews and anti-Nazis for Abwehr 140-41, 280; relations with Schellenberg 141-46, 149-50, 237-39; covers Josef Müller's operations 142; reaction to death of Heydrich (1942) 146; shows symptoms of despair 146, 149; evasion of orders to have Giraud assassinated 147-49; Himmler's attitude to 150, 238-39; and campaign against Russia 150; and Abwehr's sabotage duties 151; forecasts overthrow of Mussolini 161; collaborates with Himmler in exposure of Rote Kapelle 165 *et seq.*; and the Schmidhuber affair 170 *et seq.*; 187 *et seq.*; collaboration with Tresckow 183 *et seq.*; protects Marogna-Redwitz 188; and arrest of Dohnanyi 191 *et seq.*

Attempts to help Dohnanyi and Müller when they are in prison 199, 203-04 *et seq.*, 210; warns Stauffenberg and Schlabrendorff 208; goes to

308

hospital at Buch 218, 220-21; develops diphtheria and is removed to isolation hospital at Potsdam 221; removed to Sachsenhausen concentration camp 231, 241; discovery of his documents hidden at Zossen 232; interrogation by Huppenkothen 240, 244, and by Stavitsky 244; taken over by Gestapo 240-43; helped by medical orderly Geissler 242; paralysed 253; views sought by 'intellectuals' of the S.D. 256; treatment in Gestapo prison 258; letter to his wife from prison 259-63; self-inflicted dipththeria 260; visited by Dietrich Bonhoeffer in his cell 263, 266; removed to hospital 266; abortive plan to rescue him 266; removed to Sachsenhausen concentration camp, 'tried' and executed 267

Dulles, Allen 216

Eden, Sir Anthony 155
Erdberg, Alexander 168
Etzdorf, Hasso von 106-07
Eulenburg, Princess 166

Falkenhausen, General von 156, 214
Faulhaber, Cardinal Archbishop Michael xxiv
Fellgiebel, General Erich et seq. 152, 225
Ficht, Lieutenant-Colonel 170-71, 175-76, 198
Fish, Mildred (Frau Harnack) 166-69
Franco, General Francisco 49, 138
Freisler, Roland 87, 178, 231, 250-51
Freytag-Loringhoven, Colonel

Wessel von 61, 103, 210, 213, 236
Fritsch, General Werner von 45, 53-56, 63, 64, 102
Fromm, General Fritz et seq. xxv, 158, 181, 228

Galen, Bishop Count von xxiv
Gaulle, General Charles de 128
Geer, Minister de 121
Gehre, Captain Ludwig 188, 202, 233, 283
Gehrts, Colonel 166
Gersdorff, Baron Rudolf von 186
Gerstenmaier, Dr Eugen 180, 251, 291
Giesler, Paul 178
Giessler, Max 242
Giraud, General Henri 147-49
Gisevius, Hans Bernd 56, 59-60, 64, 80-86, 88, 94-95, 108, 126-27, 128-30, 140, 159, 187, 188, 231, 248
Goebbels, Joseph et seq. 84, 144, 209, 228-29
Goerdeler, Dr Carl xxv-xxvi, xxvii-xxviii, 52-53, 56-57, 67, 88-89, 99, 101-02, 104, 114, 117, 132, 133, 151-54, 156, 157, 160, 161, 179, 180, 209-10, 214-17, 221, 224, 228, 231, 242, 246, 249, 254-56, 273, 275
Goltz, Count Rüdiger von der 54, 119, 205-06
Göring, Field Marshal Hermann 54-55, 57-58, 59, 64, 79, 82, 95, 101, 127, 166, 180, 224, 273
Grigg, Sir James 91
Grosscurth, Colonel Hans 61, 102-03, 107, 108, 118, 119, 189, 277
Gütner, Dr Franz 69-70, 84 87, 190
Guttenberg, Baron Carl Ludwig von 189, 210, 283

310

311

the invasion of Russia 133; takes over operational command of Army 136; invades Yugoslavia 139; treatment of his generals 158-59; and fall of Stalingrad 159; escapes assassination following visit to Russian front 1943 185-86; *et seq.*; initial plans to arrest King of Italy and the Pope 210; involuntarily eludes would-be killers 216, 222; dissolves Abwehr and dismisses Canaris 219-20; survives the attempt of 20 July 1944 *et seq.*; orders 224; execution of remaining conspirators, April 1945 268
Höppner, General Erich 78, 136, 230
Honigen-Huene, Baron 151
Howard, Leslie 151
Huber, Kurt 177-78
Huppenkothen, Walther 138, 146, 232, 240 *et seq.*, 267, 268, 287-89

Ickrath, Captain 175, 282

Jackson, Mr. Justice Robert H. 129-30
Jodl, General Alfred 87
John, Hans 231, 292
John, Otto 68, 133, 202, 212, 218, 231, 290

Kaas, Monsignor Ludwig 109
Kaiser, Jacob 245
Kaltenbrunner, S.S. General Ernst 188, 219, 220, 237, 254, 256, 268, 289
Keitel, Field Marshal Wilhelm 84, 87, 92, 93, 94, 101, 128-32, 147-49, 150, 151, 188, 190, 204, 218 *et seq.*
Kjolsen, van (Danish Naval Attaché) 123
Kleffens, Minister van 121

Kleist, Peter 216
Kleist-Schmenzin, Lieutenant Ewald Heinrich von 217
Kleist-Schmenzin, Major Ewald Heinrich von 70-77, 86, 91, 251
Klop, Lieutenant 121
Kluge, Field Marshal Günther Hans von xxiv-xxv, 134-36, 154, 157, 160, 183-84, 209-10, 214, 224, 230, 231
Knobloch (warder) 245-46
Kordt, Erich 90, 106
Kordt, Theodor 77, 90
Kowalski, Colonel 182
Krauss, Dr 166
Kreisau Circle xxvi, 90, 161
Kruls, Captain 122
Kuckhoff, Adam 166-69
Kuckhoff, Greta 167-68
Kuechler, Field Marshal Georg von 160
Kuhn, Major 215
Kutzner (interrogator) 220-21

Lahousen, Colonel Erwin 60-61, 78, 92, 100, 101, 102, 130-32, 138, 147-48, 184, 210, 257, 292
Langbehn, Carl 162, 188, 212, 246
Lange (interrogator) 245
Leber, Julius 133, 216, 221, 223, 273
Leibholz Dr 155, 265, 290
Leuschner, Wilhelm 210, 216, 221, 274
Leiber, Father Robert 109-12, 123
Liebknecht, Karl 41
Leopold III, King of the Belgians 124
Leverkuehn, Paul 38, 141, 218, 292
Liedig, Franz 279
Lindt, August 124
List, Field Marshal Wilhelm 160

312

314

315